M & E

M & E Handbooks are recommended reading for examination syllabuses all over the world. Because each Handbook covers its subject clearly and concisely books in the series form a vital part of many college, university, school and home study courses.

Handbooks contain detailed information stripped of unnecessary padding, making each title a comprehensive self-tuition course. They are amplified with numerous self-testing questions in the form of Progress Tests at the end of each chapter, each text-referenced for easy checking. Every Handbook closes with an appendix which advises on examination technique. For all these reasons, Handbooks are ideal for pre-examination revision.

The handy pocket-book size and competitive price make Handbooks the perfect choice for anyone who wants to grasp the essentials of a subject quickly and easily.

THE M & E HANDBOOK SERIES

Management:
Theory and Principles

Tony Proctor
MA, M Phil, MBIM, FRSA

*Head of Department of Business and Management Studies,
Bolton Institute of Technology*

MACDONALD AND EVANS

Macdonald & Evans Ltd
Estover, Plymouth PL6 7PZ

First published 1982

© Macdonald & Evans Ltd, 1982

07121 1389 4

Filmset in Monophoto Times by
Northumberland Press Ltd, Gateshead
Printed in Great Britain by
Richard Clay (The Chaucer Press) Ltd,
Bungay, Suffolk

Preface

Management is truly a subject without bounds. Few syllabuses that I have read, textbooks that I have examined or even question papers that I have studied agree whole-heartedly about the subject matter in its entirety. It is therefore relatively difficult to be completely comprehensive in writing a book of this nature. I apologise for any inadvertent omissions that the reader may discover, therefore.

I have covered the various topics which appear most frequently in the courses to which I have referred and have also included some quantitive material relevant to those topics. It is intended that the book should be used as an introduction and a framework for study and both a comprehensive bibliography and a list of books for further reading have therefore been included at the end of the book. It is essentially intended to act as an introductory text on management theory, aimed principally at the student of management. As such it should prove to be of interest to students at BEC Higher Diploma level in particular.

I would like to thank the following professional bodies for their permission to reproduce questions from past examination papers.

Institute of Chartered Secretaries and Administrators
Institute of Industrial Managers
Institute of Administrative Management
Institute of Personnel Management
Institute of Cost and Management Accountants
Institute of Management Services
Institute of Supervisory Management

I would also like to acknowledge the assistance of Anne Proctor, BA, M Ed for her assistance in perusing the text and of Rebecca Proctor for her assistance in checking all the arithmetic calculations.

June 1982   TP

Contents

List of Illustrations

CHAPTER I

A Historical Perspective

INTRODUCTION

Management is not a nineteenth or twentieth century concept; it dates back to much earlier times. Ever since people began to form groups and to work together towards a common purpose the elements of management have been present. As the size of the groups expanded, the task of managing them became more complex and difficult; it is this that has given rise to the management theories and structures of today.

In this chapter a review is made of the development of management thinking and practice up until the end of the nineteenth century. Management is defined and a brief survey of its progress given. Some attention is devoted to the contributions of the eighteenth and nineteenth centuries to the study of management methods and to the way in which managers of this period appear to have acquired their skills. Finally, some illustrations of Victorian business management are considered.

NATURE OF MANAGEMENT

1. Management defined. Management may be thought of as the task of planning, organising and controlling any organisation or group of people. It comprises: planning work; staffing with competent personnel; directing the activities of subordinates and representing their views to superiors (and vice versa). In addition, it may involve co-ordinating various activities in order to meet over-all goals. It can also be defined as getting a job done through the medium of human effort. In 1937, Luther Gulik, an American scholar with research interests in government organisation and public administration, envisaged management as comprising seven functions:

(*a*) *planning*; deciding what to accomplish and setting short and long range goals for the organisation;

(*b*) *organising*; deciding what positions have to be filled and what duties and responsibilities are assigned to them in order to achieve work goals;

(c) *staffing*; finding the right person for each job;

(d) *direction*; informing people of what has to be done and what is expected of them in each situation. It also involves developing good morale and helping staff to improve their skills;

(e) *control*; assessing what progress has been made towards achieving set goals;

(f) *innovation*; developing new and better ways of doing things;

(g) *representation*; representing the organisation in dealing with a number of outside groups.

Another way of describing the function of management is in terms of the people such as managers, executives, supervisors, etc. in an organisation who are engaged in management activities. In the case of a small business, one manager may have complete charge of operations. He may also be the owner, or "entrepreneur". Large organisations have more than one manager; as soon as two or more managers exist, the management structure usually becomes hierarchical, with one manager having other managers accountable to him as shown in Fig. 1.

The highest level in the hierarchy, top management, is responsible for the over-all efficient running of the business. Below this level are the middle managers whose responsibilities are fairly diverse. They include plant managers, sales managers and/or heads of departments within an organisation. The layer of middle management may be so thick that one tier of middle managers might oversee another. The next level is lower or "front-line" managers who are concerned with the supervision of rank and file employees.

2. Types of business unit and their management (*see also* V,19). Business units can be divided into a number of categories.

(a) *Sole trader*. The business is owned by one person who receives all the profits and bears all the losses. The sole trader may expand by forming either a partnership or a limited liability company to raise capital and acquire management assistance. The owner's unlimited liability is a major disadvantage of this type of business.

(b) *Partnership*. The Partnership Act 1890 defines a partnership as "a relation which subsists between two or more people engaged in carrying on business with a view to profit". It sets out the rules under which partnerships should operate and considers the legal aspects of bankruptcy and dissolution. The maximum number of partners legally permitted is usually twenty.

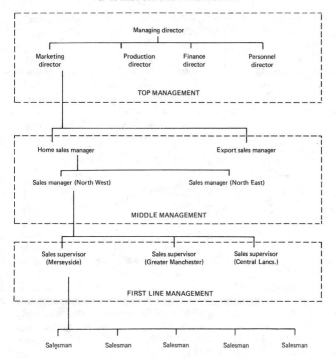

FIG. 1   *A hierarchy of management.*

Although partners work as individuals they may have joint liability for the debts incurred by any of the other partners. The Limited Partnerships Act 1907 overcame the problem of unlimited liability, introducing the limited partnership where partners are liable only to the extent of the capital they have put in, provided that there is one "general partner" whose liability is unlimited.

(*c*) *Joint stock companies.* The ownership and control of a joint stock company, unlike that of a partnership or sole trader, can be separate. Before the 1844 and 1855 Companies Acts the relationship between ownership and control was haphazard. Statutory companies, such as the East India Company, could be formed by Royal Charter or Act of Parliament, but the most common form of company was the partnership. However, investors were wary of partnership ventures on account of their unlimited liability and felt they should be liable only to the extent of the capital they had invested.

The Companies Act 1855 introduced limited liability giving investors a degree of protection, while the basis of the regulations governing present day companies is found in the Companies Acts of 1948, 1967 and 1976. The joint stock company is the most common form of company registered under these Acts. The joint stock company is jointly owned by shareholders who are each liable only to the amount of share capital they have subscribed.

Shareholders appoint a Board of Directors to manage the affairs of the company (*see* IV).

(*d*) *Public corporations.* Large-scale business units under public ownership, created by Act of Parliament, these organisations are run by a board appointed by the government. Examples are British Rail and the National Coal Board.

(*e*) *Co-operatives.*

(*i*) *Producer societies.* These are generally concerned with agriculture whereby farmers pool their resources and produce. Co-operative activities might include marketing, loan and use of equipment and transport.

(*ii*) *Consumer societies.* These are retail business units, co-operatively organised, which were originally formed, amongst other reasons, to enable members to obtain benefit from the profits made by the society in proportion to the goods purchased from it by its members. Profits were distributed to members in the form of dividends. Each member is a shareholder; shareholders appoint a management committee which in turn appoints staff to run the business.

3. Genesis. Primitive man was principally a hunter and gatherer. His first tools were probably used to hunt wild animals and to provide food and clothing for himself and his family. He lived in isolated groups but, nevertheless, there are several aspects of his life then that remain important in any formal organisation today. These are as follows.

(*a*) *Division of labour.* Generally speaking, the male members of the group would carry out the job of hunting and providing raw materials for food and clothing, while the females stayed behind to look after the family and the raw materials provided by the males. Here then was one of the basic and fundamental concepts of economic, commercial and business theory: tasks were divided amongst members of a group according to their special interests and abilities.

(*b*) *Co-operation.* The hunters in the group realised that by co-operating with each other their tasks could be completed more effectively and that the spoils of the hunt could be much greater therefore. Whereas one man working on his own might be lucky to obtain food on more than three days a week, a joint hunt would produce food every day and in a much shorter time.

(*c*) *Specialisation.* Hunters soon discovered that the most efficient teamwork could be accomplished if individuals performed different roles in the course of the hunt. One might become expert in throwing the spear at a long distance, for example, while others might have different talents, such as designing pits in which to trap larger animals. Specialisation enabled the weaker members of the group to survive, as they might not otherwise have had sufficient skills to support themselves unaided; they might have carried out other ancillary tasks such as scouting or making weapons, for example, which would have contributed to the total effort.

(*d*) *Communication and mobility.* Later, man learned to develop and use more sophisticated tools and to cultivate the land, relying less on hunting for sustenance. Nevertheless, the economy was still one of self-sufficiency or subsistence and trade or commerce was still unknown. Man still produced food or clothing solely for his family or extended family group. It was possibly the development of language and the mastery of the horse, and the improvements in communication that these brought, which eventually led him to realise the benefits of exchanging goods and services.

(*e*) *Trade.* As a result of the development of language and increased mobility, the exchange of goods and services (trading) began to take place. Eventually local trading centres (markets) grew up where producers came to exchange their surplus goods amongst themselves by barter. The development of local markets accelerated the process of specialisation: producers began to specialise in that which they were best at producing. In turn, as more people began to specialise in and produce particular goods, the markets themselves became more complex.

(*f*) *Wealth.* The exchange of goods led to the accumulation of wealth. Certain individuals were better at producing goods than others and therefore they were able to exchange their larger surplus productions for the labour of others; they began to employ others to work for them.

(*g*) *Leadership.* In a group such as that described above, one member, the leader, had to make decisions about the allocation of tasks and the co-ordination of group activities. This role was usually assumed by the member of the group with the greatest intelligence and physical strength. The development of trade and the creation of wealth, which in turn led to the employment of one individual by another, meant that leadership became less dependent on physical strength alone.

EARLY MANAGEMENT THINKING

4. The Egyptians and Sumerians. Egyptian and Sumerian records dating back several thousand years BC show that the civilisations of those times knew the importance of organisation and administration. Their systems of management appears to have evolved for the purpose of:

 (*a*) co-ordinating and organising military activities;

 (*b*) establishing a hierarchical system of government to cope with an increasing population;

 (*c*) establishing a system of accounting to record trade transactions and taxes levied; and

 (*d*) systematically planning the construction of large scale buildings (temples, pyramids, etc.) and controlling the work-forces needed to build them.

5. The Greeks and the Romans. Both the Greek and Roman cultures have had a significant influence on the development of modern management thinking.

 (*a*) *The Greeks.* The Athenian Commonwealth, with its councils, popular courts, administrative officials and board of generals provides later evidence of the early existence of a systematic form of government and administration. Socrates was one of the earliest writers on the subject of management. Plato, who despised commercial activity as "base and common", nevertheless epitomised the need for commercial and administrative skills in his description of the "Ideal State". Plato's student, Aristotle, was averse to the profit motive in business but his philosophising is none the less at the root of modern decision-making techniques. Xenophon, a contemporary of Plato, urged that commerce should be encouraged and that merchants should receive "the honour of seats of distinction on public occasions". He is renowned for what can be regarded as the first systematic book on leadership, the *Cyropaedia*, based on his own personal experience and ideas. This is still recommended by top management consultant Peter Drucker as one of the best books on the subject.

(*b*) *The Romans.* The complexity of the task of administering the Roman State and its Empire brought about considerable development of managerial techniques. The success the Romans enjoyed for several centuries in controlling their vast empire may have lain in their ability to organise. Indeed, the delegation of authority and the establishment of a chain of direct authority relationships from superior to subordinate were both noted features of Roman society.

(*c*) *The Church.* The eventual fall of the Roman Empire and the ensuing Dark Ages held back the progress of management. During this period, and up until the Renaissance, the Church held the secrets of formal organisation, a legacy from the government of the Roman Empire. There is, however, little evidence that the excellence of the Church's system of management was matched in secular fields.

6. The Renaissance. Niccolo Machiavelli's book, *The Prince*, written in 1513, represented a historic step in the development of management thought. Although his principal concern was with the government of the State and not with the administration of a business, much of the advice he addressed to the then ruler of Florence is still of great relevance to business organisations. He put forward the idea that leaders have to adapt their behaviour to the demands of a particular situation if they are to be successful. One who behaves with patience at a time when the situation demands this may be ruined if he does not adapt his policy to different circumstances. He also considered that chance plays an important part in the outcome of events and that, therefore, it is more prudent to pursue a bold strategy in times of change.

Machiavelli stressed that a leader needs support from senior colleagues if he is to reconcile the divergent interests of the groups and individuals he leads. In this context he suggested that a new leader should "lop heads" quickly when he comes to power. However, it may be prudent in such circumstances to err on the side of caution.

DEVELOPMENT OF MODERN MANAGEMENT

7. The historical perspective. Historically, as we have seen, the basic concepts of management emerged as the result of supervisory or leadership practices. Government or the State, the military, commerce and the Church all developed their own systems of management relatively independently. The development of modern management falls broadly into two periods.

(a) *Before 1700*. Documentary evidence of business management before 1700 is relatively sparse but, until well into the nineteenth century, most businesses were small and directed by their owners. Firms were purposely restricted to a manageable size as owners felt that they could not trust their subordinates. Indeed it was not uncommon for owners to be defrauded by their employees and even into the early part of the nineteenth century dishonest, absconding and alcoholic managers abounded who inflicted much damage on the firms who employed them.

(b) *After 1700*. This period was characterised in Britain by industrialisation (*see* **8**) and the emergence and development of large numbers of small businesses. It was an era in which entrepreneurship flourished, with control of the business directly in the hands of the owner.

8. The Industrial Revolution.

(a) *1750–1850*. The term "Industrial Revolution" describes the replacement in Britain of an economy based on agriculture and manual work with the population dominated by machines and their manufacture. While other countries have since followed suit Britain was the first to industrialise. The process was gradual, but it is generally accepted that the mid-eighteenth century marked the beginning of the change.

(b) *1850–1900*. Towards the end of the nineteenth century mechanisation took on greater importance as technology developed and firms began to increase their output substantially to cope with the demands of a rapidly growing population for consumer goods. Increased mechanisation and a general increase in the size of the manufacturing units, which were required to effect economies on a large scale and to facilitate mass production, led in turn to the demand for a hierarchical system of management. Firms grew so large that it was impossible for one man to manage effectively the whole enterprise, while the growth of the marketing and accounting functions in firms put even greater pressure on the need to recruit and develop specialist managers. This period, therefore, eventually saw the emergence of the delegation of management.

9. The era of mass production. Mass production techniques evolved during the period from 1900 to the 1930s. One of the most important management objectives at this time was to try to decrease unit costs of production. From the marketing point of view, therefore, the aim was to offer a standardised product at the lowest price, typified by the remark Henry Ford is reputed to have made about his Model T cars: "Give it to them any colour as long as it's black!". Few firms were interested in diversifying their product-market scope and most sought satisfaction through the growth of their own industry. Management, then, was primarily concerned with the efficiency of production.

10. The era of mass marketing. By the mid-1930s, the demand for basic consumer goods in the developed world had reached saturation point. The more affluent (chiefly US) consumers began to demand more from a product than that it should be purely functional, so that sales of cars such as the Model T Ford began to decline. General Motors began to search for ways of differentiating its products from those of its competitors, and introduced an annual model change, the first company to do so. With product differentiation came the development of promotion, advertising and selling techniques.

During this period businesses were characterised by internal conflict as power shifted from production-orientated to marketing-orientated managers. This change in emphasis had many implications for the management team. It required new problem-solving approaches and changes in organisational structure.

11. The post-industrial era. The period of industrialisation was followed by what has been called the post-industrial era, generally held to have started in the mid-1950s, and coinciding in the UK with the beginnings of large scale mergers between firms, diversification of product-market interests, the growth of management services and management science, and the early days of the computerisation of routine clerical work. Indicative of the change was the rapid introduction of new and revolutionary technologies: nuclear power, jet-propelled aircraft, electrification of the overground railway system and the growth in the electronics industry; and the decline of the weaker industries in Britain such as the cotton and motor-cycle manufacturing industries.

In the early part of the twentieth century, and even up to 1950, domestic industries were often protected against foreign competition by government-imposed tariffs and other trade barriers. In some cases this protection was directly intentional but in others the policy was intended to conserve valuable foreign currency reserves by discouraging unnecessary imports.

Since 1950, however, many international trade barriers have been removed, resulting in fierce competition in some product markets. The Japanese, for example, have come to dominate the world markets for cameras and motor-cycles and many manufacturers, previously well-established in these fields have disappeared.

The growth in world markets since the 1950s has resulted in an accompanying growth in world trade. This has led in turn to a need for much larger business organisations and it has accelerated the tendency towards mergers, creating organisational problems of even larger dimensions for management.

12. Early management theorists in the UK. The rise of management theory, as explained, is directly related to the development of industrialisation.

(a) *Matthew Boulton and James Watt.* One of the earliest attempts to systematise management thought in Britain, and perhaps the best documented, is that of Matthew Boulton (1728–1809) and James Watt (1736–1819). Matthew Boulton was a manufacturer and engineer who financed and introduced James Watt's steam engine. In coming to grips with a series of crises, these two business partners acquired the knowledge to introduce "regularity, delegation and division of functions" into their business. Their relative success in managing their own firm led them to become critical of the mismanagement of others and so to realise that their own methods could be applied elsewhere with equal success.

(b) *Robert Owen and Benjamin Gott.* Scotsman Robert Owen (1771–1858), manager of cotton mills firstly in Manchester and then in New Lanark, and Benjamin Gott (1762–1840), owner of woollen mills in Leeds, were both noted for the effectiveness of their approaches to the task of management. Owen in particular, was interested in social reform and was the first industrialist to back up theories of management's social responsibilities with a programme of action providing housing and schooling for his work force far above contemporary standards for workers' communities.

(c) *William Brown.* William Brown, joint owner of a flax-making mill in Dundee, in the nineteenth century, was also well-known for his managerial ability. He eventually adopted the role of consultant to his industry. His essays on the subject of management

(1818–23) were quite remarkable for their time. He saw that the first and most important object at his own mill was to make a profit. In order to achieve this he had organised the mill systematically into eleven departments. Each of them had their transactions recorded separately and each had a manager and supervisor who had instructions regularly to check work performance, materials used and quality, etc. Each department was examined in rotation at set intervals.

Brown was aware of the need for co-ordination between departments, particularly between sales and production departments. He also stressed, in describing the qualities a good manager should possess, that administrative and social skills were as important as personal qualities, technical and business knowledge. The effective use of administrative and social skills, he held, enabled discipline to be kept in the mill without causing undue friction between management and the workforce.

(*d*) *Charles Babbage.* One of the most significant contributors to management theory during the early part of the nineteenth century was Charles Babbage (1792–1871). Primarily a mathematician, he wrote a book, published in 1832 entitled *On the Economy of Machinery and Manufactures.* His specific interest was in the economics of the division of labour and the development of scientific principles to govern a manager's use of facilities, materials and labour to get the best possible results. Babbage's ideas on the human aspects of organisation were also ahead of his time. Generally employees were considered then to be hostile to the idea of work and certainly not to have an interest in it.

Babbage put forward the idea that there could be a mutuality of interest between worker and owner. He proposed that workers should be able to participate in the profits of a business according to the effort they were prepared to expend. Workers, he recommended, should receive:

(*i*) a fixed rate of pay reflecting the nature of their work;

(*ii*) a share in the profits; and

(*iii*) a bonus for any suggestions they made to improve productivity.

Reward, Babbage considered, should be allocated according to productivity.

13. The contribution of the eighteenth and nineteenth centuries. The relative failure of these two centuries to produce more significant contributions to management thinking probably arose for the following reasons.

(a) *The emphasis on developing technology.* Although this was a period of commercial activity, it was also one of technological innovation and businesses were founded on the basis of improved technology. It was the owners who had control of the commercial and technological aspects of their businesses and, by and large, they were technologists who saw the improvement of their business in terms of advancing technology rather than better management methods.

(b) *Individuality of approach.* Pioneers and entrepreneurs abounded and all were keen to demonstrate how they were different from one another in order to find for themselves a place within an industry. The success of a business was thought to be partially, if not wholly, due to the fact that it was different in some way from all other businesses in the locality. Since the differences between companies were emphasised, there were no incentives to look for any similarities for the purpose of putting together a set of management guidelines.

(c) *Owners' attitude to the workforce.* A fundamental change in the attitudes of business owners towards their workforces was required before any progress could be made with understanding workers' motivation and, therefore, with improving their management. It was held by most employers during this period that a reform of character was required on the part of every single workman, since their characters were derived from pre-industrialisation times and were not suited to the new industrial system.

14. Management education and training. Management as such was not formally taught in the eighteenth or nineteenth centuries: its skills were largely acquired through practical experience which was then passed on. James Watt and Matthew Boulton, for example, after giving them a basic grounding in practical book-keeping, geometry and algebra, sent their sons to gain initial management experience by overseeing small firms.

Opportunities for formal education as such had become, by the end of the nineteenth century, much more widely available, so that the number of highly successful businessmen who were entirely self-taught was small, but up until this time, managers did not generally receive a high level of education.

George Stephenson (1781–1848), Richard Arkwright (1732–92) and Josiah Wedgwood (1730–95) were among the innovators and businessmen of this period whose only formal education had been at the village school. This was a reflection both of the educational opportunities available at the time, and of the fact that many if not most entrepreneurs started as small local tradesmen or crafts-men. This gave rise to the tradition of the resourceful amateur, self-trained on the job, rather than the man specially and elaborately trained. This was true all the way from the boardroom to the bench. For most owner/managers therefore, formal education was followed by apprenticeship to a local craftsman and practical experience.

NINETEENTH CENTURY MANAGEMENT

15. Introduction. The degree of success enjoyed by firms before 1850 varied considerably; some perished and some survived. During the early part of this period firms operated under conditions where there was an increasing demand for products and services, so that anyone of reasonable intelligence, if he had the will, stood a chance of operating a firm profitably. Not surprisingly, perhaps, goods produced for the mass market were often of poor quality, while business failures were frequent.

16. Business failures. Evidence of the organisation and progress of early Victorian firms is scanty, but it is clear that some firms failed because they were not sufficiently marketing-orientated and others as a result of bad management. James Thompson (c. 1800–50) of the Primrose Works near Clitheroe in Lancashire, perhaps the leading calico printers of the time, produced short runs of exclusive prints, designed by Royal Academicians. In 1841, heedless of the warnings from his chemical manager that the business was doomed unless he changed the character of his product, Thompson refused to abandon his short runs. Other calico printers did attempt to produce for the mass market however, and in order to do so cut their costs to the bone by introducing cheaper designs, longer runs and paying lower wages. Thompson died just before his renowned works was closed.

17. Business successes. The history of Alfred Bird's firm provides an insight into entrepreneurship during the nineteenth century. One of the most interesting aspects of its development is its intro-duction of marketing management methods.

(a) *Alfred Bird.* Alfred Bird (c. 1810–79), an experimental chemist, opened a small chemist's shop in Birmingham in 1837. He had served an apprenticeship with a reputable firm of druggists and he had qualified as a Fellow of the Chemists Society. Not merely a retailer, he used to spend long hours conducting his own experiments after shutting up his shop in the evening. In 1843 he perfected a yeast substitute which later became known as baking powder.

His most famous innovation was an eggless custard in powder form. While sales of this quickly rose in volume, the demand for the baking powder was less spectacular, so he incorporated advertisements for his product into calendars which were then given away free. This represented the first use of calendars as an advertising medium.

(b) *Alfred Bird Jnr*. In 1867, Alfred Bird Jnr (1849–c. 1920) entered his father's business and became one of the first owner/managers to introduce a policy of marketing and sales promotion into a business. The first pictorial advertisements for Bird's products that resulted from this policy appeared in 1880 and, in conjunction with their originator T. B. Browne, Bird set the pattern for the twentieth century system of advertising through recognised agencies.

Alfred Bird Jnr's interests stretched beyond marketing. In the late 1880s, mechanical engineers were persuading industrialists that manual labour could be replaced effectively by machinery and, as he was always ready to consider new ideas that would make his production more efficient, he installed several ingenious machines which speeded up the packing and wrapping of his custard and baking powder.

After Alfred Bird's death, the business was taken over by his son who instituted a number of changes. The founder had been primarily a scientist who had run the business as a means of supporting himself and his family. Alfred Bird Jnr, on the other hand, was an organiser and manager. He was keen to expand the business and made a number of changes to the premises so that it became less of a shop and more of a factory.

He appointed agents nationwide to do the work of customer contact and in doing so created the basis on which the concept of the sales force was to develop. He also inherited some of his father's innovative characteristics: in the 1870s he invented Bird's Blancmange Powder, launching the product in no less than fourteen different flavours. In 1890 he introduced Bird's Egg Substitute and in 1895, Bird's Jelly Crystals, the forerunner of tablet jellies.

18. The delegation of control. The structure of nineteenth century businesses and their method of operation obviated the need for the delegation of control and therefore for a hierarchical system of management.

(*a*) *Partnerships and sole traders.* Throughout most of the nineteenth century the typical business unit was the partnership or sole trader (*see* **2**). The partnership was founded on practical professional and commercial skill and personal expertise and possessed many advantages. Ownership and control were synonymous enabling owners to avoid the dangers of delegating the running of the business to a manager (*see* **7**). The problems associated with managing an expanding business were solved by offering partnerships to conscientious and trusted employees who had proved themselves. Manufacturing and trading businesses were thus able to expand without having recourse to a corporate form of organisation. As partners generally had to buy their way into a partnership, this form of expansion was largely self-financing in that capital brought in by new partners could be used for expanding the business. Many of the production processes involved in the industry of the time were relatively simple in any case so that operations could easily be overseen by groups of partners.

(*b*) *Limited liability companies.* The principle of the owners of a business having only limited liability for its debts was not adopted finally until 1855 (*see* **2**(*c*)). In that year, however, limited companies only accounted for between five and ten per cent of the important business organisations and it was only in such industries as shipping, iron and steel that they existed in any quantity. Even in the case of those firms which had taken on limited liability status, the "partners" still held control. There is little evidence to suggest any significant divorce of ownership from control before 1900.

(*c*) *The pattern of ownership.* The pattern of ownership exhibited in the nineteenth century had several implications for the corporate strategies of the firms involved. The growth pattern was one of duplication and multiplication of existing plants and processes. Firms produced a limited range of related products and did not pursue diversification actively, which would have required the recruitment of executive talent from outside.

CONCLUSION

It is a combination of the factors which led to a growth in the size of firms and the subsequent problems that arose out of such growth that eventually led to the emergence of scientific management thought early in the twentieth century. As we shall observe in the next chapter, attention was first focused on finding more efficient means of organising labour—possibly still reflecting the old belief that man was not basically interested in work and that in order to increase his productivity, his activities needed to be formally structured and systematically organised. Later, the emphasis changed and attention was transferred to assessing the personal needs of all employees.

PROGRESS TEST 1

1. Define management. **(1)**

2. Distinguish between: (*a*) sole trader; (*b*) partnership; (*c*) joint companies; (*d*) public corporations; and (*e*) co-operatives. **(2)**

3. What are: (*a*) division of labour; (*b*) co-operation; (*c*) specialisation; (*d*) communication? **(3)**

4. What impact did the development of trade have on the demand for managerial skill? **(3)**

5. What gave rise to an increase in the importance of management skills in ancient times? **(4)**

6. What was Machiavelli's contribution to management thinking? **(6)**

7. Who were the main contributors to management thought in eighteenth century Britain? **(7, 12)**

8. Can you account for the dearth of management thinkers prior to 1900? **(13)**

9. What was the state of management education and training during the eighteenth and nineteenth centuries? **(14)**

10. Can you account for the difference in attitude to the task of management as between "founder" and "successor"? **(16, 17, 18)**

CHAPTER II

Modern Management Thinking

INTRODUCTION

In this chapter some of the contributions made by the more important twentieth century thinkers on management are reviewed. If the reader finds their language obscure, this simply reflects the difficulties which they faced in attempting to develop a new field of study and a vocabulary to match their thinking, chiefly in an American context.

The changing environment in which business organisations operate have clearly exerted considerable influence over the development of modern management thinking (*see* III) and for this reason, individual contributors have been considered chronologically. Generally, during the era of mass production (*see* I,**9**) management thought was directed towards finding the best way of performing a job and evolving management principles. But as firms became more marketing-orientated and internal conflicts arose in the era of mass-marketing (*see* I,**10**), interest shifted to the social and psychological dimensions of organisations. Later still, in the post-industrial era, the emphasis has changed to include the consideration of "strategic management" (*see* **1** (*d*))

1. Classification. While it is useful and necessary to identify and classify the different schools of thought, it is not always possible or desirable to compartmentalise thinking on management too rigidly. The reader should realise that distinctions between approaches may become blurred.

(*a*) *The classical school.* The first writers to concern themselves with the subjects of management and organisation as such (*see also* I,**9**) thought in terms of the formal structure of an organisation. They tried to formulate principles which could be applied by all managers. These writers belong to the *classical school.* Writers of this school seek to find the best way of dividing tasks, grouping them together under various departments and devising means of co-ordinating activities. Early writers of the classical school include:

(*i*) *Fayol* (*see* **2**) who formulated a series of management principles; and

(*ii*) *Taylor* (*see* **3**) who promoted "scientific management".

(*b*) *The Human relations school.* On the whole, the classical school did not take the social and psychological dimensions of the work situation into account or fully explain the workings of an organisation over a period of time. It was prevalent during the era of mass-production (*see* **I,9**) when management objectives were to find the most economic way of producing goods through the division of labour and the organisation of the work-load. The behavioural school, on the other hand, considers the needs and behaviour of the members of an organisation as well as its structure. The emergence of this school coincided roughly with the advent of the era of mass-marketing and the new marketing approach to management (*see* **I,10**). Although there are early proponents of the behavioural approach, Mayo and Roethlisberger's Hawthorne studies of the later 1920s and early 1930s (*see* **8**) mark the start of wide-spread interest in it.

(*c*) *The contingency theorists.* This school of thought suggests that organisation structures should reflect current environment circumstances. These are:

(*i*) technology.

(*ii*) innovation, and

(*iii*) uncertainty.

Major contributions to contingency theory have been made by Trist and Woodward who independently concerned themselves with the impact of technology on work organisation. In addition, Burns and Stalker together examined the impact of innovation on organisational structure, while Lawrence and Lorsch examined the problems associated with coping with uncertainty.

(*d*) *The systems approach.* A new school of thought arose in the post-industrial era which considered an organisation as a number of systems. There are a number of ways of considering an organisation from this perspective. Two such ways are:

(*i*) *the decision-making* (*information systems*) *approach.* This considers the organisation's function as being one of providing information on which decisions may be based. Writers include Simon, Cyert, March, Ackoff and Arnoff.

(*ii*) *the total systems approach.* This views the organisation as a whole system comprising various sub-systems. Different writers adopt different systems-viewpoints on organisations. A common feature, however, is the need to view an organisation as a whole and its sub-systems as interdependent and interrelated parts of that whole. Emphasis is placed on communication channels and flows of information between sub-systems, with the idea that the organisational design should facilitate information flow to support decision-making. The approach stresses the importance of identifying the need for, and use of, information and the position of the decision-maker.

The major impact of the systems approach on organisation structure has been the development of "matrix" structures (*see* IX). These recognise the fact that traditional organisation structures are inappropriate in many instances because of the problem of co-ordination across functions.

THE CLASSICAL SCHOOL

Two of the most important writers of the classical school were Fayol and Taylor. They were contemporaries, both born in the middle of the nineteenth century, and both with first-hand experience of the management problems created by the growth of large-scale enterprises towards the end of the nineteenth century.

2. Henri Fayol (1841–1925). A French mining engineer, his prime interest was in the functioning of organisations. He spent most of his working life in general management with one firm, eventually becoming its managing director. He maintained in his influential book, *General and Industrial Management*, first published in English in 1948, that all activities of an industrial firm could be considered under six headings:

(*a*) technical;	(*d*) security;
(*b*) commercial;	(*e*) accounting;
(*c*) financial;	(*f*) managerial.

His definition held that management functions comprised:

(*a*) forecasting and planning;	(*d*) co-ordinating;
(*b*) organising;	(*e*) controlling.
(*c*) commanding;	

Fayol recommended a number of guidelines or principles (still in general use) to help managers perform these functions well.

(*a*) Division of work and specialisation should be encouraged since it leads to greater productivity.

(*b*) The authority to issue commands should be accompanied by responsibility commensurate with its proper exercise.

(*c*) Good leadership must be provided to maintain discipline and order.

(*d*) There should be unity of command: each man should have only one boss.

(*e*) There should be unity of direction: a single plan should be laid down for all employees engaged in the same work activities.

(*f*) The interests and goals of individual members of the organisation should be made subservient to the overall organisational goals.

(*g*) The system of reward should be related wherever possible to the individual's wants and needs. There is no one perfect system of remuneration.

(*h*) The degree of centralisation or decentralisation (of authority and decision-making) should vary according to the individual circumstances of different organisations.

(*i*) It is essential to have both vertical and lateral communication in an organisation, but it is important in the latter case that superiors in the scalar chain (chain of command) are aware of such communications.

(*j*) To minimise lost time and unnecessary handling of materials it is essential to achieve both material order and social order in an organisation.

(*k*) In order to achieve equity a "combination of kindliness and justice" is required in dealing with employees.

(*l*) Successful businesses require stability of tenure as far as managerial personnel are concerned. A low turnover of management staff is important.

(*m*) All employees should be given the opportunity to use their initiative.

(*n*) It is the task of management to foster an *esprit de corps*. High morale in an organisation is a vital ingredient of its success. The manager has to co-ordinate effort, encourage keenness and use men's abilities without causing hostilities as a result of the rewards he offers to them.

3. Frederick W. Taylor (1856–1915). An American by birth, Taylor spent all his working life in the United States. Often referred to as the father of scientific management, he started at the Midvale Steelworks, Philadelphia as a labourer, later rising through foreman to become the company's chief engineer and subsequently consultant to the US engineering industry. His best-known work is *Principles of Scientific Management* (1911).

Taylor considered that the basic reason for hostility between management and worker was that there was a conflict of interests between them: while the workforce desired high wages above all else, management's aim was for low labour costs. He believed that it was possible for the interests of both parties to be reconciled through the medium of his "scientific" methods of management, leading to a better and more profitable business. He held that four aims of factory management should be applied to achieve this:

(a) determine the best way for a worker to do his job;

(b) provide him with proper tools;

(c) train him to follow precise instructions; and

(d) provide incentives for good performance.

The first to introduce "time and motion" studies, he determined the best way of doing a job by breaking down each job in his factory into its constituent motions, analysing these to eliminate those that were non-essential, and timing the worker as he did so. With superfluous motion eliminated, the worker's output was greatly increased, while, by measuring work in this way, it was possible to establish an optimum output for a particular job. Workers would be happy to co-operate with management in introducing the new system he held, because of the financial incentive involved and the fact that it would enable them to do their work with the minimum of effort. While Taylor's principles were sound (they form the basis of the modern subjects of work study and organisation and methods) practical difficulties have been encountered in the implementation of his theories:

(a) the definition of a good day's work is always the subject of controversy between management and workers;

(b) where an incentive scheme based on work measurement is in operation and individuals produce considerably more than the group norm or average output, management is apt to want to re-evaluate its definition of an optimum day's work. As a result, individual workers in a group do not encourage each other to exceed the group norm.

(c) some employers used time and motion studies to set high production norms in order to increase output without a correspondingly high increase in wage levels.

(d) generally, workers tend to resent having their thought processes studied, while the elimination of non-essential movements from a job make it repetitive and less interesting.

Later followers of Taylor included Gantt, Frank B. and Lillian M. Gilbreth, Bedaux, Rowan and Halsey.

THE HUMAN RELATIONS SCHOOL

Taylor's ideas were unable to halt the decline in productivity and standards of production which occurred frequently throughout industry in the 1920s. The next step, therefore, was for management to seek ways of understanding and motivating the workforce. Here it was able to draw on the work of sociologists and psychologists, the behavioural or social scientists, which had given rise to a new science: industrial psychology. This considered the worker in relation to his job environment and to his fellow workers and supervisors; these writers belong to the *human relations school*.

4. Influential thinkers. A number of influential nineteenth century thinkers created the climate in which the behavioural school of management thought was able to develop.

(*a*) *Max Weber (1864–1920).* A German sociologist, Weber approached the study of managerial behaviour through his concept of bureaucracy. He made a number of analyses of the organisation of religious, military and business establishments and from these concluded that "hierarchy, authority and bureaucracy (including clear rules, definition of tasks, and discipline) form the basis of all social organisations". In Weber's view, the manager was the individual who interpreted and applied the rules of the organisation.

(*b*) *Emile Durkheim (1825–1917).* A French sociologist, Durkheim put forward the idea that groups, as a result of forming values and norms, were able to control the conduct of individuals in an organisation.

(*c*) *Vilfredo Pareto (1848–1923).* Pareto, an Italian sociologist, viewed society as a social system incorporating many sub-systems. All systems seek to achieve equilibrium, homeostasis. If a system's equilibrium is disturbed, it will seek either to incorporate the result of the disturbance into its own structure or to reject it. Pareto's contribution was that feelings and attitudes can disturb a system's equilibrium.

5. Mary Parker Follett (1868–1933). Like Taylor, Mary Parker Follett was also interested in the management of organisations. An American, her ideas were far in advance of her time and probably for this reason were not published until eight years after her death. A graduate of Harvard and Cambridge universities, she studied philosophy, history and political science. Interested and active in social work, she was instrumental in establishing a youth employment bureau. Her interest in social work later led her to study social aspects of management.

One of the first to realise the potential of psychology as a means of understanding worker and management behaviour, she saw the management problems of her time in terms of reconciling the needs of individuals with those of the social groups to which they belong. She held that it was management's task to understand how and why such groups are formed and to co-ordinate their aims and objectives. She held that consultation with those affected by a management decision should take place before such a decision is made, leading to increased morale and improved motivation within the organisation. Orders or commands should be based on the objective requirements of a given situation and not on the whim or fancy of a particular manager. Her intention was that management should create the situation where it would be easy for workers to co-operate of their own accord.

6. Hugo Munsterberg (1863–1916). Another to consider the subject of management from the perspective of the social sciences was Munsterberg. Born in Danzig, Poland, he pioneered the application of psychology to the fields of business and industry. His influential book *Psychology and Industrial Efficiency* (1913) set out his desire to discover:

(*a*) the best way to find people whose mental abilities best suited them for the work they were required to do;

(*b*) the conditions that would motivate each individual to produce his greatest output.

Others pursuing similar lines of thought were Frank B. and Lillian Gilbreth and Walter Dill Scott.

7. Benjamin Seebohm Rowntree (1871–1954). The earliest industrialist to promote the extensive use of personnel practices, sociologist and philanthropist, Rowntree was the son of the founder of the cocoa and chocolate manufacturer, H. I. Rowntree & Co. He introduced into his firm a medical department, day continuation school, five-day week, pension plan, profit-sharing scheme, unemployment compensation, canteen and recreation facilities and in addition trained company industrial psychologists to guide both management and workers. All of these changes were introduced into the company between 1897 and 1936.

8. Elton Mayo (1880–1949). A psychologist, Mayo conducted a pioneering industrial research project known as the *Hawthorne studies* (*see also* XII,**12**) at the Western Electric Company's Hawthorne Works, Chicago between 1924 and 1932, the results of which were later summarised by his collaborators F. J. Roethlisberger and William J. Dickson in *Management and the Worker* (1939). If the findings of his research did not revolutionise management thinking (since they merely supported Pareto's earlier ideas), they focused attention dramatically on the behavioural approach to management. Originally called in to assess the potential effect on productivity levels of a proposed change in the lighting of the works, Mayo set up two groups producing the same part under similar conditions, intending to vary the intensity of light for the test group but to keep it constant for the control group. To his surprise, he found that the output of both groups rose despite variations in the intensity of the test group's lighting. Investigation revealed that productivity had increased as a result of an improvement in the groups' morale: because great interest had been shown in them and because the advice and co-operation of members of the group had been sought by the company during the experiment, workers had felt themselves to be important and it was this that had caused output to rise.

9. C. Argyris (1923–   ) and others. The Hawthorne studies showed that workers can obtain satisfaction through belonging to small, stable work groups and suggested that management could achieve its goals by establishing such groups. It also focused management scientists' interest on discovering the most important determinants of an individual's work behaviour, which are motivation, leadership, roles, groups and communication. These, along with the specific contributions of writers such as Herzberg and Maslow, are discussed later (*see* X,7, **8**)

Behavioural scientists have made many contributions to management studies since the Hawthorne investigations. An important contemporary contributor is Chris Argyris, an American academic. He draws together the ideas of both contemporary and earlier writers. He maintains that individuals are not, by and large, averse to work, a belief at one time commonly held by employers, but instead seek self-management, self-direction, responsibility and self-actualisation. He believes that organisations are not traditionally conducive to enabling individuals to achieve these goals, and thereby to benefit the organisation as a whole. He considers that this failure is due to a lack of *interpersonal competence* which results in mutual suspicion and distrust and a lack of frankness of manner and job commitment. Management, he suggests, should aim to develop the full potential of individuals and their interpersonal relationships thereby facilitating better performance of the whole organisation.

10. Chester Irving Barnard (1886–1961). An American Administrator and sociological theorist, Barnard was greatly influenced by the work of Pareto, Mayo and Roethlisberger; his book *Functions of the Executive* (1938) made a major contribution to management theory. His principal proposition was that it is the function of the executive (implying all types of managers and supervisors) to maintain a system of co-operation and co-ordinated effort in a formal organisation. Barnard distinguished a "formal" from an "informal" organisation as follows.

(*a*) *Formal organisation.* This is the set of consciously co-ordinated social interactions which have a deliberate and joint purpose.

(*b*) *Informal organisation.* This comprises those social interactions without a common or consciously co-ordinated joint purpose.

He maintained that, if a formal organisation is to function properly, it must include people who:

(*a*) are willing and able to communicate with each other;

(*b*) are willing to contribute to the action of the group;

(*c*) possess a conscious common purpose.

Further it must provide:

(*a*) the opportunity for individuals to specialise in doing that which they do best;

(*b*) a system of incentives which will motivate people to make effective contributions to the furtherance of group aims and objectives;

(*c*) a system of authority which will permit its executives to make and carry through decisions;

(*d*) a system of decision-making based on logical thought.

He concluded that, in order to work effectively, the formal organisation must be compatible with the informal. He held that the function of the executive is to:

(*a*) maintain this compatibility;

(*b*) encourage good intra-organisational communication;

(*c*) ensure that others in the organisation perform essential duties;

(*d*) formulate and implement plans of action.

Barnard saw co-operation amongst individuals as the keystone of organisational effectiveness and good leadership as the means of achieving it.

11. Elliot Jaques (1917–　). A Canadian by birth, Jaques is renowned for his *action research* undertaken in the Glacier Metal Company's engineering factory in London. He set out to study the psychological and sociological factors affecting group behaviour within the firm and to develop more effective ways of dealing with social stresses within it. In addition, since the work involved collaboration with members of the firm a further objective was to allow improvements in social interactions to take place. The kind of problems studied included worker-management co-operation on the works committee, and the quality of executive leadership at the divisional managers's meetings.

(*a*) *Role and status.* Jaques found that individuals showed a strong desire to have their role and status within a group clearly defined in a way that would be acceptable to all members of the group. He found that problems arose when role boundaries were not clearly defined and when individuals were obliged to occupy more than one role. Conflict could also arise in an individual's mind when there was a discrepancy between his own views and those demanded of him by the role he had to adopt.

(*b*) *Leadership.* Further, he found that difficulties arose in committee meetings if the senior member present did not assume the leadership role by avoiding or abdicating his authority or responsibility. All groups, he concluded, expect one of their number, usually the most senior, to assume the leadership role, and unless this happens, the group will not be able to function well. The problem with the works committee was that it was composed of people who occupied widely different positions in the firm's formal hierarchy. It was difficult for a member of the committee who did not occupy a senior position within the firm to assume the leadership role.

12. Alvin Gouldner (1920–　). Gouldner, a contemporary American sociologist, raised the problem of the dysfunctional inefficient consequences of bureaucracy. He challenged Weber's assumption that members of an organisation would carry out instructions and accept authority imposed from above unquestioningly. (Weber put forward his theories (*see* **4**) before the full emergence of trade union power). Gouldner studied the problem of how to impose authority in the face of group hostility, and the consequences of this for the organisation. Developing Weber's concept, he identified three types of bureaucracy:

(*a*) *mock bureaucracy*; here rules are laid down by external sources, e.g. an official return or report required by an outside party on the organisation concerned;

(*b*) *representative bureaucracy*; here rules and procedures are put forward and mutually accepted by superiors and subordinates;

(*c*) *punishment-centred bureaucracy*; here compliance with rules and decisions is sought through coercion. Either management or workers may impose rules: management may seek to enforce strict rules on timekeeping, for example, while workers may impose job demarcation rules.

With representative bureaucracy, deviations from the rules are treated as oversights or non-malevolent acts, but with punishment-centred bureaucracy, deviations are treated as wilful disobedience. Thus punishment-centred bureaucracies can create dysfunctional consequences in the form of conflict and strife.

Weber had pointed out that the strength of the punishment-centred bureaucracy was in creating an efficient organisation which emphasised the employment of rationally designed general and impersonal rules. But Gouldner argued that to impose general and impersonal rules is merely to impose minimum standards of behaviour which in time become adopted as usual. Thus management seeks to control by introducing more stringent rules which in turn leads to greater conflict, etc.

13. Amitai Etzioni (1929–). Etzioni, a contemporary American sociologist, was interested in why an organisation should continue to exist. His interest centred in particular on why individuals accept authority and comply with prescribed standards of behaviour. The two problems are interrelated: an organisation pursues specific objectives in order to ensure its own survival; to achieve these objectives, a firm lays down rules which its members must follow. In other words, it must have power to control the activities of its members to ensure that they comply with the over-all requirements necessary for it to achieve its organisational goals.

Etzioni's researches led him to conclude that organisations can be classified by the means which they use to ensure that their members comply with requirements:

(*a*) coercive power (e.g. concentration camps);

(*b*) remunerative or utilitarian power using material means (e.g. business organisations);

(*c*) normative or "identitive" power using symbolic means such as prestige (e.g. religious organisations, universities, etc.).

He noted that an individual's response to authority can be classified as:

(*a*) *alienative*; usually in response to coercion;

(*b*) *calculative*; usually in response to remunerative or utilitarian approaches;

(*c*) *moral*; usually in response to normative or identitive approaches.

Etzioni advocated that a business management system should be remunerative or utilitarian where an individual's response will generally be a calculative one.

THE CONTINGENCY THEORISTS

14. Joan Woodward (1916–71). The impact of advances in technology on organisations and their management is of great significance and a number of writers have considered this subject. Joan Woodward, a British researcher (1965), has found a strong positive correlation between the introduction of improved technology and certain aspects of a firm's organisation:

(*a*) the length of the line of command;

(*b*) the span of control of the chief executive;

(*c*) the percentage of total turnover paid to members of staff;

(*d*) the ratios of managers to total personnel, of clerical and administrative staff to manual workers and of graduate to non-graduate supervision in production departments.

Her research forced management thinking away from the abstract elaboration of principles of administration to a study of the constraints different technologies and their associated control systems impose on organisational structure and management.

15. Robert Merton (1910–   ) and others. Robert Merton, an American, suggested (1957) that the introduction of new technology could affect the nature of social relations between workers.

This confirmed the research findings of Trist and Bamforth (1951), Walker and Guest (1952), and Emery and Trist (1965). The key feature of the studies carried out by these men is that the introduction of new technology can of itself disrupt the psychosocial system to a point where it will not be able to operate effectively. The implication of this is that proper consideration must be given to the effects on the psychosocial system before new technology is introduced. The reason why the publication of *The Times* newspaper was suspended for such a long period (1978–79), for example, was that a satisfactory agreement could not be concluded between staff and management on the introduction of new technology.

16. Tom Burns (1913–). The contributions of British researcher Burns and his collaborator Stalker (1961) have been amongst the most notable in assessing the impact of advances in technology on management systems. They showed that while one management system was appropriate for firms operating in a stable economic and technological environment (the *mechanistic* system), another was necessary for those adapting to a rapidly changing technology (the *organic system*).

(*a*) *Mechanistic.* Mechanistic systems are characterised by rigidly prescribed organisational structure in which there are well-defined tasks and methods, duties and powers attached to each functional role. Information tends to flow vertically along the lines of authority in the organisation and there is little horizontal exchange between individuals of similar status in different departments.

(*b*) *Organic.* Organic systems, on the other hand, have a relatively flexible structure with the emphasis on horizontal forms of communication. Power, influence and status within the organisation is based more on technical know-how than position within the hierarchy.

Burns and Stalker did not propose a model system as did Weber but suggested that a firm should use that which was most appropriate for its particular circumstances.

17. P. R. Lawrence (1922–) and I. W. Lorsch. Lawrence and Lorsch thought of manufacturing organisations as having environments that might be conveniently thought of as being divided into three segments.

(*a*) a market segment;
(*b*) a research and development segment;
(*c*) a technological segment.

They suggested that each of these environments is likely to have different rates of change and each of them is likely to differ also in the length of time that elapses between the making of a decision, or taking of an action and the outcome becoming known to those who are involved in it. Lawrence and Lorsch's study of organisations suggested that, in the face of uncertainty, organisations are likely to be more efficient and effective if their structure differentiates between functions in terms of informality of structure, interpersonal relationships, time scales and goals.

THE SYSTEMS APPROACH

The impact of technological advances and the realisation that the external environment in which a firm operates shapes the needs of its management and organisational structure led to the present "systems" approach which considers organisations as a series of interconnected and interrelated systems.

THE DECISION-MAKING APPROACH

This approach considers management from the point of view of its role in producing and obtaining information for the making of organisational decisions.

18. Herbert A. Simon (1916–). A contemporary American academic with considerable practical experience, Simon began his career in local government. His prime interest was in decision-making which he considered to be the central function of management; he has made a number of contributions to management theory, but the two main ones are as follows.

(a) *Administrative man and "satisficing".* Arguing against the classical economists' doctrine of *rational economic man*, who was held to consider each option in any given situation and to choose that course of action that would yield the optimum (most profitable) outcome, he proposed instead *administrative man*, who attempts to *satisfice* (find the most satisfactory outcome) rather than optimise. He argues that decision situations are in practice so complex that it is not possible within the limits of human rationality to identify all the possible outcomes of exercising choice amongst options in a given situation. He suggests that executives should instead attempt to simplify and "satisfice". "Satisficing" is defined as pre-determining a set of criteria against which to evaluate a decision alternative, specifying acceptable limits against each criterion and selecting that option which satisfies the most criteria—bearing in mind any which are critical.

(*b*) *Computer-aided decision-making*. Simon's second contribution is closely linked to his first. He believed that with the advent of high speed electronic computers much of the work of routine decision-making could be undertaken by them—*programmable* decisions. Such decision-making was to rely on *heuristics* (the problem-solving procedure that involves conceiving a hypothetical answer to a problem at the outset of an inquiry in order to give guidance and direction to it).

The first edition of his book *The New Science of Decision Making* (1960) was published at about the time that the large-scale installation of business computers was taking place. His foresight has proved correct for much of today's routine decision-making, such as the re-ordering of stock and the pricing of goods, has been taken over by computers.

19. Richard Cyert (1921–) and James March (1928–). Cyert and March, contemporary American contributors, developed decision-making theory alongside Herbert Simon at Carnegie Mellon University in the USA; their best-known book is the *Behavioural Theory of the Firm* (1964). Their theory links that of classical economics to that of organisations in order to explain how business decisions come about, taking as the basis of their model a large, multi-product organisation operating under conditions of imperfect competition. They studied price, production volume and internal resource allocation decisions.

Cyert and March view a business unit as an information processing and decision-making system. They visualise the organisation as a coalition of individuals all pursuing essentially different goals. Individuals are assigned to different departments where they attempt to solve problems presented to them by top management's need for information on which to base its decisions. Each sub-unit or department considers its own objectives as being of paramount importance to the firm as a whole. They also suggest that most managers probably spend as much time resolving internal conflicts as they do in dealing with contacts outside the firm.

Cyert and March postulate that there are four features of the decision-making process which together explain how a decision is reached:

(*a*) *quasi-resolution of conflict*; an organisation is a coalition of conflicting interests. This results in a lack of consensus of opinion when it comes to decision-making. Organisations will employ a number of devices to circumvent unresolved divergencies of opinion, for example accepting a solution which is satisfactory, though not optimal, from the point of view of all the members of the coalition.

(b) *uncertainty avoidance*; many options considered by an organisation involve uncertainties. Firms will often avoid these and choose instead to solve first those problems that are most pressing.

(c) *problemistic search*; executives have to search to find possible answers to a problem. Such solutions are not necessarily obvious when a problem is first encountered.

(d) *organisational learning*; executives in an organisation will change or adapt its goals as a result of their past experience.

20. C. W. Churchman (1913–), R. L. Ackoff (1919–) and E. C. Arnoff (1922–). The application of quantitative methods to decision-making or problem-solving gave rise to *operations research*, or *management science*, which uses a "scientific" approach to solve management problems.

Operations research grew out of the activities of scientists who, during the Second World War, were asked to find solutions to tactical and logistical military problems. While the methods they developed were applied to non-military business management problems after 1945, Churchman, Ackoff and Arnoff (1957) were among the first contemporary writers to indicate the management applications of OR. The "scientific approach" involves:

(a) formulating the problem;

(b) constructing a mathematical model to represent the system under study;

(c) deriving a solution from the model;

(d) testing the model and the solution derived from it;

(e) establishing controls over the situation; and

(f) putting the solution to work.

THE TOTAL SYSTEMS APPROACH

21. Introduction. An organisation can be regarded as comprising a number of systems and sub-systems (*see* Fig. 2).

(a) *The operating sub-system.* At the core of the organisation is the operating sub-system which is concerned with accomplishing stated objectives effectively and efficiently. It "gets things done" such as producing goods and services, etc;

(*b*) *The co-ordinative sub-system.* This surrounds the operating sub-system and is concerned with translating objectives into operational plans and procedures and interpreting the output of the operating sub-system;

(*c*) *The strategic sub-system.* This relates the activities of the organisation to its environment.

The total systems approach views management's functions as follows:

(*a*) *external*; the role of management is basically to deal with uncertainties and above all to enable the organisation to maintain

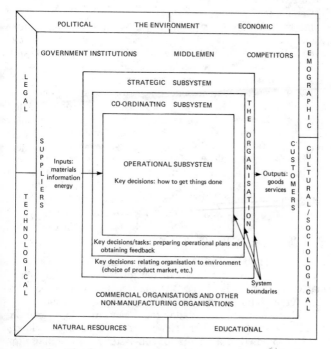

FIG. 2   *The firm and its environment: a systems viewpoint.*

harmony with its environment by successfully adapting to changing circumstances;

(*b*) *internal*; an organisation is seen in terms of a number of systems and sub-systems; it is management's role to oversee these by spanning and linking them, thus maintaining the internal stability of the organisation.

Figure 2 depicts the managerial system within the overall context of the firm and its environment. In overseeing the boundaries between sub-systems, management must relate one sub-system to the next. However, an interaction space is shown between the strategic sub-system and the influence of the environment. This is because a firm cannot interact directly with its various environments, technological, cultural, etc. but only with other organisations or groups which represent those environments or are themselves more directly influenced by them.

Demographic, cultural or sociological factors, for example, may influence new customers or employees with whom or through whom management has to deal. Each new generation has a somewhat different set of values and attitudes from its predecessor. These factors influence its demand for products and services and its expectations of employment, for example.

The influence of environmental factors is strongest at the strategic boundary of the organisation with its environment interaction space. However, their influence can permeate to reach the co-ordinative and operational sub-systems; a change in the availability of natural resources such as the discovery of natural gas, for example, can radically affect manufacturing processes (part of the operational sub-system) and create new problems for management to solve at that level. Again, the introduction of computers (a change in the technological environment) can, for example, reduce the dependence of the co-ordinative sub-system on clerks for the administration and planning of control systems, creating new problems for management.

22. F. E. Kast and J. E. Rosenzweig. Kast and Rosenzweig (1974) are contemporary proponents of the total systems approach to management. They hold that "the management system spans the entire organisation by directing the technology, organising people and other resources, and relating the organisation to its environment". The organisation is viewed as an open sociotechnical system composed of a number of sub-systems. The organisation receives:

(*a*) inputs of energy, information and materials from its environment;

(*b*) these inputs are transformed by it into

(*c*) outputs which are returned to its environment.

The organisation is not viewed simply as a social or technical system but as a structuring and integration of human activities around various technologies. These technologies influence the nature of the inputs received by the organisation, the transformation processes, and the systems' output. In addition, the social system determines the effectiveness and the efficiency of the utilisation of that technology.

Kast and Rosenzweig hold that the internal organisation comprises several major sub-systems.

(*a*) the *goals and values* sub-system;

(*b*) the *technical* sub-system: the knowledge required for task performance;

(*c*) the *structural* sub-system: the manner in which the tasks are divided and co-ordinated;

(*d*) the *psychosocial* sub-system: the manner in which groups and individuals interact and collaborate; and

(*e*) the *managerial* sub-system.

STRATEGIC MANAGEMENT

Emphasis has shifted away from the operational function of management to its strategic function, i.e. away from how best to perform a job towards the setting of goals and deciding what an organisation ought to be doing.

23. Igor Ansoff.

(*a*) *Introduction.* In order to obtain a better insight into how firms adapt to rapidly changing environmental influences, interest in recent years has moved to the construction of a behavioural theory of *strategic management*. Ansoff's (1979) far-reaching theory is one such in which he seeks the answers to five basic questions.

(*i*) What are the patterns of organisational behaviour in a turbulent environment?

(*ii*) What determines the differences in those behaviour patterns?

(*iii*) What factors contribute to success and failure?

(*iv*) What determines the choice of a particular mode of behaviour?

(*v*) What is the process by which organisations move from one mode to another?

(*b*) *Strategic thrust.* Ansoff's view is that firms which perform satisfactorily are better able to cope with environmental turbulence than those which do not. Satisfactory performance is seen to be the result of adopting the most appropriate form of "strategic thrust" (*see* IV) for a given circumstance, at the same time having an organisation competent to administer that thrust. A strategic thrust can be:

(*i*) entrepreneurial; or
(*ii*) marketing.

Thrust strategies may range from having fixed product markets and simply serving those markets at one extreme, to opening new markets, pioneering new products and marketing concepts and creating new technologies at the other.

(*c*) *Power structure and leadership.* Ansoff points out that the type of power structure within an organisation and the resulting form of strategic leadership can have considerable consequences both for the choice of strategic thrust and for the competency of the organisation to carry out its chosen thrust strategy. Just as Cyert and March (1963) showed how operational decisions can result from a quasi-resolution of conflict, reflecting the fact that an organisation is a coalition of conflicting interests, Ansoff shows that decisions relating to choice of strategic thrust can be affected in the same way.

The most "successful" firms are those which adopt a strategic thrust moderately ahead of its industry; he noted that "the firms which 'stick their necks out' by making premature innovations perform poorly, so do those that lag behind the majority".

(*d*) *Implications.* His theory has important implications for management today. Smaller enterprises can often make straight-forward decisions in an efficient way because there will be fewer interpersonal conflicts to resolve. This was the case in the nine-teenth century when ownership and control were often vested in one individual.

The ensuing separation of control from ownership and the devolvement of decision-making to lower echelons of management have created very real problems of conflict of interest. This has been exacerbated by worker participation in key decisions and representation at board level. Government intervention has also forced top management to reconsider its strategic policies from time to time.

CONCLUSION

The subject of management thinking is a jungle of ideas, theories and philosophies through which the student must find his or her way; while it is possible to categorise earlier writers as "classical", "behavioural" or "systems theorist", it is difficult to do so with the more recent researchers. However, the aim has been to introduce the student to the various kinds of management thinking and to the contributions of the most important writers.

PROGRESS TEST 2

1. Differentiate between the "classical school", the "behavioural school" and the "systems school" in terms of their respective approaches to the study of management. **(1)**

2. What contribution did Henri Fayol make to the understanding of management functions? **(2)**

3. Why do you think that Frederick Taylor has been called "the Father of Scientific Management"? **(3)**

4. How valuable were Mary Parker Follett's contributions to management theory? **(5)**

5. How important were the Hawthorne studies in bringing a new dimension of understanding to managerial problems? **(8) (9)**

6. What contribution did Chester Barnard make to management theory? **(10)**

7. What do you understand by the systems approach to management? **(18–22)**

8. What is meant by "strategic management"? **(23)**

CHAPTER III

The Environment

INTRODUCTION

In this chapter the nature of the external environment of a business organisation and how it can influence management behaviour is outlined. Management operates, not in a vacuum, but within a framework of economic, legal, political, socio-cultural and technological activities.

TYPES OF ENVIRONMENT

1. The proximate environment. A business organisation can be regarded as a resources conversion system. Inputs to the system take the form of finance, labour, materials, etc. and outputs, goods and services. The proximate environment is concerned with how and where to obtain the various resources which are employed in conversion processes and whence and how the system's output should be distributed. These resources are:

(a) sources of labour supply;
(b) sources of finance;
(c) sources of materials;
(d) customers and middlemen.

In addition, there are a number of proximate bodies which have a direct influence on management activities:

(a) trade unions;
(b) competitors;
(c) local communities.

2. The general environment. We can consider the general environment of a business organisation under five headings, all of which are constraints on management activities:

(a) economic;
(b) legal;
(c) political;
(d) socio-cultural;
(e) technological.

THE PROXIMATE ENVIRONMENT

3. Sources of labour supply. More detail is given to the sources of labour supply in XIII, but it should be stated here that the availability of labour is clearly a constraint on the efficient running of an organisation. Skilled labour (i.e. managers, supervisors, skilled tradesmen, technicians, etc.) can be obtained from a variety of sources. These include:

(*a*) retraining existing employees;

(*b*) students who have completed courses at colleges and universities;

(*c*) competitors;

(*d*) other organisations which employ individuals with the right kind of skills;

(*e*) the unemployed.

Suitable skilled labour may be in short supply in different regions or parts of the world. In certain areas of the UK there is a large supply of labour with specific skills: in London, for example, there are many people with secretarial and clerical skills. In other locations, however, there may be a shortage of people with the skills a company may require: the developing countries have a chronic shortage of most types of skilled labour.

Employment statistics in the UK show that London and the South East are areas of relatively low unemployment while the West of Scotland and the North East of England have much higher figures. Central government has recognised the need to provide assistance for areas of high unemployment and various Acts of Parliament have been passed which enable financial inducements to be made to persuade firms to move to these areas. These inducements include:

(*a*) the provision of regional development grants for purchasing plant and equipment;

(*b*) depreciation allowances;

(*c*) loans at favourable rates; and

(*d*) a weekly subsidy paid towards the salary of every male employee of the firm.

In addition, the Industry Act 1972 made provision for selective financial assistance for projects likely to provide employment in such areas.

In the UK, central government has also actively encouraged

workers to relocate, and even, through its Skillcentres, to retrain.
It has also encouraged industrial training and education throughout the country. Both Tyne and Wear and the West of Scotland
regions, for example, have created educational facilities which aim
to provide a pool of labour equipped with the necessary skills.

4. Sources of finance. While sources of finance are covered in detail
in a later chapter (*see* V) the supply of finance can be a considerable
restraint on management activities. Finance affects a firm directly
and indirectly.

(*a*) *Directly.* In the first place, the availability of capital for
investment in plant, machinery and premises affects management
plans for expansion and renewals. This is dependent on government economic policy and on the willingness of individuals to
subscribe share capital. Not only is its availability important, but
also its cost. When the cost of capital is comparatively low, management is able to invest and expand, but when it is high plans for
expansion and renewals may be curtailed.

(*b*) *Indirectly.* Financial constraints may also affect the management of a business enterprise indirectly; for example a manufacturer's customers (wholesalers, retailers, or other firms) may
have difficulty in raising finance to pay for the goods or services
they require. This will have an adverse effect on the demand for
the manufacturer's output and on the firm's marketing effort.
Finally, the manufacturer's profitability will be adversely
affected if the ultimate consumer has insufficient cash to buy his
goods.

5. Sources of materials. Because they were originally sited close
to the sources of raw materials they needed, many industries, such
as steel, have now become concentrated in specific regions. While
in many cases the sources of raw materials around which they
were grouped are now depleted, other factors have since persuaded
firms to stay and to bring in their raw materials from elsewhere.
Given adequate transportation systems and economic transportation costs, the proximity of materials need not of itself determine
the location of an industry or firm.

There are, however, other problems associated with the availability of material supplies. If it were possible for a firm to perform
all the tasks necessary for it to maintain its output, material supplies
would not be problematical. However, this is not usually feasible
and, except in the case of a cottage industry such as the knitting

industry of the Hebrides, for instance, such a situation is rare. If we take as an example a firm manufacturing toy cars, each retailing for about £2, three different materials will be used:

(a) metal alloy;
(b) plastics;
(c) paint.

This firm is not involved with the production of any of these three materials and in addition has to buy moulds with which to produce its cars. The firm's ability to produce must depend, therefore, on the availability of all these materials; if any of them is unavailable, it may not be able to continue to manufacture and eventually may go out of business.

Moreover, a dramatic escalation in the price of any of these materials may force management to raise the price of its product. Plastic, for example is a by-product of the petroleum-refining industry, itself dependent on the oil-extracting industries of various parts of the world. A restriction in the availability of crude oil will eventually cause a rise in its price, with a resultant rise in the price of plastics. This may cause management to consider alternative materials for the manufacture of its model cars.

A further problem is that in some industries there may be only a few or even one supplier of certain materials. It frequently happens in the UK motor industry, for example, that car assembly is halted by the manufacturer's inability to obtain particular components from an outside supplier. Management may seek to alleviate this by having more than one source of supply, but this may result in a higher price being paid for supplies: smaller quantities ordered will mean less favourable terms.

6. Customers and middlemen. Two marketing features of the last twenty-five years have been the changes in retailing and distribution channels and the ever-present changes in consumer requirements. The business philosophy of marketing is to supply to the market goods or services which the consumer wants to buy. Management must therefore be constantly aware of changes in consumer demands and must be able to modify its existing products or create new ones to meet them. Any manufacturer that does not will find it difficult to remain in business.

A striking example of customer-orientated marketing is provided by John Bloom's now defunct Rolls Razor company. Operating in the UK in the early 1960s, this small company managed, if only for a short time, to obtain a twenty-five per cent share of the domestic washing machine market in the face of competition from other large and well-established firms. His success was attributed to the fact that he produced a simple machine at a modest price, and marketed it aggressively, which, at that time, the larger firms were not attempting to do.

Unless a manufacturer engages in direct selling and distribution to its markets, it will have to depend on middlemen to carry out these functions. Here, the ultimate responsibility for promoting its products is outside the company's control. It is vital, therefore, that management selects the best possible channels of distribution for its output and market.

7. Trade unions. Skilled workers in British industry are generally represented by a union which reflects their craft rather than the industry in which they work. This has given rise to a multiplicity of unions. Workers in the newspaper industry, for instance, are represented by no less than four print unions, the NGA, NATSOPA, SLADE and SOGAT, as well as by the NUJ and others. An agreement negotiated with one union may not be acceptable to another whose interests may conflict with it. Management's task in dealing with trade unions can therefore be extremely complex.

8. Competitors. A firm's management decisions will be affected by its competitors in the markets in which it operates. There are three types of market:

(a) *Atomistic* markets are where there are many producers and where product differentiation may or may not exist. Product differentiation occurs when consumers regard the products of different firms in the same industry as being imperfect substitutes for one another. This type of market is common in the UK. Examples are the markets for clothing and fresh fruit and vegetables.

(b) *Oligopolistic* markets are where there are few producers, where product differentiation may exist, and where there may be substantial barriers to new firms entering the market. Competition in oligopolistic markets where product differentiation does exist is characteristically cut-throat. Examples are the markets for washing powders, still films and motor vehicles.

(c) *Monopolistic* markets exist where one supplier fulfils all the needs of a particular market. Few firms enjoy a complete monopoly as many governments consider this to be against consumer interest.

Monopolies are only encouraged in the UK for the supply of essential goods or services, where they are State-controlled. Examples are the markets for the postal and telecommunications services, and rail transport.

Market structure influences management behaviour in the following ways:

(a) *Atomistic.* Where market conditions are atomistic, for example, marketing information is often difficult to obtain; it may even be impracticable to assess the size of the market. Marketing decisions are therefore taken under conditions of great uncertainty. On the other hand, because the market is fragmented, there will be a large number of firms, each actively competing with each other, making it relatively easy for a new entrant to obtain a modest share of it.

(b) *Oligopolistic.* Competition under oligopolistic conditions can vary from the severest forms of cut-throat competition to those of tacit collusion between firms. In EEC countries and the USA open collusion in the form of trade cartels is not tolerated, as it is felt to be against the best interests of the consumer.

(c) *Monopolistic.* Monopolies are generally considered to restrict competition to the disadvantage of the ultimate consumer and successive government have legislated to ensure that a proposed merger or acquisition is not against the public interest. Top management must therefore take this into account when planning a step such as this. While monopoly power can lead to increased efficiency through economies of scale, the onus on management is to show that its activities are not against public interest.

Firms contemplating diversification are often faced with the problem of assessing the strength of competitors in the product-markets they intend to enter. The existence of competitors with large resources can be a barrier to entry for a firm of modest means, particularly in an oligopolistic market where marketing or investment costs may be high. Generally, it is easier to compete in an atomistic market; few firms would attempt to challenge Procter & Gamble and Unilever's domination of the soap powder market, though a small firm intending to produce machine tools might feel it could easily achieve a 5 or 6 per cent share of that product market.

9. Local communities. Management also has to consider the needs and requirements of the local communities that surround its factories. In particular, noise and pollution levels require considerable attention. A problem arose when a chemical manufacturer in the north-east of England received complaints from local housewives that its plant was dirtying the washing that they hung out to dry. The firm found that it would have been extremely difficult to control pollution in the short term, but hit on the idea of providing local housewives with a free laundering service instead.

THE GENERAL ENVIRONMENT

10. Economic.

(*a*) *The economic climate*. The economic climate has a considerable influence on management behaviour. When employment levels are high and demand for goods and services is great, management's prime task is to keep pace with it. When the economy is depressed, however, management has to seek alternative markets, reduce costs and streamline the organisation. Alternating booms and slumps were characteristic of the era before the Second World War. These extremely sharp fluctuations caused great hardship in general and severe problems for business management in particular.

(*b*) *Government intervention*. Largely as a result of the work of the economist John Maynard Keynes (1883–1946), governments in the UK in the past thirty years have been able to come to grips with the boom-slump syndrome and have developed an arsenal of weapons with which to control or smooth fluctuations in the economy. For example, consumer spending can be stimulated by reducing taxes whilst in the same way it can be curbed by increasing them.

(*c*) *Indicative planning*. In a mixed capitalist economy such as that of the UK the purpose of government intervention through the exercise of fiscal controls is to provide in the long term a means of achieving economic growth. It is thus designed to sustain the internal long range plans of individual business firms. The marketing plans of a house builder, for example, will assume a certain level of purchasing power in the economy. Government economic policy will generally help to ensure the availability of that purchasing power.

Indicative planning such as this, where government and industry collaborate in co-ordinating their aims and exchange information about their intentions is, in theory, an excellent means of controlling a mixed economy. However, in practice there are, apparently, insuperable difficulties which prevent the efficient operation of such a policy. Government may be prevented from carrying out its chosen policies by a balance of payments crisis, for example, and by the ensuing debts to other countries which may have helped to support its currency. Moreover, whatever the government in office, there will always be some sectors of the economy whose aims will conflict with those of central government and who will attempt to frustrate its aims.

11. Legal. Successive governments have become increasingly concerned not only with the economic but also the legal framework within which a company may operate. The legal infrastructure impinges on a business in several ways. Its purpose is to protect the various *publics* of an enterprise from being wilfully or unwittingly harmed by its actions. Different organisations have different publics but those of the model car manufacturer considered previously would be:

(*a*) customers;
(*b*) middlemen;
(*c*) local communities;
(*d*) employees;
(*e*) competitors.

A firm could harm any of these publics in a variety of ways.

(*a*) *Customers.* It could supply customers with shoddy, unusable, dangerous or unreliable goods.

(*b*) *Middlemen.* It could threaten to withhold supplies to middlemen who do not conform to its marketing requirements, such as the retail price of its products.

(*c*) *Local communities.* It could pollute the environment of the immediate community surrounding its factories, deprive it of amenities or cause unnecessary irritation. There may be pollution of waterways by discharged effluent, excessive noise, unpleasant smells, etc.

(*d*) *Employees.* It could force unreasonable working conditions or terms of employment on its employees.

(*e*) *Competitors.* It could engage in unfair marketing practices to give itself an advantage over its competitors.

There are therefore many different ways in which a firm can act against its publics. The legal infrastructure is designed to prevent this from happening.

Some specific examples of the legal infrastructure created by various Acts of Parliament are as follows.

(*a*) *Wages Council Act 1959*. Under this and the subsequent Employment Protection Act (1975) certain basic conditions of employment are laid down. Industries too small or too scattered to have allowed trade unions have become established. Wages inspectors visit such employers periodically and any found to be failing to implement these minimum standards may be prosecuted.

(*b*) *Resale Prices Act 1964*. This prevents manufacturers from forcing their retail prices on middlemen, unless they can show exceptional reasons for doing so.

(*c*) *Monopolies and Mergers Act 1965*. This enables the Department of Trade to refer to the Monopolies Commission any merger which is considered to strengthen a firm's monopoly position.

(*d*) *Redundancy Payments Act 1965* (as amended by the Employment Protection Act 1975). This gave employees the right to receive redundancy pay (*see* (*m*)).

(*e*) *Misrepresentation Act 1967*. This established protection for those who enter into contracts in good faith, but subsequently find that a key statement made by the other party to the contract was falsely, but unwittingly, made.

(*f*) *Trade Descriptions Act 1968*. This stipulates that every trade seller must substantiate any claim made on behalf of his goods.

(*g*) *Restrictive Trade Practices Act 1968*. This amended an earlier (1965) Act prohibiting collective agreements concerning prices, conditions of service and processes of manufacture thought to be against the public interest.

(*h*) *Equal Pay Act 1970*. This requires that equal pay should be provided for men and women working for the same employer and doing the same or broadly similar work.

(*i*) *Contracts of Employment Act 1972* (*as amended by the Trade Union and Labour Relations Act 1974*). This requires that all employees should receive details of terms of employment (including rates of pay, holiday entitlement, length of contract, etc.) within thirteen weeks of taking up employment (*see* (*m*)).

(*j*) *Fair Trading Act 1973*. This sets out to impose further control on monopolies and restrictive practices and generally to ensure consumer protection against unscrupulous traders.

(*k*) *Supply of Goods* (*Implied Terms*) *Act 1973*. This guarantees the consumer certain basic rights in any transaction for the purchase of goods.

(*l*) *Health and Safety at Work etc. Act 1974*. This requires employers to comply with certain minimum standards for working conditions.

(*m*) *Employment Protection (Consolidation) Act 1978*. This Act replaces the Redundancy Payments Act 1965, the Contracts of Employment Act 1972, the Trade Union and Labour Relations Act 1974 and the Employment Protection Act 1975, and brings together all their provisions under one piece of legislation.

(*n*) *Race Relations Act 1976*. This, with specific exceptions, makes it illegal to discriminate on grounds of race in matters, among others, relating to employment.

(*o*) *Sex Discrimination Act 1975*. This requires employers not to discriminate on grounds of sex or marital status in respect of recruitment, training and promotion.

(*p*) *The Employment Act 1980*. This made picketing "in contemplation or furtherance of a trade dispute" lawful. This legal protection was not extended to "secondary picketing" however.

It should also be noted that UK businesses are also subject to European Economic Community law. In certain cases, this has meant alteration to British law, particularly company law. Other important EEC legislation affecting British firms relates to customs duties, agriculture, transport, the movement of labour and capital between member countries, and the regulation of the coal, steel and nuclear industries. Another important aspect of EEC law concerns competitive practices; under EEC legislation, collusion between firms leading to price-fixing, restrictions on production, marketing, investment, sources of supply or bargaining rights are prohibited.

12. Political. Central government influences management by imposing financial and legal controls to achieve the overall goals of economic growth and prosperity. However, it can be influenced by various independent political pressure groups.

(*a*) *CBI*. Management itself is able to apply pressure through the CBI (Confederation of British Industry).

(*b*) *TUC*. The trade unions may also apply pressure through the TUC (Trades Union Congress).

(*c*) *Others*. These are two of the most effective, but other groups may also try to forward their aims by pressurising government to legislate. Conservation groups, for example, press for greater control of industrial pollution. If government legislates for this, it may require firms to introduce measures which could increase the cost of production and hence retail prices. Car exhaust antipollution laws in the US, for instance, have increased the price of automobiles. Other consumer groups may demand higher standards of quality, safety and service.

13. Socio-cultural. The socio-cultural environment has social, cultural, demographic and educational characteristics.

(*a*) *Social* characteristics include social structure, family patterns and occupational structure.

(*b*) *Cultural* characteristics include ideologies, beliefs, values and norms.

(*c*) *Demographic* characteristics include the age, sex and geographical structure of the population.

(*d*) *Educational* characteristics include the level of basic literacy and the extent to which higher and further education is provided.

All these characteristics are dynamic and change with time. Socio-cultural characteristics influence the business environment in the following ways. They affect:

(*a*) patterns of consumer expenditure;
(*b*) the size of and skills of the labour force;
(*c*) attitudes towards work and business.

(*a*) *Patterns of consumer expenditure.* These have changed considerably during the course of the present century. Rising living standards have created a demand for "luxury" goods undreamt of fifty years ago. Most homes in the UK now have at least one television set, many of them colour sets. Higher educational standards have created a demand for mini-computers and pocket calculators; cars, once the prerogative of the affluent, are now owned by thousands of families. Moreover, shorter working hours, increased holidays and more disposable income have created a demand for new leisure products and services which, even thirty years ago, did not exist. Changes in consumer demands influence the types of goods and services that manufacturers produce and hence can create new industries and destroy existing ones. The general rise in the educational standards of the population has made it more critical of the goods and services it consumes. Management has to keep pace, therefore, with changes in consumer demand.

(*b*) *The size and skills of the labour force.* Changes in education and training standards have had a considerable impact on the size of the skilled labour force in the UK. Technical and business education developed rapidly during the late 1960s and throughout the 1970s. In 1960, only a handful of courses in commercial subjects at degree level was available; there are today more than a hundred courses in Business Studies alone. Polytechnics did not exist then and the number of students in full-time higher education actively following technologically-based courses was much lower than it is today; part-time education was the accepted way of studying for most business and technological qualifications.

(c) *Attitudes towards work and business.* Rising educational levels have introduced changes in values and in attitudes towards work and authority; individuals now expect to have more say in what they do at work and are no longer likely to accept authority unquestioningly. These changes are particularly important for management since they may create problems of motivation and control. The phenomenon of the middle-management drop-out, who is willing to accept a lower level of salary and responsibility in preference to the struggle for higher position, has become common-place. Additionally, one of the after-effects of the "permissive society" has been that a greater emphasis is placed on individuality, "doing your own thing", than on conforming to authority.

14. Technological. Technological developments influence organisations in a number of ways.

(a) *Output and processes.* They enable the development of new products to take place and therefore the development of new or different skills and production processes. This may, in turn, impel management to acquire new marketing skills. This means that firms which operate in industries characterised by a high degree of technological innovation, such as the computer industry, will often experience organisational difficulties, and a flexible or organic management structure will be required to cope with the problems created by innovation.

(b) *Staffing levels.* The influence of technology is not necessarily confined to the organisation's output or its production processes. The advent of high-speed electronic computers, for instance, has enabled management to handle, store and analyse much more easily the data on which it bases its decisions. This has had a striking impact on the staffing levels needed for routine clerical work; in some cases management has been able to replace whole departments of clerks with a single machine. At the same time, however, new jobs will be created for other personnel such as computer operators, etc.

(*c*) *Communications.* Improved technology has also revolution-ised communications. Its effect is felt in two different ways:

(*i*) *transportation*—innovations such as supersonic passenger aircraft and the high speed train have made it possible for manage-ment to considerably reduce time spent on travelling;

(*ii*) *telecommunications*—innovations such as the telex system and videophones have made efficient personal contact possible even at long distances.

PROGRESS TEST 3

1. Differentiate between the proximate and the general environ-ment. **(1) (2)**

2. What kinds of labour supply problems does management encounter? **(3)**

3. How might management try to insure itself against the problems arising from shortages in the supply of materials? **(5)**

4. What impact do changing consumer wants and needs have upon management? **(6)**

5. Describe the management problem that arises as a result of having to deal with more than one trade union at a time. **(7)**

6. How can market structure affect business behaviour? **(8)**

7. In what ways does management have to meet the needs of the local community? **(9)**

8. In what ways can central government regulate the economy? **(10)**

9. What kinds of laws have been enacted which have a bearing on the business activities of an organisation? **(11)**

10. What are political pressure groups? What relevance do they have to management? **(12)**

11. Suggest ways in which the socio-cultural environment has changed during the last decade. Examine its implication for management. **(13)**

12. Comment on the way in which technology, and technological change in particular, might affect management. **(14)**

CHAPTER IV

Strategic Management

INTRODUCTION

In this chapter top management's strategic function (*see* II,**23**) is considered together with the nature of business objectives. Profit-making and non-profit-making organisations are compared since they differ in their aims and objectives and the methods by which they seek to achieve these.

THE AIMS AND OBJECTIVES OF ORGANISATIONS

1. An organisation. This can be considered as a group of individuals with a common purpose. These individuals, in both profit and non-profit-making organisations, pursue a number of objectives independently but each has a common objective, survival. Non-profit-making organisations are distinguished from profit-making organisations by the way in which they seek to survive.

(*a*) *Sources of income.*

(*i*) *Profit-making organisations.* A profit-making organisation, such as a woollen manufacturer, obtains its income from its commercial activities. Its survival is dependent, therefore, on the success of its commercial activities. Undertaking these activities entails formulating strategies which will enable the firm to adapt successfully to its constantly changing environment.

(*ii*) *Non-profit-making organisations.* Non-profit-making organisations such as charities, hospitals, educational institutions and most public corporations receive only part of their income from commercial activities and rely instead largely on income from government subsidies and other sources. Schools and colleges for instance rarely engage in commercial activities, almost all their income is derived from public funds; whereas nationalised industries on the other hand, while subsidised from public funds, also undertake commercial activities.

(*b*) *Corporate strategy.* The extent to which an organisation has to undertake commercial activities determines its corporate

51

strategy and its top management's approach to business management.

(*i*) *Profit-making organisations.* The top management team in profit-making organisations is geared to searching for new ways of generating profit to ensure the continued survival of the firm.

(*ii*) *Non-profit-making organisations.* Top management in non-profit-making organisations tends to be much less "strategically" orientated and concentrates instead on ensuring that the organisation functions smoothly and provides the highest level of service for the least cost. This is not to say that non-profit-making organisations are not, or should not, be concerned with strategic thinking, but that it is, in practice, uncommon for them to do so. However, some of the principles of strategic planning are now being applied in non-commercial organisations, as in the case of a university which, finding that certain courses failed to attract adequate student numbers, mounted different courses to attract students in larger numbers.

2. Corporate growth strategy. A business organisation must be able to fulfil certain criteria if its development is to be successful.

(*a*) *Vertical integration.* Early business entrepreneurs such as Alfred Bird & Son (*see* I,**17**) sought to obtain income and profits by producing a particular good or range of goods for an expanding product-market. At its inception, Bird's business was no more than a small chemist's shop in his sole charge, but because of the level of his training and personal aspirations, Bird, assisted by his son, was eventually able to expand the original retail business into one that also undertook manufacturing processes. This form of growth strategy is known as *vertical integration*.

(*b*) *Product development.* Throughout the nineteenth century and following on from this initial strategy, Bird's firm sought to consolidate its position by adding to its product line a series of new products (*product development*) similar to those which it had originally manufactured.

(*c*) *Increased market penetration.* At the same time the firm also vigorously promoted both its existing and new products in order to gain additional sales in the market, developing new marketing methods to achieve *increased market penetration*. This form of growth strategy was fairly common in the nineteenth century as most markets were rapidly expanding in size and because it allowed the owner/entrepreneur to retain control of his business.

(*d*) *Market development.* During the twentieth century other means of growth and expansion have been used by most firms, including Birds. Mergers, diversification and multi-stage programmes of vertical integration have been commonplace. In 1946, for example, Bird's was merged with the General Foods Corporation of America; overnight it became part of a multinational organisation offering a wide range of products to a number of different markets, engaging in both retailing and manufacturing and in a variety of service industries. A growth strategy involving expansion through the medium of new markets such as this is known as *market development*. New markets may be either new geographical markets or new market segments.

(*e*) *Diversification.* Growth via new products and new markets simultaneously is referred to as *diversification*. The alternative growth strategies discussed above are outlined in Fig. 3.

3. Strategic management. The structure of an organisation (particularly its top management) and its growth are closely interrelated, as studies of the development of large British firms in the twentieth century and the impact their method of growth has had on their

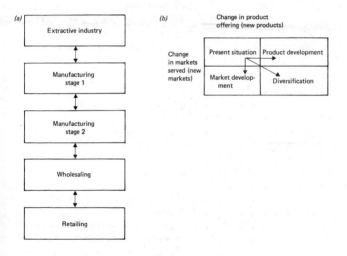

FIG. 3   *Growth strategies: alternative approaches.* (a) *By acquisition; and* (b) *by marketing policy* (*either by offering new products or by developing new markets for existing products*).

organisational structure have shown (Derek Channon, 1973). Strategic management is concerned with managing the growth or survival of an organisation. According to Ansoff (*see* II,**23**) the responsibility of strategic leadership rests with two groups:

(*a*) the shareholders, who define their expectations, and

(*b*) general management, whose role is to fulfil these expectations.

In other words shareholders express their wishes which general management interprets and converts into appropriate strategic action, while the technologists carry out the instructions under the guidance of management. Before the turn of the present century, strategic leadership was in the hands of entrepreneurs, since ownership was not divorced from the control of a business. The entrepreneurs determined the objectives and policies of their organisations and their future planned development. They tended not to diversify the product-making scope of their businesses but aimed instead at maintaining a share of a growing market.

However, the creation of public limited companies, and the consequent divorce of ownership from control in private business, led to the appointment of executive directors and general managers to run businesses. While shareholders are the legal owners of a business, they will not necessarily have the capacity to run it and so will appoint a board of directors to do this for them. A share-

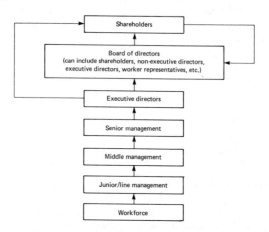

FIG. 4 *Management structure in a medium-sized business.*

holder may be appointed a director, while directors themselves may be executive or non-executive, that is, participating (or not) in the day-to-day running of the company.

Figure 4 illustrates the management structure of a medium-sized business. The board of directors may include:

(*a*) a number of major shareholders;

(*b*) non-executive directors enlisted for their expertise, or other contributions; and

(*c*) executive directors: members of the senior management team.

The chief executive is usually a member of the board of directors which will sometimes include worker representatives.

TOP MANAGEMENT

4. Board functions and leadership. Leadership of the board of directors is in the hands of the chairman. It is essential, therefore, that there should be a good working relationship between the chairman and the managing director or chief executive of the firm. Sometimes, the managing director and the chairman are the same person. The main responsibilities of the board of directors include:

(*a*) giving approval to initiating long range company planning and strategy, company objectives and major policy decisions;

(*b*) ensuring that an adequate supply of capital is available to finance operations;

(*c*) ensuring that the firm complies with all legal requirements;

(*d*) authorising large capital expenditure;

(*e*) engaging and selecting senior executives and approving management promotions;

(*f*) ensuring that there is an effective system of executive development;

(*g*) maintaining an effective organisation structure;

(*h*) providing leadership for the company as a whole;

(*i*) guarding the interests of shareholders and deciding on dividend policy;

(*j*) appraising company performance and exercising control;

(*k*) dealing with all matters relating to potential mergers, take-overs or acquisitions and keeping shareholders informed on such matters; and

(*l*) offering professional advice to executives.

Drucker (1968) maintains that, while the board of directors is legally considered to represent the owners, having all the power to do so, in reality, in most of the large companies its powers are in effect carried out by executive management. This may arise through the emergence of an "inside" board, comprised exclusively of executive management.

Nevertheless there are some real functions which, in Drucker's view, only a board of directors can perform. These are:

(a) approving decisions relating to what the company's business is and should be;

(b) approving company objectives and the means employed to measure the extent to which these have been achieved;

(c) critically appraising company fiscal policies;

(d) giving judgment on matters relating to organisational problems;

(e) ensuring that the strengths of individuals are effectively put to use in the organisation; and

(f) ensuring that its rewards to managers, its management tools and management methods strengthen the organisation and direct it towards its objectives.

Drucker feels that it is important that the board of directors should include individuals whose background is different from that of executive management. This is because "what is needed on a board is not people who agree with management ... but people who are likely to see things differently ... and to ... question the assumptions on which the chief executive team acts".

5. The chief executive. The chief executive of a business firm is usually referred to as the managing director; his task is to implement the policies, plans and decisions of the board of directors and to suggest to the board any revisions that may be necessary from time to time. Peter Drucker considers that the activities that make up the chief executive's job when taken together are too diverse to be performed by a single individual and that all the characteristics that make the ideal chief executive are unlikely to be found in one man. A chief executive needs to be:

(a) a thought man;

(b) a man of action;

(c) a front man; and

(d) a first-rate analyst and synthesiser.

He concludes that the chief executive's function (except perhaps in the smallest business) can only be carried out by a team. It is not unknown therefore to find business organisations managed by "chief executive teams". One of the leading British banks, for example, employs two chief executive teams. In this case:

(a) the Chairman and his deputy are concerned with the setting of basic objectives; whilst

(b) the joint general managers have been concerned with policies, practices and personnel.

The speed with which the one-man chief executive is, in practice, being abandoned in company after company amply supports Drucker's view. While there may still be a chief executive officer in these companies in fact the job is usually discharged by a group, working as a team.

Despite the predictions of Drucker and other like-minded writers other experts are sceptical of the idea of a "plural chief executive", controversy over which continues to exist. Koontz and O'Donnell, for instance, have noted that "small and medium firms will shy away from plural chief executives.... A few firms have tried this form.... Most of these have abandoned the idea".

6. Divisionalisation. As firms grow in size they become more complex and consequently more difficult to manage. Large companies are often broken up into separate divisions, therefore, each of which carries out a specific aspect of the business, with each division having its own board of directors. Alternatively a firm (which becomes the holding company) may come to control a number of subsidiary companies through a series of mergers and acquisitions and these can be compared with divisions (*see also* IX,11).

Since each division or subsidiary operates on the basis of powers delegated to it by its main board of directors, an effective relationship must be established between main and divisional boards. Divisional or subsidiary chairmen are usually ex-officio members of the main board, which enables a two-way communication of ideas and directives to take place. In other instances, the main board may send certain of its members to specific divisions either as chairmen or as liaison directors, under a local chairman.

7. Top management in non-profit-making organisations. Ansoff has noted (1979) that strategic leadership in non-profit-making organisations has been rare:

There is no group, comparable to general management in the firm, which is formally responsible and accountable for strategic leadership. Management of non-profits is expected to stay away from strategic change.... Deans are expected not to meddle in curriculum and research planning nor hospital managers in design of medical care. The job of administrators is to ensure smooth functioning of the organisation and to secure maximum possible subsidies.

Nevertheless the position and outlook is changing rapidly. The anticipated reduction in the number of full-time students in the 1990s, for instance, means that universities, colleges and other educational institutions are already experiencing the need to think in terms of re-adjusting and re-aligning their product-market scope to meet the needs of society.

Libraries, hospitals and nationalised industries face similar environmental problems. Almost entirely supported by public funds, the National Health Service is faced with a dilemma. With its limited resources it must choose between caring for the sick ("patch and repair" operations) and preventative medicine which depends largely on research work. Nationalised industries such as the power corporations, face fuel shortage problems in the near future. All these cases are examples of the need for strategic management.

STRATEGIC OPTIONS

8. Growth and survival strategies. In order to ensure its survival, a business organisation must keep abreast of market developments and keep in touch with the changing demands of its environment as well as with the activities of its competitors; in other words, it has to run in order to stand still. It does not necessarily have to grow in size, however, beyond the point at which it can give satisfaction to its owners, in order to survive. Many small retail establishments founded at the beginning of the present century have survived as successful businesses without recourse to large scale expansion. Their survival is, no doubt, largely attributable to their ability to keep pace with changes in consumer demands.

Philip Kotler in 1972 identified the major growth or survival strategies which an organisation can employ and these are considered in the following sections.

9. Market penetration. This involves increasing the usage of present products by present customers in present markets. This strategy is one which may both lead to growth and ensure survival. In atomistic markets (where there are many buyers and sellers) the activities of the highly ambitious firms are unlikely to have a marked effect on the sales of the less ambitious firms until the point of market saturation is reached. Even then it is likely that the least *efficient* firms will suffer most rather than the less ambitious firms.

Eventually, however, as mergers and takeovers have illustrated in the past, it is likely that the smaller firms will be overwhelmed. In the UK in the 1920s and 1930s for instance, there were many car manufacturing firms: Austin, Morris, Armstrong-Siddeley, Alvis, Rover, Sunbeam, Ford, Vauxhall, Singer, Humber, Riley, Triumph, Bentley, Rolls-Royce, Aston Martin, Daimler, etc. were all in competition with each other. Today only a handful of these major manufacturers are left. Increased market penetration can be achieved by:

(*a*) encouraging existing users to use more, e.g.

   (*i*) offering "packs" instead of single items, or "two for the price of one";

   (*ii*) continuously introducing new models or versions of the product to the market and thereby increasing the rate of product obsolescence; and

   (*iii*) encouraging users to put the product to other uses;

(*b*) attracting the customers of competitors, i.e.

   (*i*) showing that a product is demonstrably different from (and preferably better than) that of its competitors; and

   (*ii*) expending more effort on promotion;

(*c*) attracting new customers for the product, i.e.

   (*i*) devising methods to induce trial;

   (*ii*) varying the price to bring in price-sensitive customers; and

   (*iii*) advertising new uses for the product.

EXAMPLES

(*1*) *A profit-making firm.* A manufacturer and marketer of convenience food products such as instant soups may increase customers' rate of usage by: offering a price reduction if a box of eight packets is bought instead of a customary six packets; introducing new flavours of soup; stressing that instant soups are not just for use at lunch time, but can be used at supper time, or for parties or picnics as well; establishing a strong brand image through TV advertising; establishing sharper brand differentiation through the inclusion of specific ingredients; or offering free-trial satchets at supermarkets. (*2*) *A non-profit-*

making firm. A library may increase customers' usage of its facilities by: permitting users to borrow material (books, records etc.) in larger quantities and for longer periods; continually introducing new material or technology into its archives which make its existing stock redundant or obsolete (e.g. installing microfilms in the reference section) or which replace or add to existing information resources; promoting other uses for library services e.g. as a centre for local news; showing that the services it offers are different from or better than those offered by other information sources; making its services better known to the public through school visits and contacts with local firms; encouraging non-users to visit the library by mounting exhibitions related to specific topics of local interest and making the public aware of the services of the library at such exhibitions; or promoting completely new uses for the library, such as a book exchange service.

10. Market development. This strategy involves selling the present product in new markets. This can be brought about by:

(*a*) geographical expansion, which can be regional, national or international;

(*b*) opening up new market segments i.e. developing specific product versions to appeal to a particular market segment, choosing alternative distribution channels, or advertising through different media.

EXAMPLES

(*1*) *A profit-making firm.* The convenience-food manufacturer may seek expansion by developing markets outside its locality. Birds initially saw its market as being within a few miles' radius of its Birmingham works. The advent of the railway system widened the firm's geographic vista and it quickly began to serve national markets, while its subsequent acquisition by General Foods gave it access to international markets. It may alternatively try to develop products which will satisfy the requirements of specific market segments. Bird recognised that some people were allergic to the eggs from which custard was originally made. His invention of the eggless custard, therefore, was a response to the needs of a specific market segment, one of the first products in what was to become an entirely new industry: instant foods. (*2*) *A non-profit-making firm.* A library may find it difficult to achieve the expansion of its geographic markets since by definition most of them are intended to meet the needs of a local community. But a library may attempt to appeal to other segments of its market. Most libraries carry large stocks of books (as well as journals, sheet music, record albums etc.) which they lend out but they may often be unaware of the identity of the principal users of their services, who might at first sight appear to consist of readers of fiction and children's books; but in addition the libarary may well be able to meet the specific requirements of local students, unaware of the facilities that their local library can offer.

11. Product development. This strategy involves developing new products for present markets. This can involve:

(*a*) new product features;
(*b*) variations in product quality;
(*c*) new models or sizes of existing products.

EXAMPLES

(*1*) *A profit-making firm.* A convenience food manufacturer may seek to: introduce a variety of goods complementary to instant soups e.g. such as instant puddings; offer its products in a new variety of different flavours; "magnify" the nature of its product (e.g. make a stronger flavoured soup); "minify" the nature of its product (e.g. make a blander-flavoured soup); introduce new ingredients into products, thereby effectively creating new products; or combine a number of product ideas e.g. the ice-cream-centred, jam-roll/pudding. (*2*) *A non-profit-making organisation.* A library may introduce a variety of different lending services for its customers in addition to its traditional book-lending service, e.g. record albums, paintings, films, slides, etc. It might also offer a wider variety of its existing products, e.g. different types of fictional or non-fictional books; books with larger print for those who have eyesight difficulties; or a "package" to cover a particular subject, e.g. a books and records package on the development of the piano concerto, for example.

12. Integration. Broadly, integration can be either backward or forward.

(*a*) *Backward integration.* This occurs where a firm takes over the activities of organisations which supply it with goods or services. A large retailing organisation may decide to acquire a manufacturing organisation for instance, or a manufacturer of finished products may decide to acquire another manufacturer further back in the production chain. The same principle can apply equally well to non-profit-making organisations. It is advantageous for an organisation to expand in this way if it has in some way experienced unsatisfactory service in the past from its suppliers or if there is some danger that its supplies will cease.

EXAMPLE

A shoe manufacturer decided to acquire a shoe-making machinery manufacturer which was running into financial difficulties. If this firm had failed the shoe manufacturer would have found it extremely difficult to obtain an alternative supply of new machines.

(b) *Forward integration.* Under this strategy, a manufacturing organisation for instance acquires a wholesaling or large retailing organisation. Similarly, a manufacturer may consider acquiring another manufacturer concerned with producing goods at a later stage in the production chain. Such a strategy, particularly where a retailing organisation is acquired, enables the manufacturing organisation to gain greater control of the marketing of its product to the eventual customer.

EXAMPLE

A paint-manufacturing firm decided that it wanted more control over the marketing of its products to the ultimate consumer; it acquired a large number of retail outlets which enabled it to do this.

13. Horizontal integration, or diversification. Diversification occurs where an organisation seeks to obtain increased sales by developing new products for new markets. It can achieve this either by generating and developing new ideas internally or it may seek to acquire a controlling interest in another firm which serves product-markets it wishes to enter. Many of the large food manufacturing firms in the UK diversified through horizontal integration, taking over firms at the same stage in the production/marketing chain as themselves, since their own internal systems for developing new product markets were weak or absent.

Ansoff suggested in 1965 that firms diversify when their objectives can no longer be met within the product-market scope that they have created for themselves. Diversification may also take place, even if a firm has met its past objectives and has unexploited new products, if cash retained after integration exceeds the amount from expansion in the conventional way. Diversification may offer a company greater profitability.

Horizontal integration may also serve a number of other important purposes. It may enable a firm to extend its:

(*a*) technology or know-how;
(*b*) materials;
(*c*) plant utilisation;
(*d*) marketing resources; and
(*e*) goodwill.

14. Conglomerate growth strategies. Whilst all the above growth methods are concerned with developing products and markets related to an organisation's existing products, market and distribution channels, a conglomerate strategy is one which involves the acquisition of unrelated businesses. Such mergers and acquisitions may simply do no more than reflect the high aspiration level of the organisation concerned; the 3M company, for example, claims that it will enter any field of business that promises to be profitable; there are, however, other advantages in pursuing this type of growth policy.

(*a*) *Financial.* Two firms may combine if one has cash resources and the other product-market opportunities, but neither has both.

(*b*) *Skill advantage.* Two firms may combine if one has skill resources and the other has product-market opportunities, but neither has both.

(*c*) *Stability.* Two firms may combine if their products are complementary to one another (reflecting seasonal variations in demand, for example) so that they can be much more effective together than in competition.

(*d*) *Political.* Mergers and acquisitions in industry may also take place for "political reasons" to remove a rapidly growing competitor or to cut down on the number of firms which can supply to a competitor, for instance. Alternatively, it may simply be to gain greater control over the marketing of goods and services.

15. Impact of strategy on organisational structure. The rapid growth of many large firms over the period 1950–70 following strategies of diversification has laid even greater emphasis on the strategic and policy-making roles of top management. Diversification necessitates the introduction of a multi-divisional structure to allow top management to delegate the detailed management of operations so that it can concentrate on strategic decision-making. As diversification increases, top management becomes increasingly divorced from day-to-day operations and may loose the detailed knowledge necessary to determine divisional product strategies.

The implications of developing multi-divisional structures for a business organisation are, therefore, that corporate and strategic objectives and policies have to become institutionalised to guide the divisional general managers in their decision-making. Executive power in the holding companies is delegated to the general managers and to the boards of directors of subsidiary companies.

16. Courtauld: an example. At the turn of the twentieth century Courtauld, the textile manufacturing firm, was a major producer of mourning crêpe. Its success in the previous century had rested on the great demand for its product, falling silk prices and the entrepreneurial expertise of its founder in the early part of that century.

As the market for mourning crêpe declined in the early 1900s, the firm undertook backward integration and embarked on the manufacture of artificial silk: viscose fibres. The parent firm founded an American subsidiary in 1910 and then between 1920 and 1940 expanded rapidly as the demand for viscose fibres grew. Overseas companies in France and Canada were founded and a joint venture undertaken in Germany and a share in an Italian firm was obtained.

The parent firm encountered difficulties in the early 1940s when it was forced to sell off its American subsidiary, a major contributor to profits. In addition most of its British and European interests suffered war damage. In 1940 a joint venture with Imperial Chemical Industries Ltd was undertaken to finance the development of nylon, marking Courtauld's entry into the synthetic fibres market, although in the early post-war period, the firm also concentrated on building up its non-synthetic fibre interests. It succeeded in achieving a dominant position in the viscose fibres market, eventually acquiring its main rival, British Celanese.

However, the relative success which the firm enjoyed in the early post-war years was mainly attributable to the fact that it was operating in a seller's market; its top management appears, with hindsight, not to have taken sufficient account of future market changes. By the middle of the 1950s it was apparent that synthetic fibres would eventually replace viscose; unfortunately the earlier joint venture with ICI, which had resulted in the creation of a new company, British Nylon Spinners Ltd, was of no use as the new company had since become independent. Neither Courtauld nor ICI, therefore, could gain access to the technology they had helped to develop. ICI was already highly diversified and had even acquired patents to polyester fibres, so its position in the textile market was reasonably good. Courtauld, however, was not, and the firm began to research acrylics fibres to ensure a share of the new market for itself. By 1958 profits were under severe pressure and it was becoming necessary to take action quickly. Top management's strategy was to diversify; as a result the firm began to acquire companies which manufactured paint, packaging, plastics, and foundation garments.

Towards the end of 1961 ICI made a takeover bid for Courtauld. It was unsuccessful, but proved extremely expensive to Courtauld in terms of the cost of persuading their shareholders not to sell out. It has since been argued that had the board of directors made known, through better public relations, the company's true financial strength and its expansion plans a takeover bid might never have been made. Evidence suggests that the older members of the board of directors were keen to sell out to ICI, whereas the younger element, led by Frank Kearton, had other views.

After the takeover bid had been fought off, Kearton took over the running of the company, embarking on a major programme of acquisition, building up considerable interests in the spinning, dyeing and finishing, weaving and knitting, hosiery and garments industries as well as limited interests in wholesaling and retailing. The company recognised that its expertise lay in textiles and that if it had not had time to develop new products, forward integration could be an effective alternative strategy. Nonetheless it continued with its research programme and was soon able to launch its own nylon fibre.

CORPORATE PLANNING

17. Corporate planning teams. Many large diversified companies found that reorganisation following acquisition, mergers and other large scale expansion strategies was complex. Several of those that ran into difficulties turned to management consultants for help and it was on the advice of such consultants that these firms adopted multi-divisional structures. An offshoot of such reorganisation was the development of *corporate planning teams* whose principal job it was to aid top management in its strategic decision-making.

Corporate planning has to take into account every aspect of an organisation's operations. It involves:

(*a*) assessing the impact that future environmental influences will have on the firm and its operations;

(*b*) systematically setting preferably quantified objectives for the organisation as a whole over the period ahead;

(*c*) appraising company strengths and weaknesses;

(*d*) determining suitable strategies which are capable of enabling the organisation to achieve its objectives;

(*e*) preparing detailed plans (both short and long term) which cover every aspect of the business and which, when put together, represent a master plan for total administrative action.

Since planners have to advise top management on strategic and tactical planning, the corporate planning team should be directly responsible to the chief executive; in particular, it should be able to suggest different courses of action and be able to identify all the arguments for or against any particular line of action. Its ability to assess the risks involved is critical and it should be able to offer recommendations to top management, with whom the final responsibility for decisions must rest.

Corporate planning teams are expected to be conversant with modern management science techniques. Progress in the area of mathematical modelling of business problems has meant that some firms are now using corporate models and computer simulation to assist in corporate planning.

18. Small organisations. The size of an organisation must be considered in relation to that of another; it is therefore difficult to draw an exact dividing line between large and small firms. The diversified enterprises mentioned in this chapter for instance are all amongst the 300 largest firms in Britain at the present time.

Smaller organisations basically face the same strategic management problems as larger ones, the essential difference being that more tasks will devolve on to the managing director or chief executive. He is unlikely to be able to consult a corporate planning team, nor will he normally have assistant managing directors to help him. In such cases non-executive directors may be particularly valuable in bringing skills to bear which the organisation might not otherwise be able to utilise.

19. Steps in corporate planning. Corporate planning is concerned with the relationship between an organisation and its environment and is expressed in the *master plan* of the organisation. The master plan comprises four elements.

(*a*) *The economic mission.* This determines the type of business that the organisation is best fitted to perform. In formulating its economic mission, a firm must first consider all its options and the inherent potentials of each. Next it must consider what would be expected of an organisation wishing to pursue successfully each of the options identified and what its own *capability profile* is in this respect. The organisation is then able to predict how well it might fare if it were to pursue one or more of the identified options. As a result of this it can then specify the options it might usefully pursue and thereby decide what its economic mission should be.

(*b*) *The competitive strategy.* This determines the correct product-market and sales approach combination which will enable the economic mission to be accomplished. It will first be necessary to identify suitable product-market opportunities and to assess the strength of competition in these markets. The organisation can then specify what modifications to its capability profile will be required to enable it to exploit successfully its identified product-market opportunities. Finally, the organisation must conduct an assessment of its resources to see which alternatives may be feasible to pursue.

(*c*) *The programme of action.* This determines the most efficient means of implementing a competitive strategy and involves making specific plans in the areas of marketing, production, research and development (R & D), finance and general management and developing an overall plan which can integrate the sub-plans.

(*d*) *Re-appraisal.* This determines the degree of success with which the preceding three phases have been implemented, when put into practice and must find answers to three questions.

(*i*) Is it necessary to search for a new economic mission?

(*ii*) Are the competitive strategies employed working successfully?

(*iii*) Is a new programme of action warranted?

PROGRESS TEST 4

1. Differentiate between a profit-making and a non-profit making organisation. **(1)**

2. What do you understand by "corporate strategy"? **(2)**

3. Define "top management". **(3)**

4. What are the functions of a board of directors? **(4)**

5. Is it possible for the function of the chief executive to be shared by several individuals? Explain. **(5)**

6. What is meant by divisionalisation? **(6)**

7. What is the role of top management in non-profit-making organisations? **(7)**

8. What is meant by "increased market penetration"? **(9)**

9. What is market development? **(10)**

10. Explain how product-development may benefit a non-profit-making organisation. **(11)**

11. Differentiate between "backward" and "forward" integration. **(12, 13)**

12. How may a firm achieve horizontal integration and what would be the purpose of it? **(13)**

13. What are "conglomerate" growth strategies and how may they benefit an individual firm? **(14)**

14. What impact has diversification had on the organisation structure of the larger British firms? **(15)**

15. What are the functions of a corporate planning team? **(17)**

16. Outline the stages in corporate planning **(19)**

CHAPTER V

Managing the Activities of a Business

INTRODUCTION

To achieve the objectives laid down for it by the board of directors and transmitted through the chief executive, a business organisation must carry through a number of programmes and activities. In this chapter these activities are examined. Later chapters cover specific aspects of these activities in greater depth.

1. An overview. Consider the activities of an engineering firm:

(*a*) *marketing*: advising production what to produce and ensuring that goods reach the customers;

(*b*) *production*: producing tangible goods;

(*c*) *purchasing*: which is concerned with buying-in goods directly used in production or which can be used to further production (thereby becoming part of the organisation's capital assets);

(*d*) *research and development*: discovering better ways of producing existing goods and developing new or improved products;

(*e*) *finance*: ensuring that an adequate supply of money is available to allow the organisation to function effectively;

(*f*) *personnel*: ensuring that all jobs in the organisation are suitably staffed so that production, marketing and administrative work can take place.

MARKETING MANAGEMENT

2. The task of marketing management. The Institute of Marketing defines marketing as: "The management process responsible for identifying, anticipating and satisfying customer requirements profitably".

Marketing, brand, product, advertising, distribution, sales, marketing research, public relations, sales promotion, merchandising and new product managers are all involved in the marketing function. These titles will generally reflect the various types of marketing decisions that have to be taken, but a few, such as brand manager and marketing manager will have more general responsibility. Perhaps the simplest way to look at marketing management is from the point of view of the types of decisions that are made. Such decisions involve:

(a) *products*: what kinds of products to produce and in what quantities;

(b) *price*: what prices to charge for them;

(c) *distribution*: what is the best way to distribute them;

(d) *promotion* (including advertising and personal selling): what is the best way to promote them.

3. Product management.

(a) *The product life-cycle*. The products and services a firm supplies to its customers are perhaps the most important aspects. If a firm's product fulfils a demand and is given sufficient marketing effort then that product is likely to be successful; however, the best marketing is unlikely to make a success of a poor product. Sometimes the demand for a firm's output appears to be inexhaustible. Mars Bars, for instance, have been sold in a form which has remained basically unchanged for the last twenty-five years. If Mars Ltd was able to produce a number of similar and equally successful products its product management problems would be few. Unfortunately not all products will retain their profitability over a period of time as successfully as the Mars Bar. All products are therefore said to have a *life cycle* (*see* Fig. 5).

Sales and profits associated with a particular product, product line or even product range, tend to diminish with time. Profitability

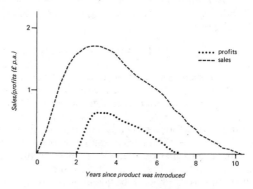

FIG. 5   *The product life-cycle.*

tends to decline in advance of sales, which may be attributable to fiercer competition, increases in selling costs or reductions in price to stimulate demand. Product life cycles vary in length considerably; the life cycle of products such as fashion clothes may only be a matter of months, whilst others such as the petrol engine last much longer.

(b) *Extending the product life-cycle and increasing the product range.* Marketing management must find ways of extending the length of a product's life cycle and at the same time look for new ones with which to replace it. Tractor manufacturers for instance will introduce periodic model modifications to encourage users to trade in their old vehicles for more up-to-date ones. Such modifications may take the form of a larger engine size, improved engine design, or additional power take-off features. Car manufacturers add new features to their existing models and bring out completely new models from time to time. Marketing management's task is to keep in touch with changes in consumer tastes and values and to ensure that these are incorporated into its product offerings.

(c) *Managing the product mix.* Few firms produce and market one product, one product line or even a single product range. Updating and improving product features is often complex and is further complicated by the dynamic nature of the profitability of the *product mix* (i.e. the total number of products produced and marketed). All products, their modifications and variations are at different stages in their respective life cycles and hence will tend to generate different levels both of profits and sales. A buoyant firm seeks to achieve at least stability in terms of its profits and sales and preferably growth as well. Managing the product mix in such a way that these objectives can be attained is not a simple job, especially if a firm produces and markets hundreds of product variations. In most firms the product mix is never in perfect balance; some products are bound to attract a disproportionately large amount of resources and yet contribute substantially less to profits than would seem reasonable. Marketing management has to check for this and recommend appropriate action as necessary. However, it may be difficult to do this if, for instance, there is profit and sales interaction between different products in the mix. The withdrawal of a less profitable product (or increasing its price) may well reduce the sales of a much more profitable product bought by customers who also buy the less profitable products.

4. Pricing.

(a) *Price strategy.*

(i) *Consumer price consciousness.* Price is an important factor which customers take into account when considering whether to buy a product, or when choosing between different brands of the same product. In theory price and sales are inversely related, provided that quality is constant: the lower the price, the greater the sales ought to be. In fact consumers are generally only price conscious over a certain range; if a product's price falls below a certain level they will infer, irrespective of the truth, that it is of less than the minimum acceptable quality and sales will decline as a result.

Again, there are occasions where an increase in price may lead to an increase in sales as when a product is priced too low for a particular group of customers.

(ii) *Price skimming.* Pricing strategy may also vary with the stage a product has reached in its life cycle. When colour televisions were first introduced to the UK market, they were too expensive for most people to buy. This was (partly) a result of management's pricing policy. It was felt that it would be more profitable initially to sell at a higher price in smaller quantities (price skimming) than to sell in large quantities with a much smaller profit margin.

(iii) *Undercutting.* Another pricing strategy for a firm entering a new product market is to sell at a lower price than that charged by its competitors. This can lead to the firm capturing a large share of the market; often its new customers may be retained even if competitors later cut their prices in response. This strategy may have the effect of forcing financially weak competitors, unable to compete, out of that particular market. The new entrant may then be able to increase its control of the product market, eventually raising prices to generate a higher level of profits for itself.

(iv) *Special offers.* Minor variations in price play an important role in marketing tactics. Firms can gain temporary advantages over competitors by instituting price cuts or special discounts for a limited period. The marketing manager has to judge what impact price cuts may have on profitability and must of course be able to anticipate the response of the firm's competitors. It is argued that price manipulation is inferior to employing promotional gimmicks (two for the price of one, free gifts, coupons, etc.) which can be discontinued easily with relatively little unanticipated effects on sales; price *reductions*, however temporary, must inevitably lead to future price *increases* which may incur customer disapproval.

(*b*) *Price-setting.* Although many firms set prices on a *cost plus* basis (at a level sufficient to cover costs and provide for a reasonable level of profitability), pricing, when used for strategic purpose as outlined above, should be carried out on a different basis. In setting prices, marketing management has to take into account not only the production costs, but also the strategic implications, cost and profit interactions between products, channels of distribution through which the product is sold (and middlemen's costs and margins) and the interaction between pricing and promotional strategies.

Whilst they can appear complex, pricing decisions are often in reality, much more simple. A firm contemplating entry to a market for the first time will often base its entry decision on whether a reasonable level of profit can be attained by simply charging the same price as its competitors. It may decide that entry is not worthwhile if the level of profitability is too low.

5. Distribution management.

(*a*) *Distribution management.* Many firms treat distribution as separate from other marketing activities, even to the extent of having a completely separate department with its own manager. Such departments' functions may include:

(*i*) sales order invoicing;
(*ii*) stock control of raw materials/finished goods and packages; and
(*iii*) warehousing and transport.

This is essentially physical distribution management and is solely concerned with the physical process of getting goods to customers.

(*b*) *Channel management.* This is a term which describes *strategic distribution management*; it involves choosing the channels of distribution which will best enable goods to be sold to customers in the quantities required. Innovation in channel strategy can often lead to a product becoming very successful. Tupperware was successfully introduced to the British market direct to the consumer through the medium of neighbourhood house-parties. Other examples of direct distribution methods include John Bloom's legendary cheap washing machine of the early 1960s which was sold by direct mail, and Hoover's vacuum cleaners which were sold on a door-to-door basis. Burco Dean also achieved a competitive advantage in the 1970s when it began to sell tumbledryers through discount warehouses as opposed to the traditional retail outlets used by its competitors. Not only can costs to the consumer be effectively reduced through the selection of efficient channels but also new customers can be attracted. Record albums (and more recently cassette tapes) were traditionally sold through specialist music retailers or the music departments of large department stores; today they can be bought in local supermarkets along with the weekly shopping. Whereas housewives may not previously have had the time or opportunity to visit the traditional outlets, it is now much easier for them to buy records and cassettes.

(*c*) *Distribution costs*. Distribution costs form a high percentage of the total price that the consumer pays for a product—as high as 30 per cent for some products. In consequence, firms seek to reduce distribution costs as much as possible provided that an acceptable level of service to the customer can be maintained. Management has to balance the cost of holding finished goods in stock against its ability to supply customers with goods at short notice. In addition it must weigh the ability to supply customers in the shortest time against the additional costs that this generates. In practice, however, generally unacceptable service results in lost sales.

6. Promotion management.

(*a*) *Types of promotion*. Selling, advertising, sales promotion (holding trade shows and exhibitions as well as using samples or premiums) and merchandising (setting up store displays and other points of sale promotions) are all forms of promotion. Personal selling and advertising are perhaps the two most widely used methods, since they are suitable for most products.

Management has to decide which combination of the various promotional tools (advertising, personal selling, etc.) will be the most effective. This is not easy, as it is difficult to measure accurately the effectiveness of any of the individual elements of promotion. Moreover, the interaction between these elements and their various combinations present almost insoluble problems for management in the rationalisation of expenditure.

(*b*) *Choice of method*. A manufacturing firm wishing to market its goods therefore faces a bewilderingly wide array of promotional options.

It must decide for instance how much effort should be put into personal selling as opposed to advertising; advertising is more cost-effective than personal selling over a large number of communication contacts, but personal selling is much more effective in terms of actually gaining a sale. The choice of method is also dependent on the channels of distribution the manufacturer adopts. The direct-selling method can be extremely expensive and here advertising may be used simply to create awareness of the product and the direct-selling method.

Most manufacturers of consumer goods usually supply their goods to middlemen, who then arrange for them to reach the customer. These middlemen may be large retailers who buy direct from the manufacturers or wholesalers who sell to small retailers. A retailer, however, may not be prepared to stock a particular line of consumer goods unless the manufacturer undertakes to advertise it nationally.

Producers of non-consumer goods tend to rely more on personal selling than on any other form of promotion. Unlike the larger consumer-goods markets where consumer-orientated advertising can be very cost-effective, the non-consumer market is much smaller in terms of numbers of customers. Moreover, in this market the information which must be conveyed to the customer is often highly technical and therefore difficult to communicate through advertising.

(c) *Typical promotion decisions.* The following are examples of the types of promotion decisions that have to be made.

(*i*) What part of the company's marketing communications objective are advertising, personal selling, sales promotion and merchandising individually suited to perform and what level of expenditure is appropriate for the different elements?

(*ii*) What mix of advertising media should be used, with what weight and with what frequency?

(*iii*) How should the entire promotional plan be phased throughout the year to take account of the needs of individual product groups for support?

(*iv*) What messages and forms of presentation should be used?

(*v*) What is the best way of determining how effective promotional efforts have been?

If personal selling is involved, the sales manager has to be concerned with planning salesmen's activities in addition; motivating them; organising the deployment of the sales force; planning sales itineraries; etc.

MARKETING RESEARCH

7. Marketing Management's need for information. Marketing managers require essential information for the purpose of planning and control:

(*a*) *Demand analysis.*

(*i*) Buyer behaviour and characteristics—what do they buy; who buys; where do they buy; why do they buy; how do they buy?

(*ii*) Market characteristics—size; potential segments; etc.

(*b*) *Competition.* Who are the competitors; what are their characteristics, strengths and weaknesses; etc.?

(*c*) *General environment.* Economic/government controls; consumerism; technological; etc.

(*d*) *Internal environment.* Marketing; production; financial and technological skills and resources.

(*e*) *Product.* What product attributes are important; how should it be differentiated from competitive offerings; how important is packaging; etc.?

(*f*) *Distribution.* Who should handle the product; what forms of physical distribution are appropriate; etc.?

(*g*) *Pricing.* What is the customer prepared to pay for the product; how should the product line be priced; etc.?

(*h*) *Promotion.* How much should be spent on promotion; how should it be allocated between the elements of the promotional mix?

(*i*) *Measures of the firm's performance.* Sales by product line; market share; level of customer awareness of the firm's advertising; etc.

In making decisions marketing managers make use of their own experience and judgment and can also make use of information provided by marketing research. The purpose of marketing research is to provide information for decison-making.

8. Marketing research. This is the systematic obtaining of information useful to management in making marketing decisions. It involves:

(*a*) assisting management to analyse, define and structure a problem or decision situation;

(*b*) devising a systematic way of obtaining information which will help management solve a particular problem;

(*c*) undertaking the systematic collection of that information om primary (involving sample surveys or experiments) or condary sources;

(*d*) analysing the data so obtained to provide information which ill help resolve a particular problem;

(*e*) recommending to marketing management a course of action ased on an interpretation of the information obtained.

EXAMPLE

A manufacturer wishes to promote its consumer product in a market segment which hitherto it has not attempted to serve. To do this it must launch an advertising campaign (message and visuals) which will have the greatest possible impact on its intended audience. Preliminary marketing research is first undertaken to identify those aspects of the product most likely to appeal to the audience and, therefore, what the most appropriate advertising theme should be. A number of different advertisements are then created on the basis of the marketing researchers' recommendations and individually tested out on a sample of the target market audience. This part of the research attempts to discover which particular advertisements are most easily recognised, recalled and associated with the product and establishes that the advertisements will be properly understood by the intended audience. If the outcome of marketing research is satisfactory and a suitable advertising campaign agreed, the manufacturer launches his product.

Acquiring information. Information can be obtained in a variety f ways, such as:

(*a*) *From existing records* (secondary data).

    (*i*) Previous research studies and company records.

    (*ii*) Commercial research reports.

    (*iii*) Trade magazine or industry reports.

    (*iv*) Government reports.

(*b*) *Through the collection of new data* (primary data).

    (*i*) Mail questionnaires.

    (*ii*) Telephone questionnaires.

    (*iii*) Personal interviews.

    (*iv*) Observation.

    (*v*) Experimentation.

    (*vi*) Simulation.

It is preferable to make use of all existing records before contemplating the collection of new data. Often the types of data already available may not be suitable for management's purposes. They may be out of date or they may give the wrong type of information. Before deciding to embark on the collection of new data one has to consider the costs and benefits of doing so. Additional information may reduce the uncertainty surrounding a decision but one has to be sure that the benefit it provides is worth the cost of collecting it in the first instance.

Choice of data collection method depends upon a number of factors—and the principal ones are cost of data acquisition and accuracy of the data provided.

10. Collecting primary data.

(a) *Surveys.* A survey may be conducted in person, over the telephone or by post. In nearly all instances a survey requires the construction of a questionnaire which is either completed by the interviewer or by the respondent. By and large surveys involve asking respondents direct questions. However, provided that the interviewer supervises the completion of the questionnaire, projective techniques (word association tests etc.) and attitude scales may be included. Surveys can be a fairly inexpensive way of generating a large number of responses.

(b) *Retail audits.* Marketing research consultants such as A. C. Nielsen Ltd specialise in undertaking retail audits. Essentially this involves the regular measurement of retail trading activity in a sample of retail outlets. A representative sample of outlets is selected and visits are made at regular intervals to inspect current stock levels in selected product categories and to examine deliveries of goods to the outlet and inter-branch transfers. This enables sales per outlet to be calculated.

(c) *Consumer panels.* These are representative groups of consumers which agree to provide data on a continuous basis about a particular product or service. Every week the individual or household concerned completes a diary indicating purchases and returns it to the reseach agency. Data collected in this way can be used to measure brand loyalty and brand switching behaviour. Periodically, panels are changed to overcome problems of bias which may result from continually completing the diary. Attwoods Ltd and Audits of Great Britain Ltd are amongst the foremost providers of the service in the UK.

(d) *Experimentation.* The most common form of experimentation in marketing research is the "split" or "matched" sample.

EXAMPLE

A retail audit of sales over a period of four weeks is conducted in a supermarket in one part of a town. No in-store promotions are offered on brand X in this particular store during the four weeks under consideration. At the same time a retail audit is also conducted at a similar store in the town where brand X is sold. The two stores are virtually identical in every way and the amount of shelf space given over to the product is identical. In the case of the second store, however, special in-store promotions are employed during the whole of the four week period. In the case of both stores competitive promotional activities are about the same level. The purpose of the experiment is to determine the effectiveness of the promotional expenditure of brand X. By holding all the other possible influences constant, the difference in sales between the two stores over the period in question is attributable to the promotional effort in the one store.

The above is a very simple marketing experiment involving only one variable. Certain types of experimental design can allow for more than one factor to be tested at the same time.

PRODUCTION MANAGEMENT

11. Types of production process. There are three basic types of production process:

(a) *Job production* is where products are produced to specific orders and are of the "one off" variety. Examples of this are: processes involving the construction of a passenger or cargo ship; the assembly of a large electrical transformer; or the building of a block of offices or factory premises.

(b) *Batch production* is where the demand for a product is substantial (more than a "one off") but not sufficiently large to warrant large-scale continuous flow production. Examples are the production of drugs, books and car batteries.

(c) *Flow-line or mass production* is where the demand for a product is such that a continuous flow of production is the most economical way of producing the goods. The many manufacturing processes falling into this category include motor vehicle manufacture and assembly, vegetable canning and record player manufacture.

The nature of the product and the quantity and frequency of its production therefore dictate the production process. The advantages of large-scale continuous flow production are that it greatly reduces the costs associated with setting up and taking down a production line, and that it allows automation of part or all of the production process with added cost savings.

Automation has a number of advantages.

(*i*) Higher output can be achieved by running machines continuously over two or three shifts per day.

(*ii*) Separate tools or jigs are not required.

(*iii*) Setting up time for job is shorter.

(*iv*) It is easier to achieve consistent quality and therefore to minimise wastage.

(*v*) There is less need for quality control inspections.

(*vi*) Manpower levels are reduced as, therefore, will be labour relations problems such as strikes.

(*vii*) Workers are released from the tedium of performing boring and repetitive tasks.

The biggest drawback to automation is the high cost of the initial capital investment. It is imperative to ensure that plant and machinery are fully utilised in order to earn a fair return on the investment.

12. Simplification and standardisation. A manufacturing business's production system aims at producing a quality product with the minimum of cost. The costs of producing both consumer and non-consumer products can be considerably reduced by standardising and simplifying the component parts of the final product. Simplification reduces the variety of components and standardisation improves their interchangeability.

EXAMPLES

(*1*) *Standardisation*. Standardisation of components in the motor car industry has led to the establishment of "unipart" spares. Customers benefit in two ways: firstly through lower prices, reflecting savings in cost; secondly, through better availability of spares. Standardisation can also have considerable advantages for a firm which buys its components from outside suppliers; it will not have to depend upon a single supplier since alternative sources can be used. (*2*) *Simplification*. The traditional motor car engine has overhead valves operated by pushrods resting on the camshaft. The "overhead camshaft" engine (where the camshaft is placed on top of the valves) eliminated the need for pushrods.

While the management of production processes, then, primarily involves choosing the most appropriate production process for the product and its market, it also involves accomplishing cost savings through product standardisation and simplification.

13. Factory location and layout. Management is seldom able to choose an ideal site for its factory, but it does, however, have control over factory layout.

(*a*) *Factory location.* Management has to choose between available sites, taking into account:

(*i*) the purchase or rental price of the premises (including local rates);

(*ii*) whether the government offers financial inducements to firms to set up a factory in a given area (development areas);

(*iii*) whether suitable labour can be obtained in the vicinity of a proposed site or, alternatively, whether suitable accommodation is available for employees of the company if a change in factory siting is under consideration;

(*iv*) the relative cost of local labour;

(*v*) ease of access to the site and the availability of local commercial services; and

(*vi*) the possibility of extending the premises in the future.

(*b*) *Factory layout.* Management is concerned with efficiently converting possibly scarce resources into marketable products. This can be greatly assisted by good factory layout. Factors to take into account include:

(*i*) making the best use of available space;

(*ii*) keeping power costs to a minimum;

(*iii*) eliminating the unnecessary movement of materials during the production process;

(*iv*) planning the layout of machines and the flow of materials in such a way that production is made easier and speedier.

14. Production planning and control.

(*a*) *Planning.* In order to co-ordinate labour and machines in the most cost-effective way, production planning and control are necessary. Here initial production targets are set which are subsequently related to performance. This task is complex, involving the co-ordination of many activities. Management has to schedule the sequence of production operations for the firm's various products and compose a corresponding set of time schedules for the completion of each operation. Also work has to be allocated to specific groups to which machines and materials of the right type and quantity must be made available.

(b) *Control.* Management cannot assume that it will be possible always for its production plans to be followed to the letter; production may be held up if materials are not delivered in time or, if delivered, are allowed to lie unattended. Machine breakdowns or industrial action may interrupt production while staff may be unavoidably absent from work during key production phases. Provided that management is aware of the problems and knows the cause of a production hold-up it can take remedial action.

To facilitate production control, progress chasers are employed to ensure the various stages of production run to time. Management can also employ a number of other control aids including flow charts showing the planned sequence of operations and Gantt charts showing how actual is related to target performance.

15. Quality control. At all stages in the production process a quality control system should ensure that materials, partly finished and finished goods are of an acceptable standard. Quality control is also known as "inspection". Materials are inspected when they arrive at the factory and at the many stages through which they pass before leaving the factory as finished goods. Since it would be impossible to check all materials and items a system of statistical sampling is used.

Quality control ensures that:

(a) consistent standards are maintained;

(b) sources of faulty materials and products are identified;

(c) wastage costs can be obtained.

16. Plant maintenance. Production management also has to be concerned with maintaining its plant and equipment which must be serviced regularly to avoid disruptive breakdowns; this may involve shutting down part of the plant for short periods. Careful scheduling of maintenance work is required to keep loss of production capacity to a minimum.

PURCHASING

17. Purchasing. The purchasing department is responsible for obtaining the materials and components which enable the firm to carry out its routine manufacturing operations, and for buying office furnishings and fittings and any other capital equipment. The buyer's role varies considerably from company to company. In some organisations purchasing officers merely place orders on behalf of other departments but, in others, the purchasing officer actively advises other departments in the firm on matters relating to purchasing decisions. Much depends on the company's policy and the skills and competence of the individual purchasing officer.

(*a*) *The role of the purchasing department.* The purchasing department may be required to carry out any of the following functions:

(*i*) ensuring that goods purchased are in the right quantities and of the right quality;

(*ii*) ensuring that orders are placed in sufficient time to ensure that production and other operations are not delayed. This often involves setting a minimum level for stocks of raw materials and component parts and replenishing whenever that level is reached. Close contact with the stock control sections is therefore essential for the buyer.

(*iii*) ensuring that purchases are made at the most favourable terms, often an onerous task. Prices for certain raw materials—particularly metals—fluctuate considerably, making it difficult for the best time to buy to be estimated. Further, buying supplies considerably in advance of production needs will tie up capital and stock for uneconomic periods of time. It may be expensive to leave capital lying idle in this way and its cost has to be compared with any price advantage gained by buying early.

Buying is therefore a specialist activity calling for considerable commercial acumen as well as a wide knowledge of industries and materials. It is concerned with value for money as well as the technical suitability of materials bought and their obtainability when required.

(*iv*) Ensuring that other members of the organisation are kept informed of new developments. This is because the purchasing department is usually in contact with a wide range of suppliers and their industries and will often be in the best position within the firm to know of alternative materials, products and production methods.

(*b*) *Factors influencing suppliers purchase of supplies.* In making purchasing decisions the industrial buyer is influenced by many factors.

(*i*) *Materials and equipment.* In the case of buying heavy machinery, its economy of operation, productivity, durability and labour or time saving features must be considered. The purchaser of materials must ensure their quality, uniformity, purity and value for money.

(*ii*) *The supplier.* Important features will be: the reliability and accessibility of the supplier; price and the ability to offer a reliable delivery and after sales service; and the ability to give a continuous supply service under all conditions. Most, if not all of the above points apply also to other sorts of supplies.

RESEARCH AND DEVELOPMENT

18. Research and development.

(a) *Function and role.* Research and development (R & D) is concerned with the technical development of products, materials, components, production processes and production equipment. Its object is to find more economical ways of manufacturing existing products (and modifying existing ones) so that cost-savings can be effected, and to develop entirely new ones to meet change in consumer demand. The Japanese Seiko watch manufacturing company for instance pioneered the mass production of highly accurate clockwork watches and later did exactly the same thing for LCD (liquid crystal display) electrically powered watches. The R & D departments of most of the leading watch manufacturers are now concentrating on developing an LCD watch which can be powered by solar energy.

With the currently fast pace of technological innovation, R & D departments are rapidly becoming a key element in the determination of the relative success or failure of an organisation in coping with its environment. One major problem is the lack of communication that R & D departments may frequently have with marketing management and top management. This may be due partly to the traditional view role that sees the R & D department as remote "boffins". R & D may come under criticism for projects which seem to have no commercial value or for using up resources on projects which, when they do materialise, are unable to repay their investment costs. Perhaps one of the best solutions to this problem is to make the R & D department directly responsible to the chief executive.

(b) *Work.* R & D is a specialist activity and should be staffed by suitably qualified individuals. All development work usually involves three stages.

(i) *Research.* This can be either *fundamental*, seeking knowledge for its own sake with little thought for its practical application, or *applied*, finding ways of using this knowledge for practical purposes.

(*ii*) *Experimental and development work*. Here, research find-ings are developed and proved on a practical scale on pilot plants or prototypes.

(*iii*) *Implementation*. This involves the initiation of full scale production of the proven prototype on a commercial scale.

Small firms may lack the resources to carry out their own fundamental research but instead may solicit the help of a university or college. Such an association can often be extremely beneficial to both participants.

Where a firm's development engineers or chemists are working on new product ideas it is essential that they maintain close contact with the firm's marketing staff to ensure that the ideas they research and develop have real commercial viability.

FINANCIAL MANAGEMENT

19. Establishing and financing a business. A business may take the form of (*a*) a sole trader, (*b*) a partnership or (*c*) a limited company (*see* I,2). The sources of finance available for setting up a business depend upon the form of business organisation to be adopted.

(*a*) *Sole trader*. Most if not all of the sole trader's finance has to be provided by the owner of the business. The amount of finance required is relatively small but loans may be difficult to obtain because of the risks associated with lending to one person operating a small business. Unless such a business is well established a bank is unlikely to lend money. Every year many owners of small businesses are made bankrupt although the amount of money owing is often quite small.

(*b*) *Partnership*. A partnership's initial capital is provided by the partners. Generally, the restrictions on the availability of loans from banks that apply to sole traders also apply to partnerships. However, if new partners admitted to the firm are required to put up capital as a condition of partnership the amount of capital available is expanded. Partners may take an active part in the running of the business or they may be "sleeping" or "dormant", where they do not, having a purely financial interest in it. Partners are jointly and severally liable for debts of the Partnership.

(*c*) *Limited company*.

(*i*) Private limited company. This type of company can raise capital in the form of "shares" and "loans". Shares entitle the subscriber to part-ownership of the business dependent on the number of shares held and also receive a share of the profits of the business. Loans on the other hand confer no such rights on the lender, who instead only receives interest on the sum loaned.

(*ii*) *Public limited companies.* These are companies which may invite the public to subscribe capital. Such companies, provided that they are sufficiently buoyant and that the economic climate of the country is favourable, find it relatively easy to obtain capital for expansion in this way. A public company will often have begun as a private limited company so that potential investors can estimate the soundness of their investment on the basis of the company's previous performance. Where a public company is founded "from scratch" potential investors must exercise care. Firms in such a position often enlist the names of well-known figures in the business world as directors to bring credibility to the venture. Loans can also be obtained from banks and other financial institutions (*see* **22**).

20. Types of capital. A company may raise capital either by issuing shares or by obtaining loans; most firms use both methods.

(*a*) *Share capital.* A company raises capital by issuing shares either to allow it to commence business or, in the case of an existing business, to allow it to expand. There are several different types of share.

(*i*) *Ordinary shares, or "equity capital" shares.* The holders of *equities* are the true risk bearers or entrepreneurs of the business since they are only entitled to participate in the profits that the company has made after all the other shareholders have received their dividends and all other payments have been made. Ordinary shareholders do not receive a fixed rate of interest on shares. They receive instead a proportion of the amount of profit that is available after all other payments have been met. The Directors, for instance may decide to retain some of the profit to reinvest in the firm in the form of new plant and equipment. In times of prosperity, therefore, ordinary shareholders do well, but when profits are low they may receive little or nothing.

(*ii*) *Cumulative preference shares.* Preference shares carry a fixed rate of dividend which is paid in priority of ordinary shares. Any arrears of dividends owing to preference shareholders must be paid before ordinary shareholders receive their dividend.

(*iii*) *Non-cumulative preference shares.* Dividends on these shares are paid out of current profits only. Arrears of dividend are not paid.

(*iv*) *Participating preference shares*. These shares carry the right to a fixed dividend plus a share of the profits after the ordinary shareholders have been paid a certain rate.

(*v*) *Redeemable shares*. This is not a permanent loan; the company undertakes to redeem the shares at a fixed or determinable time, but often at a premium.

(*b*) *Loan capital*. Loan capital is distinguished from share capital in that it is in the form of loans or *debentures*. Unlike shareholders, lenders of money are not members of the company, and have no say in the way in which it is run; they are creditors. Loan capital must be repaid before a fixed date and the company pays interest on the loan. The term *debenture* is not defined in law but it is commonly understood to mean loans to companies. There are a number of different types of debenture.

(*i*) *Registered debenture*. Here one individual or company lends money to a firm. This may well be a bank.

(*ii*) *Debenture stock*. Here individuals lend money to a firm. This takes the form of stock issued to the public in the name of the Trustees who look after the interests of the lender.

(*iii*) *Loan stock*. This comprises unsecured debentures.

(*iv*) *Convertible debentures*. Holders of these debentures usually have the right to convert them into ordinary shares at a later date. In other respects, however, they are similar to other forms of debentures and receive a fixed rate of interest.

In addition to raising capital in the above ways, a firm which is operating profitably can also retain some of its profits to finance an expansion or investment programme. Whether or not a firm raises additional capital by borrowing or by raising more share capital depends to some extent on the purpose for which it is required (*see* Fig. 6 and Table I). One of the problems of issuing additional shares is that it can lead to management losing control of the firm's policies. In instances 1 and 2 in Table I, *A* owns 60 per cent of the firm's shares and can thus effectively exercise control over it since he has the greatest voting power. In instance 2 the firm has extended its capital base from £2.1m to 2.4m to finance a planned expansion. The additional capital is raised both by increasing retentions from profits and by increasing the amount of debenture holding. Effective control of the business is held by A since his share holding is still 60 per cent. In instance

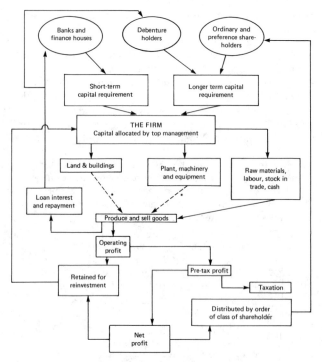

*Depreciation charged to production is shown as a broken line to distinguish it from normal cash flows

FIG. 6 *Cash flow in a business* (*public limited company*).

TABLE I. TYPE OF CAPITAL AND CONTROL IN A FIRM IN A NUMBER
OF DIFFERENT INSTANCES

	Instances		
	1	2	3
Share capital	£1m	£1m	£1.3m
Debenture capital	£0.6m	£0.7m	£0.6m
Retained profits	£0.5m	£0.7m	£0.5m
% of shares owned by *A*	60	60	45
Control exercised by	*A*	A	not A
Total capital	£2.1m	£2.4m	£2.4m

3 the extra capital is raised by issuing additional shares with the result that A's shareholding drops to 45 per cent. This could mean in theory that if all the other shareholders were to act in unison, A could be outvoted. In practice a shareholding of less than 50 per cent is often sufficient to gain control since such a shareholder can enlist the help of other shareholders so that together they control the majority of the shares.

21. Gearing. The decision on how to raise capital is therefore an important one for management. The firm has to balance the costs against the benefits of the various methods and ascertain the financial mix most appropriate for the company. The right mix will result in the lowest average weighted cost to the firm.

In making the "mix" decision, financial management has to take into account such factors as the purpose for which the capital is required (short or long term finance), the state of the capital market (variations in interest rate), the relative costs and availability of the different sources, and the firm's corporate attitude towards risk.

It should be noted that, whilst raising capital through increasing the number of ordinary shares may be "cheaper" than issuing debenture stock upon which a fixed interest has to be paid irrespective of profits, such action can lead to a loss of control by shareholders who have a vested interest in the running of the business. The degree to which control is lost is, of course, dependent on the amount of additional capital required.

Gearing, then, is the ratio of a company's fixed interest borrowings to its equity (i.e. of debentures, loans and preference shares to ordinary shares). It is important that this ratio should not be too high since a high ratio may lead to large variations in the share price during periodic fluctuations in the economic climate. Under such circumstances the risk of a company failing during a severe decline in trade is increased—ordinary shareholders are unlikely to be attracted to the company during times of recession since the dividend will be low or non-existent, owing to the high percentage of prior charges that have to be met. Moreover, even preference shareholders would be taking substantial risks—if profits were severely reduced even fixed dividend payments might not be made. In addition a high ratio means that even a small change in profit can make comparatively large changes in the dividend paid to equity holders; hence investment in such a firm would be highly speculative.

22. Sources of finance.

(*a*) *Finance houses.* Financial institutions such as clearing banks, insurance companies, superannuation funds, unit trust and trade unions lend large sums of money to businesses. Such establishments are able to lend money because they all have an excess of income over expenditure.

(*i*) *The clearing banks.* The clearing banks, receive customers' money which is placed with them for safety, convenience and to some extent to gain interest. These banks estimate the amount which is likely to be demanded by customers at any one time, investing the remainder. Most of these investments are short-term projects where capital is recoverable at short notice should the bank's customers' withdrawals be exceptionally heavy.

(*ii*) *Others.* Insurance companies and superannuation funds can make more long term investments since they are much less likely to need to call back their invested capital at short notice. It should be noted, however, that in recent years the clearing banks themselves have diversified into insurance, superannuation funds and even leasing and so are now offering many other non-traditional services as well as financial advice.

(*b*) *The Stock Exchange.* Another source of capital is the London Stock Exchange which enables the buying and selling of stocks and shares to take place at their current value and without any delay. A firm (or an individual) wishing to buy or sell securities instructs its stockbroker as to what shares are to be bought or sold. These instructions are passed to one of the members of a jobbing firm who deals on the floor of the Stock Exchange and the appropriate transaction is conducted on the client's behalf. The Stock Exchange is also concerned with exercising control over the issue of new securities or shares, vetting any new issues before approving them. The work of actually issuing securities is carried out by *issuing houses*; firms wishing to raise share capital have to contact such an establishment.

(*c*) *Merchant banks.* These are large organisations which can offer several services to businesses. They can act as issuing houses or more simply in an advisory capacity. A merchant bank may also lend capital.

23. Financial accounting. Financial accounting is concerned with recording and analysing revenues and expenditures associated with all transactions which extend outside the business. It enables the extent of sums owing from debtors and to creditors to be established and permits the valuation of assets. Accounts are published to meet the legal requirements of the various Companies Acts, to provide information for the owners, management and potential investors/lenders on how the company is performing. Two important accounting documents are:

(a) *the Balance Sheet*—this gives a static picture of the business at any point in time, showing assets owned by the business and the claims which may be made against them (liabilities);

(b) *the Profit and Loss Account*—this shows total expenses and income over a period of time together with the net profit available for disposal.

A careful examination of these accounts can enable management to monitor an organisational unit's:

(a) overall profitability;
(b) utilisation of assets in producing sales;
(c) financial gearing and
(d) ability to meet its financial commitments (liquidity).

ABC Co. Ltd

BALANCE SHEET (Simplified)

Balance sheet at 31st December 19–

LIABILITIES	£000		ASSETS	£000	
Share capital			Fixed assets (at cost *Less* depreciation)		
Authorised and issued shares					
5,000 8% Preference shares at £5 each	25		Premises and land	112	
100,000 Ordinary shares of £1 each	100	125	Plant and equipment	65	177
Revenue reserves			Current assets		
Unappropriated profit		50	Material stock	20	
Shareholders interest			Finished stock	19	
			Debtors	45	
			Cash	14	
					98

Loan capital				
Debentures 10%		50	*Less* Current liabilities	
			Creditors	50
			Net current assets	48
		225		225

ABC Co. Ltd
Profit and Loss Statement
Profit and loss statement year ending 31st Dec 19–

	£000	£000
Sales		320
Cost of goods sold		
Direct materials	70	
Direct wages	30	100
Gross profit		220
Less expenses		
Indirect wages and salaries	35	
Depreciation	20	
Other expenses	80	135
Operating profit		85
less Debenture interest		5
Pre-tax net profit		80
less tax		40
Net profit after tax		40
less preference share dividend		2
Net profit for ordinary shareholders		38
less ordinary share dividend		20
Retained earnings (for reserves)		18

Accounts must be interpreted with great care as there are many pitfalls to be guarded against. For instance, in examining a balance sheet and applying financial ratios, management must be fully conversant with how the figures have been derived.

24. Commonly applied financial ratios.

(*a*) *Return on investment* (*ROI*). Several methods of determining ROI are employed. One such method, used as a measure of overall managerial performance is shown below:

$$\text{ROI} = \frac{\text{Operating profit}}{\text{Total assets}} \times 100\%$$

However, the ROI is only of value if it can be compared with the ROI figures for past periods or other companies. A decline in ROI is a sign of a weakening position since it means the firm's assets are realising less and less in terms of its profits. Care must be taken when comparing figures for different organisations to ensure that the figures are calculated from the same base and in the same manner.

(*b*) *Profitability analysis.* If a declining rate of return on investment is identified it is important to find its cause. The customary approach is to examine how the firm utilises its assets in producing sales and how it makes a profit. The decline in the firm's fortunes may be because sales are declining or not growing at a rate commensurate with the growth of its assets. The utilisation of assets is measured by examining changes in the sales to assets ratio over a period of time. A decline in this ratio can occur when a firm makes a heavy capital investment in new processes or equipment or acquires less efficient firms as part of a diversification programme. On the other hand a declining ROI can result from increased direct or indirect costs. This can be ascertained by analysing the profit and loss statement, showing the major items as a percentage of sales.

(*c*) *Liquidity.* Rough indicators of a firm's ability to meet its commitments are as follows.

(*i*) *Quick ratio or liquidity ratio.* This denotes a firm's ability to meet its immediate liabilities and is expressed as:

$$\frac{\text{Debtors} + \text{cash}}{\text{Current liabilities}}$$

(*ii*) *Current ratio.* This is expressed as:

$$\frac{\text{Current assets}}{\text{Current liabilities}}$$

Both of these ratios should ideally not be less than 1.

The above measures are a useful guide to outsiders trying to judge the financial state of a company. The receipts and disbursements statement in the cash budget, however, is the best measure of a firm's liquidity. It reveals:

(*a*) the rate at which assets are converted to cash;

(*b*) the availability of cash in relationship to need; and

(*c*) the amount of cash required to satisfy that need.

25. Management accounting. Management needs more information than can be produced or provided by financial accounting. The costing department can provide information which will be useful in management decision-making. The basic categories under which costs are considered are as follows.

(*a*) *Prime costs.*

(*i*) *Direct materials* (directly used in manufacture).

(*ii*) *Direct labour* (which comprises the wages of those who are directly involved in producing goods or providing a service).

(*iii*) *Direct expenses* (expenses directly relevant to producing goods or providing a service).

(*b*) *Overhead costs.*

(*i*) Indirect materials.

(*ii*) Indirect labour.

(*iii*) Indirect expenses.

Management accounting provides data on which pricing policies can be based and enables costs to be allocated for all items which contribute towards the operation of the business. This in turn enables a system of planning and control to be implemented.

Management accounting is concerned with:

(*a*) *budgeting*: planning future business activities and placing monetary values on the plans;

(*b*) *operational control*: making sure that the work is carried out without wasting resources (money); and

(*c*) *evaluation*: assessing what has been achieved in relationship to what has been planned.

There are two ways, apart from expansion, in which a firm can increase its profitability:

(*a*) either by increasing revenues from existing products; or

(*b*) by reducing expenditure (costs).

Management attempts to control costs by tracing them to the actual point at which they are incurred. Such points are termed *cost centres* and may comprise a machine, a number of machines or some other unit to which direct costs can be attributed (*product centre*). Indirect costs are first allocated to a *service centre* and then reallocated to a product centre. Machine maintenance, for example, is first charged against a service centre and then reallocated against each machine. In this way it is possible to know exactly what costs are incurred at each centre over a specific period of time and to evaluate this against the budgeted amount.

Management accounting, also reveals which of the items in a company's product mix are most profitable so that their sales can be expanded and the less profitable ones withdrawn if necessary. In addition the kind of information it provides enables management to monitor how costs are being incurred and changes in these costs. The subject of the profitability of the product mix is discussed further in VIII.

PERSONNEL MANAGEMENT
(*see also* XIII)

26. The personnel officer. Not all organisations have a personnel officer. The role may be shared between several managers; in some cases a labour officer may have the task of hiring blue collar workers. Some of the many factors which have given rise to the growth of personnel management in business organisation are:

(*a*) the continued growth of trade unions and the need to develop organisational specialists capable of advising top management on how to deal with trade union negotiations;

(*b*) the legal requirement to provide training as outlined by the Industrial Training Act 1964;

(*c*) the growing recognition that it is necessary to give attention to human relations in industry.

The duties of the personnel officer include:

(*a*) recruitment of staff;

(*b*) training and education of staff;

(*c*) overseeing worker safety and welfare; and

(*d*) advising management on trade union negotiations.

27. Recruitment of staff. The personnel officer consults with all levels of management in the firm to ascertain both present and future staff requirements and, in conjunction with the appropriate manager, undertakes to interview and select staff. Another personnel function is dealing with personal staff problems with which line management staff cannot easily deal. If a conflict between a superior and a subordinate cannot be resolved the personnel officer may be able to arrange a transfer for the subordinate. The personnel officer also keeps all employee records and deals with dismissals.

28. Training and education. This involves arranging induction programmes for new employees and on-the-job training. In addition the personnel officer has to arrange, where necessary, for younger employees to attend day or block release classes at colleges of further education. Some large firms have their own training schools for teaching trade apprentices. ICI has its own management training establishment where both commercial apprentices and all levels of management undergo periodic training, retraining or simply attend refresher courses. Many other large companies also have their own management training establishments while smaller firms can take advantage of short courses run by universities, polytechnics and private management colleges. The personnel officer has to advise management of the availability and suitability of such courses.

29. Industrial relations. Discipline is necessary to allow an organisation to function effectively and to work towards its organisational objectives. This involves setting out a system of rules and regulations which channel behaviour towards the accomplishment of organisational goals. These rules must be demonstrably fair. Enforcement of organisational rules requires a system of punishments for non-compliance. These may take the form of reprimands, suspensions or dismissals.

Most organisations now have members who belong to trade unions. The function of trade unions is to represent employees collectively on matters relating to:

(*a*) wages and salaries paid for services rendered;

(*b*) conditions of work and fringe benefits;

(*c*) the representation of employees when rules have been infringed and punishment administered; and

(*d*) the sponsoring of legislation relevant to the protection of employees' jobs.

In most organisations there are formal procedures for dealing with disputes. Shop stewards representing the trade union and the employees are the first link in the chain of negotiation. Trade unions negotiate directly with top management so that unless the personnel officer is a member of the top management team his role can only be advisory.

30. Workers' safety and welfare. The personnel officer may oversee the operation of the welfare department. The welfare department customarily has a full-time qualified nurse in regular attendance together with a number of auxiliaries. As occasion demands, a doctor may be brought in on a consultative basis. In large organisations trained social workers may be employed on a full-time, and psychologists on a consultative, basis. Every organisation should have a safety officer; his duties are to ensure that all employees are trained in accident prevention and to inspect premises and plant to ensure that they are safe.

31. The company secretary. The role of the company secretary, who is generally directly accountable to the chief executive, varies from company to company. In some organisations he or she may also occupy the role of chief accountant. The company secretary is usually responsible for:

(*a*) maintaining certain statutory books (e.g. the register of members) and for making periodic returns (e.g. the annual return).

(*b*) arranging directors' meetings, preparing agenda papers and minutes and ensuring that appropriate action is taken following decisions taken at such meetings; and

(*c*) general administration services (mailroom, messengers, typing pool, janitors, etc.).

PROGRESS TEST 5

1. What is the "marketing concept" and how does this relate to the task of marketing management? **(2)**

2. What do you understand by the product life cycle? **(3)**

3. Is there always an inverse relationship between sales and the price charged for a product/service? Explain. **(4)**

4. Distinguish between "channel management" and "physical distribution management". **(5)**

5. What are the elements of the promotion mix? **(6)**

6. What are the functions of marketing research? **(7)**

7. Indicate the ways in which secondary marketing information may be obtained. **(9)**

8. What are the different ways of collecting primary data? **(10)**

9. What are: (*a*) consumer panels; (*b*) retail audits? **(10)**

10. Give examples of three different types of production process. Under what circumstances would one type be used in preference to another? **(11)**

11. Distinguish between product simplification and product standardisation. **(12)**

12. What are the main factors to be taken into account when considering the most suitable site for a factory? **(13)**

13. What is the function of a progress chaser? **(14)**

14. What is the function of a quality control inspector? **(15)**

15. Why does the status of a purchasing officer vary from organisation to organisation? **(17)**

16. What is the purpose of R & D? **(18)**

17. How does the way in which a sole trader seeks to finance his business differ from that of a public limited company? **(19)**

18. Distinguish between the different types of share and loan capital in a public limited company. **(20)**

19. What do you understand by the term "gearing"? **(21)**

20. What are the principal sources of finance which a public limited company can approach? **(22)**

21. Explain the purpose of the management accounting function in a firm. **(25)**

22. What are the role and duties of a personnel officer? **(26)**

23. Comment on the role of the personnel officer in industrial relations. **(29)**

24. What is the function of the company secretary? **(31)**

CHAPTER VI

Planning

INTRODUCTION

This chapter examines the nature and describes the process of planning; a distinction is made between corporate and functional planning and their relationship is discussed.

1. Definitions. Planning is a technique "whereby the skills of a variety of specialists can be brought to bear on a problem before the formal stage of decision-making is reached" (Herbert Simon, 1959). "Planning is the primary task of management. It must occur before any other managerial function because it determines the nature of those functions. Planning is more than forecasting. It involves the process of choosing an objective, charting a course, and moving along that course to the attaining of the objective" (Robert Fulmer, 1978). The planning process involves:

(*a*) selecting objectives;
(*b*) communicating objectives;
(*c*) identifying premises;
(*d*) surveying and assessing resources;
(*e*) establishing policies;
(*f*) choosing alternatives;
(*g*) taking action;
(*h*) making rules and procedures;
(*i*) establishing budgets; and
(*j*) establishing timetables.

Strategic (corporate) planning has also to be distinguished from *functional* (conventional) planning. The former is the process of determining how an organisation can make the best possible use of its resources in the future, while the latter concentrates on making the best use of current resources. Corporate planning focuses on ways in which these resources can gradually be altered to allow the enterprise to become more successful in the future.

THE PLANNING PROCESS

2. Selecting and communicating objectives.

(*a*) *Definitions.* "The purpose of a business is the production
and marketing of economic goods and services. But to accomplish
these purposes, a number of enterprise objectives may be necessary
and, in turn, a number of supporting goals by departments and
sections" (Koontz and O'Donnell, 1976).

(*b*) *The objectives hierarchy.* Objectives in an organisation may
be seen as a hierarchy (*see* Fig. 7). In the case of a shoe manufacturing and marketing business, its over-all objective is to produce,

FIG. 7   *A hierarchy of objectives.*

in specified quantities, shoes of a certain type, quality or design,
which will appeal to certain markets. At the next, lower, level
in the hierarchy there may be objectives for researching and
developing new ideas for shoes and shoe materials; and objectives
for marketing and producing shoes. Suppose the corporate objective of the firm is (amongst other things) to sell £10m worth of
shoes at the retail level in a given year. Passing down through
the different levels in the hierarchy of objectives, this will eventually
mean that a particular salesman has to sell *y* pairs of shoes in
that period. Further down still in the hierarchy the purchasing
officer's objective will be to obtain enough raw materials to enable
this level of production to be achieved. (It is not intended to
suggest that any one set of objectives is less important than another,
merely that it is subordinate to it.) Fig. 7 illustrates a hierarchy

of objectives. The financial objectives are at the base of the pyramid as it is necessary to obtain finance before any of the other objectives can be achieved. At the next level there must be sufficient personnel available to enable the organisation to function, and so on.

(c) *Managing objective.*

(i) *Multiplicity.* Managing a system of interrelated objectives is complicated by the fact that there will probably be a multiplicity of them. A firm may set objectives, for instance, for sales and return on investment figures; the periodic introduction of product modifications and new products; penetration of overseas markets; the achievement of a dominant position within its industry; and at all times improving the value that society puts on its operations. Management should avoid becoming preoccupied with one objective to the detriment of others.

(ii) *The time-scale.* Another factor in the management of objectives is the time scale. An organisation may set long, medium and short range objectives, all of which may need to be interrelated. The identification of the shorter range objectives will follow from an evaluation of the priorities of the longer range objectives.

(d) *Clarity of objectives.* If objectives are to be useful to management, they must be:

(i) *specific enough to be measured*; such an objective might be to produce 15,000 pairs of shoes of type K via process A using machines p and r and employing four operatives during week 26 without allowing overtime work; or to sell 4,000 pairs of shoes of type K in area D through outlets type L using salesman y in weeks 20 to 26, subject to a constraint of £D selling expenses;

(ii) *measurable in terms which the nature of the objective demands.* For example, if the intended effect of advertising is to create customer awareness of a product then objectives should be set in terms of creating a given level of awareness, not in terms of achieving sales. Similarly, the success of an advertising campaign should be assessed by measuring how much awareness has been created, not how many sales have resulted.

3. Development of management by objectives. Early management writers such as Fayol, Urwick and Barnard emphasised the idea of management by objectives. But it was not really until the mid-1950s that steps were taken to put these ideas into practice. The General Electric Company of America was one of the first companies to do so.

As firms grow, so arises the need for them to develop formalised methods of planning and control; without clear objectives managing is haphazard and it becomes difficult to assess an individual's performance effectively or efficiently. Large organisations therefore need a formalised planning process.

Management by pre-determined objectives enables everyone to understand what they are working towards. While over-all objectives are determined by top management, each subsequent level in the hierarchy or link in the network should be able to negotiate or renegotiate its particular objectives with the preceding level or stage. It is important that managers and their subordinates alike know exactly what their objectives are and have a say in setting them. Whilst this may seem to be desirable and even obvious, it does not always happen. Employees often do not know what is expected of them and have little opportunity for discussion with their supervisors.

For example, a sales manager in an expanding market anticipates that since overall sales are certain to expand from year to year it is reasonable to expect each salesman to increase his sales from period to period. He must not overlook the fact, however, that it may be more difficult for a salesman in one particular area to expand his sales at the same rate as a salesman in another area; it will be more difficult, for example, to gain new insurance business in slum clearance areas than in new "middle-class" housing estates. Nevertheless, it is not unknown for a sales manager in such a position to apply a simple rule of thumb: "Overall sales are expected to be 10 per cent up on last year; all salesmen should therefore increase their sales by 10 per cent in the coming year." The sales manager should instead talk to each of his salesmen individually and agree a reasonable target with each of them, bearing in mind the type of areas in which each salesman operates and the fact that over-all sales are expected to be 10 per cent up on the previous year.

FORECASTING

4. Identifying premises. Premises are the assumptions on which plans are based, they may be internal to the organisation or external to it and can vary with time.

(*a*) External premises comprise:

(*i*) the economic, technological, political, social and ethical conditions in the environment;

(*ii*) the conditions which influence demand for the products or services of the organisation;

(*iii*) the factor market (land, labour, location, materials, capital, etc.).

(*b*) Internal premises comprise:

(*i*) capital investment in plant and equipment;

(*ii*) decisions already taken which relate to strategies, policies and major programmes;

(*iii*) the inflexible dimensions of organisation structure;

(*iv*) the beliefs, attitudes and skills of top management.

Both external and internal premises may be quantitative or qualitative.

(*a*) Quantitative dimensions infer any premises that can be expressed numerically, e.g. available machine hours, availability of bank credit etc.

(*b*) Qualitative dimensions infer any premises that cannot be expressed numerically, e.g. public attitudes towards the company, etc.

5. Futurism. Fayol wrote of *prevoyance* being the essence of management and recommended quinquennial and decennial forecasts as well as annual ones. Futurism, then, is the systematic forecasting of premises.

(*a*) *Methods of estimating future premises.* Several methods are used to estimate future premises. Some firms do not take into account the fact that premises may change over time necessarily. In those firms which do attempt to take changes in premises into account in the planning process the degree of systemisation, or sophistication, with which this is done varies considerably. Some managers will largely rely upon their own subjective interpretations of the economic climate, though they may also draw on information from previously published sources; at the other extreme organisations may utilise the economic, social and political forecasts of outside experts and in addition employ a wide range of complex techniques and methods to assist them in making their forecasts.

(*b*) *Factors affecting future premise estimation.* The size of the firm and the nature of its business is critical; large, widely diversified enterprises are more likely to employ fully systemised forecasting methods and corporate scanning mechanisms than smaller firms with narrower product-market scopes. Whilst managers in small firms are recommended to think through the process of planning carefully, usually they would not be able to employ expensive forecasting methods in identifying future premises.

6. Economic forecasting. Reasonably accurate indicators of future economic premises can be obtained from government sources such as the Export Credits Guarantee Department (ECGD); the National Economic Development Council (NEDC); and certain international institutions such as the Economist Intelligence Unit; major banks, etc. A company should first study the broad forecasts of national and regional economic trends and then assess what effect these will have on the various industries which it serves. Finally, the effect of economic conditions on these industries has to be related to the impact they will have on the firm itself. In this context it is worth noting the usefulness of "input-output" tables which show the interrelationship of industries and their sharing of the gross national product (GNP) through the process of sales and purchases between industries.

7. Technological forecasting.

(*a*) *Function.* Rapidly changing technology and its implications for R & D in firms and in the development of new products has necessitated the development of ways of forecasting new technological advances. Obviously the firms which have most need of this are those operating in areas of high and changing technology such as electronics. Here, technical personnel can be encouraged to anticipate future developments and, through frequent contact with outside organisations, to estimate how current scientific developments may influence the future state of a particular technology. The effect these changes may have on their own company and its product markets can then be indicated. This is one way in which R & D can be involved in top management planning. Even in the smaller company there will be an individual or several individuals with sufficient technical or scientific knowledge able to provide similar information.

(*b*) *Method.* Perhaps the best known technological forecasting technique is the *Delphi technique* named after the Oracle at Delphi in classical Greece. This method employs *cybernetic arbitration.* Expert opinions are systematically solicited, collected, evaluated and tabulated. Open discussion is avoided since certain dimensions of social interaction may distort group feelings—one person may emerge as a charismatic leader and unduly influence others. A carefully designed programme of personal interrogations is employed, often using questionnaires, and participants are given information feedback at each stage about the other experts' opinions.

Top management in a firm which manufactures domestic appliances, for instance, may be interested to know when a technological breakthrough allowing cooking by laser beams is likely to occur. The group of individuals participating in the exercise are asked to make their predictions with supporting arguments. When all responses have been received the process is repeated, but this time the information obtained in the first round is circulated among the participants. The process continues until a reasonable consensus of opinion is reached.

8. Social and political forecasting.

(a) *Demographic.* Only demographic forecasting (i.e. predicting shifts in the socio-economic characteristics of populations) has received significant attention from the business world. Clarks Shoes of Street in Somerset, for example, closely monitors UK trends in the number of children of various ages and fluctuations in the average number of children in a family.

(b) *Other.* It is also important to forecast other changes in society. For the multi-national firm or for the firm which conducts a considerable amount of its business on an international scale these other factors are equally important. The political stability of a particular area of the world will have considerable implications for a company's present or intended manufacturing, assembly and marketing operations in that country. Changes in social tastes and mores, too, have direct implications for marketing management in different regions throughout the world.

9. Demand (sales) forecasting for products and service.

(a) *Definition.* A sales forecast is a prediction of expected sales of products or services, assuming that a given marketing strategy is employed, for a specific period of time and in a specific geographic area.

(b) *Importance.* The importance of the sales forecast cannot be overemphasised:

"One of the major planning premises in the typical business enterprise is the sales forecast ... it underlies ... new product, production and marketing plans, and it also reflects conditions of the market which are external to the firm. Because it sets the framework on which most internal plans are constructed, it must be regarded as the dominant planning premise of an enterprise" (Koontz and O'Donnell, 1976).

(*c*) *Application.* Sales forecasting is customarily associated with business planning but is also relevant to non-business enterprises. For example, a hospital has to anticipate the demand for its beds; a college has to anticipate the demand for its courses and a museum or art gallery has to anticipate the number of people likely to visit a particular exhibition. However, for simplicity we will consider the application of sales forecasting in a manufacturing firm. There are a number of ways of forecasting sales.

10. Jury of executive opinion. This represents a combination and averaging out of the many different views which top managers in the firm will express. Research has shown that "subjective" estimations can be equally as valuable as more "objective" methods provided that a sufficient number of subjective estimates are taken into account and that the persons making those estimates are well informed and are capable of making sound judgments.

(*a*) *Advantages.* This method has many advantages. The elaborate and expensive preparation of economic studies and statistics is not required; it allows experience and judgment as well as inanimate data to be brought into play. This kind of forecasting is perhaps most useful in a small organisation or where the number of products under consideration is relatively small.

(*b*) *Disadvantages.* It is difficult to break down forecasts by product, time period, area, organisational unit, etc.

11. Salesmen's opinions. Here, salesmen and their supervisors are asked to make estimates of sales by product for individual areas or customers. These estimates are then reviewed by senior sales staff, sometimes in the light of information on business conditions provided by top management. Similarly, information may also be obtained from marketing research staff.

12. Users' expectations. Such an approach is quite feasible where the number of users is likely to be small. The main limitation of this method is therefore that it is difficult to apply where the number of users is large, although the use of statistical sampling techniques can make this possible.

13. Statistical methods.

(*a*) *Extrapolation.* This involves analysing collected data, allowing the identification of trends and, therefore, predictions of future performance to take place. It involves utilising past changes in only the variable of interest as a basis for future predictions.

Extrapolation of historical data can take a variety of forms but there are three basic methods:

(*i*) *Naive method.* This uses the value of the most recent periods as a basis for forecasting the next period. It is most useful for short-term forecasting and where sales data changes slowly over time (*see* XVI).

(*ii*) *Time series analysis.* This is useful for forecasting anything from three months to three years ahead. It assumes that the original data of a series are composed of: a secular trend (**T**), a cyclical component (**C**), a seasonal component (**S**) and an irregular component (**I**). It is usual to express the relationship between the components and actual sales in the form of an equation: Sales in period $t = T \times C \times S + I$.

The technique involves decomposing data in order to obtain measures for trend, cyclical and seasonal factors. The method is fully discussed in XV.

(*iii*) *Growth curves.* These are useful in predicting sales over longer periods (say three to ten years) and concentrate solely on the underlying trend which the data throws up. Most growth curves are "S" shaped, reflecting the fact that during the first years of a product's life, growth will be slow but in the middle years relatively fast (*see* Fig. 8). As the product reaches market saturation point (the point at which all potential buyers will have purchased the product at least once) the growth rate again slows down. There are however a variety of other curves and methods of deriving equations from them (*see* Kotler (1976) and Battersby (1970)). Note that growth curves are only useful in predicting sales where it is known that the point of market saturation has not yet been reached.

(*iv*) *Exponential smoothing and moving averages. See* XV.

(*b*) *Lead indicators or correlation analysis.* This is where management is able to infer likely sales in advance of actual sales from an independent indicator; obviously a longer lead time is more convenient than a shorter one. New housing developments in a particular area for instance, can be used as a lead indicator of likely future sales of new furnishings and carpets in that area.

Lead indicators can be industrial and economic statistics from which it is possible to obtain an indication of the value or direction of the variable that is of interest to the forecaster. The forecaster has to use common sense in searching out likely lead indicators. To facilitate this it will probably be necessary to run a *correlation*,

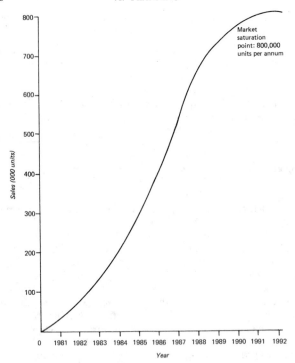

FIG. 8   *A typical S-shaped growth curve.*

or *regression analysis* (for a good account of these techniques, *see Statistics,* W. M. Harper, 1982); this is to quantify the relationship between the lead indicator and the variable of interest to the firm. Lead indicators can be useful in estimating the turning point of a trend (for a good discussion of this technique, *see* Firth, 1977).

(c) *A mathematical model.* This is an extension of (*a*) and (*b*) above. Such models can allow for economic and demographic variables as well as the fluctuations in the marketing effort expended by the firm. The scope of this book does not allow a detailed discussion of mathematical model, for which *see* Firth, 1977.

Parker and Segura (1971) forecasted the sales of a home furnishings company using a *regression model* which included two lead indicators and a measure of economic activity. Housing starts for the previous year (H_{t-1}), sales of the previous year (S_{t-1}), disposable income for the present year (I_t) and time (T) were used as predictor variables. The equation:

$$S_t = 33.51 + 0.033\ H_{t-1} + 0.373\ S_{t-1} + 0.672\ I_t - 11.03\ T$$

was based on 22 years of data and gave a good fit to the data.

Statistical methods bring a degree of objectivity to forecasting; however, in the final analysis they should be used purely to give weight to ideas subjectively held. In practice, therefore, both objective and subjective methods of forecasting should be used in conjunction with each other.

14. Surveying and assessing resources (resources forecasting). After objectives (and external premises) have been formulated, management must next consider whether it has acquired or how it can obtain the necessary resources to achieve them. From IV it will be recalled how Courtauld, faced with falling profits, decided that it needed additional resources to achieve its medium- and long-term objectives and thus ensure its survival. In consequence it acquired a large number of smaller firms which together provided those resources.

15. Establishing policies. "A policy is a general plan of action that guides the members of the organisation in the conduct of its operation" (Kast & Rosenzweig, 1974). Fulmer (1978) suggests that policies are means that prevent a company from acting purely according to the dictates of circumstance. Brech (1963) goes as far as to look on policy as the foundation of good management practice. In all cases the ultimate responsibility for determining both objectives and policies rests with the board of directors (or, in the case of a nationalised enterprise, the State).

The *general* or *over-all policy* of an organisation represents its social outlook and attitudes. These could be to contribute to:

(*a*) the economic needs of the community through the products and services it produces;

(*b*) the welfare of its employees;

(*c*) the advancement of the social life of the local community in the neighbourhood of its works or factories; and to

(*d*) ensure that every action it takes contributes towards assuring its survival.

Strategy is the direction in which human and material resources are applied to afford the best possible chance of attaining a particular objective. The key factor in strategies and policies is that it should give a unified direction to plans. Over-all (*corporate*) strategies and policies must be translated into operational (*tactical*) plans. An excellent example of the need for a successful inter-relationship between tactics, strategy and policy is illustrated by an unsuccessful venture which the Volkswagen company made into the medium-sized luxury car market. The company's over-all policy was to expand and the strategy chosen was to enter the medium-sized luxury car market. Its tactic was to incorporate a new rotary engine, developed by NSU, into the design of its car; this tactic proved to be the ruination of the venture as the engine was in-adequately engineered (Koontz and O'Donnell (1976)).

The following are examples of marketing, production, financial and personnel policies.

(*a*) *Marketing.*

(*i*) *Product.* Producing a limited range of products or extend-ing the range to include related products or even complete diversification.

(*ii*) *Price.* Pricing one's products in relationship to those of one's competitors, i.e. below, or the same as their prices.

(*iii*) *Distribution.* Distributing consumer goods through cer-tain specified retail outlets so as to reflect the desired quality image of the product.

(*iv*) *Promotion.* Giving pre-eminence to a particular feature of the firm's products or services in all its promotions, e.g. the high level of its after-sales service.

(*b*) *Production.*

(*i*) Choosing between making or buying in certain types of component parts for the firm's products.

(*ii*) In batch production, specifying an acceptable range for the length of a production run.

(*iii*) Choosing between producing to order and for stock.

(*iv*) The maintenance of stock levels.

(*c*) *Financial.*

(*i*) *Capital procurement.* Obtaining finance for different under-takings.

(*ii*) *Cash and depreciation allowance policies.*

(*iii*) *Working capital.* Deciding how much credit should be given and can be obtained.

(*iv*) *Distribution of profits.* The retention and distribution of profits; deciding how retained profits should be employed.

(*d*) *Personnel.*

(*i*) *Selection and training.* Fixing the length of probationary service; the qualifications required for particular types of work; making internal versus external appointments to fill vacant positions.

(*ii*) *Wages and salaries.* The level of remuneration.

(*iii*) *Sickness benefit policies.*

(*iv*) *Relations with trade unions.* Handling different types of grievance.

(*v*) *Relations with the public.*

16. Choosing alternatives. Before decisions can be made, alternative courses of action must be identified. Planning involves not only setting objectives and stipulating premises but also identifying alternative ways by which those objectives may be attained. Until an array of alternative courses of action are identified, effective decision-making (*see* VII) to achieve objectives will not be possible. Choosing between alternatives is a search process for which an operative management information system is necessary.

17. Taking action. As soon as alternative courses of action are identified, that which appears to be the most appropriate can be selected. Decisions must then be communicated effectively to those who have to carry them out. It is not sufficient merely to communicate the nature of a decision; the reason for making it must also be made clear to those who receive the directions. Planning often fails because a decision taken at one level is not supported by compatible decisions taken at lower levels in the organisation, when lower level of management fail to understand company strategies. The following is an illustration:

EXAMPLE John Brown works as a salesman for a firm which manufactures and sells pharmaceutical products. His boss sets him the target of selling 500 boxes of a new drug during the month of September 1980 to retail chemists. In addition he has to sell them a further 4,500 boxes of different kinds of drugs in that month. John finds in practice that it is easier to sell more of the existing drugs to the chemists (he sells 4,750 boxes of them) than to persuade them to take the new ones of which he sells only 250 boxes. In consequence, while he achieves his overall target of 5,000 boxes he only sells half the target number for the new drug.

If all the firm's salesmen did the same it would not be able to meet the demand for its existing products while unsold stocks of its new product would begin to build up.

18. Making rules and procedures. "Established procedures may be viewed as a chronological sequence of steps to be taken in order to accomplish a specific objective ...; procedures are policy decisions made in advance ... rules are guides to action rather than to thinking" (Fulmer, 1978). The following plan for a market research interview clearly illustrates the difference between rules and procedures.

Rules.

(*a*) Do not smoke whilst carrying out the interview.

(*b*) Always ensure that your appearance is tidy.

(*c*) Avoid introducing red herrings into the interview. It can be time consuming and detract from the purpose of your visit.

(*d*) Always address interviewees in a formal manner and avoid familiarities.

(*e*) Carry with you several writing implements.

Procedure. Explain to the interviewee who you are, whom you represent, and the purpose of the interview. Show him your letter of introduction and let him have time to read it. Emphasise to him that he is not being pressurised into answering questions and that he is free to participate in the interview or not as he chooses. Seat the interviewee in a comfortable chair preferably so that no light shines in his eyes, etc.

Rules and procedures can do much to facilitate the carrying out of a plan. They must be unambiguous and of course capable of being carried out. There is little point in having a rule that all sales reports should be submitted to head office on the last day of the month, for instance, as it will not be clear whether the reports have to arrive at head office, or whether the salesmen are to despatch them on that day. Moreover, the last day of the month may fall within a holiday period or a weekend, thereby making it difficult to observe the rule.

19. Establishing budgets. Budgeting is defined as setting targets to be achieved over a given period of time and quantifying them. Budgets form an integral part of management by objectives and

enable all members of an organisation to know what is expected
of them. Budgets are also part of the central control function
since they enable subsequent performance to be measured against
predetermined targets. They are closely related to plans and there
are a number of different types of them:

(a) *Revenue and expense budgets.* These express plans in money
terms. The most important of these is the sales budget, the formal,
detailed expression of the sales forecast, which is used as the basis
of budgetary control. The sales budget stipulates targets to be
achieved by

  (i) product;
  (ii) time period; and
  (iii) geographical area and customer.

Expense budgets control expenditure on such widely different
items as labour, materials and travel.

(b) *Time, space, material and product budgets.* These specify
production targets together with the amount of man hours (by
trade, craft, etc.), machine hours (by different machines), materials
(raw materials, bought-in components, packaging etc.) and space
required to achieve production targets.

(c) *Capital expenditure budgets.* These cover expenditure on
specific capital items such as plant, machinery, equipment, stock,
etc. Capital expenditure budgets must be carefully related to long-
range planning objectives since investments in plant, equipment,
etc. will tie up capital for a considerable amount of time.

(d) *Cash budgets.* These are essentially a forecast of receipts
and payments and therefore can be used to indicate the availability
of cash to meet financial obligations as they become due. In
addition cash budgets will show the availability of excess cash
enabling planning for the investment of surpluses to take place.

(e) *Balance sheet budgets.* These anticipate the state of the
organisation's capital account assets and liabilities at any future
time, as well as providing a means of checking the accuracy of
the other budgets. Budgets are considered further in chapter VIII.

20. Establishing timetables. "Time costs money" is a well known
adage. Frederick Taylor's "scientific" management methods were
aimed at reducing the amount of time and therefore the cost
required to perform a specific task efficiently. This principle gave
rise to an area of study known as *method study.*

Planning involves formulating procedures which in turn implies
that tasks should be carried out in a certain order. Some procedures

may be grouped together and carried out independently of others. For example, salesmen can obtain orders for goods independently of (though in conjunction with) the actual production of those goods. Management's task is to synchronise all the various plans and budgets as well as to ensure that finance to carry them out is available exactly when required; if it arrives too late the task or project may be delayed; too early, and it will tie up capital unproductively. In addition, manpower has to be available to produce the goods outlined in the production schedules. If, for instance, a future increase in production is anticipated, additional staff will be required to handle it. The manpower plan should therefore allow for the recruitment of new staff in sufficient time to allow them to be trained first. Production and sales budgets are key budgets whose synchronisation is essential. A production department's inability to satisfy the demands of a marketing department is a frequently quoted source of conflict. This may be alleviated, however, if both departments keep within their respective budgets, and synchronise them.

21. The interrelationship of corporate and functional plans. This can be illustrated by the following example.

(a) *The company.* A small (fictitious) company, Czarina Electronics, manufactures two types of small transformer for industrial use, two types of electronic module for digital wrist-watches and a range of LCD and LED (light-emitting diode) pocket calculators. It employs a workforce of eighty, has five directors and made a return on capital employed of 52.8 per cent in 1980 on a sales turnover of £2m.

The directors envisage that in ten years the company will have become a public limited company, quadrupled its annual sales turnover, yet maintained its rate of return on investment at over 20 per cent p.a. It does not envisage diversifying its product market scope into areas which are dissimilar to those in which it operates, but expects to gain much greater penetration of the pocket calculator market and also to launch a new range of pocket-sized computer-based electronic games.

The firm's directors base their overall strategy on economic reports and scanning of the technological press which confirm that these product markets have a considerable future in the 1980s. Furthermore they believe that this move would be in keeping with a trend towards a greater emphasis on intellectual leisure pursuits and pastimes.

(*b*) *The R & D plan*. Its long-range R & D plan involves building up a small team of experts in micro-computer programming. The firm envisages R & D product development in electronic games to be the key element in the firm's future success. The short-range R & D plan (one year) allows for finalising technical specifications and the building of a prototype pocket-sized electronic LCD display chess game.

(*c*) *The Marketing plan*. Long range marketing plans include the development of a small marketing management team of perhaps two or three. It realises that market research will be of enormous assistance in directing R & D effort and includes, even in its short-range plans, provision for a full-time marketing research and marketing planning assistant. The marketing department currently operates a small sales force which it plans to treble in size over the next ten years. At the present time it has no executive director but hopes to recruit one within three years. Long-range product planning centres on the development of the computerised games and more elaborate pocket calculators. The short-range product plan is to launch the computerised chess game in 1980.

The venture into games means that the firm will have to obtain new distributors capable of handling its new product. The implication of this for the 1981 sales force plan is that an additional salesman will have to be hired to solicit suitable new accounts. To date the firm has never undertaken any form of advertising, leaving the promotion of its consumer-oriented products in the hands of its distributors. The long-range plan includes provision for consumer advertising to promote the new range of games.

The firm's pricing policy has always been to charge the same as competitors and it has never undertaken price leadership. It does not envisage a change in its pricing policy.

(*d*) *The production plan*. The long-range production plan indicates the need for increased capacity. This will require the development of additional factory space on land adjoining the present factory in 1986/87 with an annexe to the factory to be fully operational by 1988. This is planned on the basis of the long-range sales forecast which indicates that existing factory space will be insufficient to handle the anticipated increase in production. The short-term plan includes replacement of the firm's existing batch production system for manufacturing calculators with a continuous process system. The projected sales volume for the next five years indicates that considerable economies of scale of production will be possible.

(*e*) *The personnel plan.* Manpower planning provides for an increase in the size of the labour force to enable the envisaged expansion to take place. It is also hoped to take on two commercial apprentices in 1983.

(*f*) *The financial plan.* Financial plans are critical for the success of the company's projected growth strategy. It is planned to finance the expansion in the short term (1981/4) out of retained profits, but in the longer term it is proposed that the firm should go public in 1985/86. A manual system of budgetary control was introduced in 1980 and there are plans to improve the nature of the management information system in the next few years.

22. The structure of a plan—a marketing example. The following is an example of the structure of an annual marketing plan.

(*a*) *A statement of over-all marketing strategy.*

(*i*) *Objectives.* All major goals should be stated in quantifiable terms.

(*ii*) *Strategy.* A statement of how it is proposed to attain these goals should be made.

(*iii*) *Premises.* A statement should be made of all major assumptions and the basis on which they are made.

(*b*) *Recommendations for appropriations.*

(*i*) A summary statement should be prepared:

(1) total monetary appropriation;
(2) estimated sales in units;
(3) expenditure per unit;
(4) anticipated profit, shown as a percentage of net sales
and
(5) items (2) and (3) for the previous period's budget for comparison.

(*ii*) The itemised budget should be broken down into monthly, quarterly and annual periods. Note that expenses should be shown by major category, e.g. advertising: TV, newspaper, journals, posters, etc. Each expense item should be accompanied by a brief note explaining its purpose e.g. "TV advertising in March/April to create awareness of new brand X".

(*iii*) Each itemised expense must be compared with th

previous period's budget figure and any differences explained. This should be presented separately from (*ii*) above.

(*iv*) A summary of the major budget items (in money terms) should be presented, comparing them with the previous period.

(*c*) *A statement of product strategy*. This should show proposed product deletions, modifications and additions, including the timing of deletions and introductions; as well as unit sales, revenues and profit objectives associated with modifications and new products.

(*d*) *A statement of sales strategy*. This should indicate the intended direction of the selling effort. It should state specific objectives for:

(*i*) levels of service provided to existing customers;

(*ii*) number of new accounts to be opened;

(*iii*) rates of introduction of new products to existing accounts; and

(*iv*) specific targets for obtaining orders from sales calls including individual sales targets for salesmen and area managers. It should further indicate how the sales force is to be deployed in the coming period and include details of all proposed sales promotion schemes.

(*e*) *A statement of advertising strategy*. This should indicate which media are to be used, the timing of the campaign, and the proportion of weight in the advertising mix given to each element. Specific communication objectives should be shown for each listed campaign.

(*f*) *A statement of sales promotion strategy*. This should be itemised as in (*e*) above. A note should be made of how it is to be linked to the advertising strategy.

(*g*) *A statement of distribution strategy*. This should be considered under the headings of "channel strategy" and "physical distribution strategy". The former should outline any intended changes in strategy and their intended effect (in both quantitative and qualitative terms). The latter might include a programme for improving methods of handling and transporting stock.

(*h*) *A statement of marketing research strategy*. This could outline objectives for:

(*i*) obtaining data which can regularly be fed into the marketing information system;

(*ii*) testing products, markets, operations or concepts.

NETWORK ANALYSIS

23. Critical path method. Planning can involve the detailed consideration of specific projects as well as the formulation of over-all strategies and the periodic structuring of business operations. A firm may need to launch a new product or a museum set up a special exhibition, for instance; here, considerable benefit can be obtained by systematically planning out in advance the procedures necessary for a successful completion of the assignment. A technique, known as *critical path method* (CPM) has been developed for this purpose. Its functions are twofold:

(*a*) to find the most efficient time arrangement for a number of activities that are worked together to achieve a single result;

(*b*) to establish the most cost-effective method of achieving (*a*) above.

24. PERT. (Programme evaluation and review technique). This is another network analysis technique similar to CPM. The main difference between the two methods is that PERT activity times are estimated as closely as possible while in CPM they are known with certainty. A full discussion of PERT and CPM is outside the scope of this book but interested readers are referred to Moskowitz and Wright's *Operational Research Techniques for Management*.

PROGRESS TEST 6

1. Define planning. **(1)**
2. What are the elements of the planning process? **(2)**
3. What do you understand by the phrase hierarchy of business objectives? **(2)**
4. In what way should objectives have clarity? **(2)**
5. Explain the concept of management by objectives. **(3)**
6. Identify the basic premises of which a business enterprise has to be aware in the process of planning. **(4)**
7. What do you understand by the term "futurism"? **(5)**
8. Comment on the importance of economic forecasting in business planning. **(6)**
9. Explain the "Delphi Technique". **(7)**
10. Why are social and political forecasts important to a business firm? **(8)**

11. Explain some of the different methods available by which to forecast demand for products and services. **(9–13)**

12. What is meant by the term "policy"? **(15)**

13. Differentiate between "rules" and "procedures". **(18)**

14. Indicate the different types of budgets which may be found in a manufacturing firm. **(19)**

15. Indicate how you think a marketing plan might be structured. **(22)**

16. What use are such techniques as CPM and PERT in planning? **(23, 24)**

CHAPTER VII

Decision-Making

INTRODUCTION

There are no hard and fast rules about how decisions should be
made but there are a number of theories which attempt to explain
the process and a number of techniques for reducing the incidence
of poor ones.

DECISION-MAKING THEORY

1. Definition. Decision-making is the conscious act of exercising
choice amongst a number of options. For management, those
options are usually courses of action, such as choosing between
making a particular component part or buying in that part from
another manufacturer.

2. Decision-making under conditions of uncertainty. Making
decisions entails working with uncertain quantities—something
which the human mind is perhaps ill-equipped to do. Ambrose
Bierce in his *Devil's Dictionary* light-heartedly describes indecision
as the chief element of success, reasoning that if fewer decisions are
made, the number of wrong ones taken will be correspondingly
fewer. There is only one way to do nothing, he holds, but there are
many ways of doing something and only one of them can be the
right way.

The error in Bierce's reasoning is of course that there will
frequently be several satisfactory solutions to a problem. It is
often preferable to choose a satisfactory solution to a problem,
therefore, than to make no decision at all.

3. Costs and benefits. Whatever decision is to be taken, it should
be made on the basis of the costs and benefits to the company
associated with each *option* or course of action.

(*a*) *Types of costs and benefits.* Costs and benefits can be social
or emotional, tactical or strategic as well as financial; any cost

120

or benefit which may appear to be associated with the implementation of a decision option should therefore be taken into account.

(*b*) *Comparison and evaluation*. Values must be assigned to each cost and benefit to enable it to be evaluated and weighed against each other; there is no simple way of comparing unlike elements. It is relatively simple to assign numerical values to financial costs and benefits and to compare them with each other, but less easy to compare financial costs with social and emotional benefits, for instance. Judgments of the latter type must always be subjective. Finally, decision options can only be properly evaluated if adequate relevant and reliable information is available.

All decisions, including those mentioned in **4**, are subject to an appraisal of their costs and benefits. A given level of advertising therefore incurs a cost and has benefits in terms of eventual increases in sales. Similarly the price of a product which is below its optimum level incurs opportunity costs (i.e. lost benefits) while the benefits associated with a given price are the revenues generated at that price.

4. The contribution of economic theory.

(*a*) *Relationship between price and sales*. Some managerial decisions involve exercising choice over a continuous range of values rather than discrete values. Pricing decisions, for example, involve choosing a particular price to charge for a product or service from a range of possible prices. Economic theory suggests that in general there is an inverse relationship between price and sales: the lower the price, the higher will be the sales. However it also shows that the relationship is not linear; after a certain point successive reductions in price by a given amount do not result in equal increments in sales (or revenue). Economic theory also maintains that beyond a certain point diminishing returns to scale are achieved.

(*b*) *Marginal analysis*. Many other managerial decisions, such as how much to spend on advertising or determining the optimum size of a production run, for example, are subject to this theory. In practice, then, it is difficult to quantify the relationship between changes in price, advertising etc. and revenue. The relationship between costs and economies of scale on the other hand is somewhat easier to estimate since fewer uncertainties are involved. This approach to decision-making is known as *marginal analysis* and is intended to elicit optimal decisions.

5. Expected pay-off. Mathematical approaches to decision-making incorporate the concept of *expected pay-off*. This can best be explained by an example.

EXAMPLE

A firm makes a profit of £2 per unit on each unit sold and currently sells 50,000 units per year. The firm expects that if it cuts its price to customers and reduces its own profit margin to £1 per unit it may increase sales to 150,000 units per year, i.e.

Sales (units)	Profit at present price (£2 per unit)	Profit at new price (£1 per unit)
50,000	100,000	50,000
100,000	200,000	100,000
150,000	300,000	150,000

The firm estimates that in the coming year there is a 50 per cent chance that sales will increase to 100,000 units, irrespective of any price cuts, and a 5 per cent chance that sales will rise to 150,000 units. A survey suggests that if a price cut is introduced there is an 80 per cent chance that sales will increase to 100,000 units and a 15 per cent chance that they will rise to 150,000 units in the coming year. The figures in the table below denote the profit anticipated at each of the three levels of estimated demand for the product.

	Estimated demand for product			EMV £
	50,000 units (£)	100,000 units (£)	150,000 units (£)	
Maintain price	100,000 (0.45)[3]	200,000 (0.50)[3]	300,000 (0.05)[3]	160,000[1]
Price cut	50,000 (0.05)[3]	100,000 (0.80)[3]	150,000 (0.15)[3]	105,000[2]

[1] $100,000 \times 0.45 + 200,000 \times 0.50 + 300,000 \times 0.05 = 160,000$.
[2] $50,000 \times 0.05 + 100,000 \times 0.80 + 150,000 \times 0.15 = 105,000$.
[3] The number in brackets represents the "chance" or "probability" that this will happen.

The expected pay-off, or *EMV* (expected monetary value), is obtained by multiplying the numerical value assigned to every possible outcome (estimate of profit) by the probability that it will occur and then summing all the values. In the example it is clear that a price reduction is not desirable since the EMV (expected profit) is much lower.

One disadvantage of this approach is that it requires the estimation of probabilities, which can be difficult. In some cases, however, probabilities may be estimated in the light of past experience (*extrapolated*). Assume that a firm needs to reduce the risk of machine breakdowns. It knows there is a probability that metal fatigue will set in after its machines have been in use for a certain length of time. Management will know that the probability of a particular component failing increases with time and it may decide that all similar components have to be replaced when there is a 50 per cent chance that failure can occur. To determine the precise point (*level of probability*) at which a component should be replaced it is necessary to calculate the respective costs and benefits of replacing the component after different lengths of service, taking into account the probability and cost of breakdowns.

5. Decision trees. Decision trees extend the concept of expected pay-off in that they allow the decision-maker to anticipate the effect decisions made now will have on future decisions, given that a decision made now will lead to another in the future. The potential outcomes of the second decision are thus dependent on the earlier decision. Suppose, for example, a manager has to decide whether to undertake further research and development (R & D) on a project. We assume he has three options:

(*a*) to go into production without further R & D;
(*b*) to undertake further R & D; or
(*c*) to drop the project altogether.

The second option will eventually involve the manager in making a further decision: whether to continue with the project. If he believes that further R & D work will increase the probability that it will eventually be worthwhile to produce and market his product, he may well wish to continue with the R & D work. Thus the outcome of the future decision has a bearing on the earlier decision that has to be taken.

Decision trees enable the decision maker to "map out" in advance all the possible outcomes and sequences of alternative decisions, thereby clarifying all the options before the decision is taken. They are useful where a number of options are available and where a number of possible outcomes is associated with each option. Examples of these are: a new product launch; a purchasing decision; deciding on where to drill for oil; deciding whether or not to undertake marketing research, etc.

To use decision trees it is necessary to obtain estimates of probabilities that events will happen. Intricate decision trees therefore require a knowledge of probability theory. The example below incorporates the idea of conditional probability and illustrates the usefulness of a decision tree in deciding whether further information can be of help prior to making a final decision.

EXAMPLE

A firm is considering whether to test market new product A or to introduce it immediately on a national basis. A test market will give the firm's competitors advance notice of its intentions. Relevant data for the decision is shown in Fig. 9. Letters (a)–(z) in the text below correspond with letters in Fig. 9 (letters (j) and (o) have been omitted for convenience).

The firm considers that if its product were to be introduced nationally without a test market there is a 0.60 probability, i.e. a 60 per cent chance (a) that it will be successful and earn a net

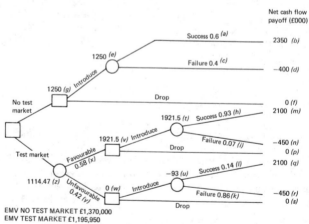

EMV NO TEST MARKET £1,370,000
EMV TEST MARKET £1,195,950

FIG. 9   *Decision tree: whether to test-market a new product.*

cashflow of £2,350,000 (*b*) over its lifespan. The firm also estimate, however, that there is a 0.40 probability (*c*) that the product will not be successful and will create a net cash outflow of £400,000, (*d*) if it is introduced. The EMV is thus:

$$0.60 \times 2,350,000 + 0.40 \times -400 = 1,250,000 \quad (e)$$

The alternative is to drop the product with a pay off of £0 (*f*). Since introducing the product without a test market has a higher EMV than that of dropping the product altogether we record the EMV of the former at point (*g*). The firm knows from past experience that test markets are good indicators of probable market demand. Indeed it estimates that there is a 0.90 probability that the test market will predict the national result correctly and only a 0.10 probability that its prediction will be incorrect. These results are shown as follows.

Outcome of marketing new product A	*Test market result*	
	Favourable	Unfavourable
Success	0.9	0.1
Failure	0.1	0.9

The firm now has to estimate the *conditional probabilities* to assess the values of the various outcomes associated with test marketing the product. For example, given that the test market is favourable what is the probability that the product actually will be a success (*h*)?

The possible outcomes of the test market, and the eventual success or failure of the product are summarised in Fig. 10. The four areas (*EFJC*, *GHDJ*, *KBHG* and *AKFE*) represent the expected frequency proportions (probabilities) with which each type of test market report can occur. The probability that the product will be a success, given a favourable test market, is estimated at:

$$\frac{\text{Area EFJC}}{\text{Area EFJC} + \text{Area GHDJ}} = \frac{0.90 \times 0.60}{0.90 \times 0.60 + 0.10 \times 0.40} = 0.93 \quad (h)$$

In the same way we calculate the other probabilities in the decision tree at this stage.

Probability of failure, given a favourable test market:

$$\frac{\text{Area GHJD}}{\text{Area GHJD} + \text{Area EFCJ}} = \frac{0.40 \times 0.10}{0.40 \times 0.10 + 0.90 \times 0.60} = 0.07 \quad (i)$$

Probability of failure, given an unfavourable test market:

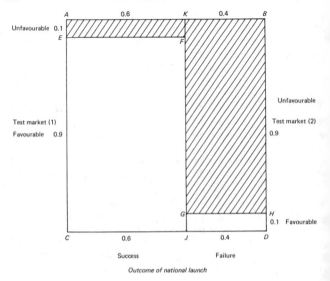

FIG. 10   *Conditional probabilites.*

$$\frac{\text{Area KBHG}}{\text{Area KBGH} + \text{Area AKEF}} = \frac{0.40 \times 0.90}{0.40 \times 0.90 + 0.60 \times 0.10} = 0.86 \quad (k)$$

Probability of success given an unfavourable test market:

$$\frac{\text{Area AKFE}}{\text{Area AKFE} + \text{Area KBHG}} = \frac{0.10 \times 0.60}{0.10 \times 0.60 + 0.40 \times 0.90} = 0.14 \quad (l)$$

Next we insert the payoffs for each of the outcomes associated with launching nationally after a test market ((m), (n), (p), (q) (r) and (s)). The firm considers that if a test market is conducted the best payoff will drop to £2,100,000 and the worst to a net loss of £450,000. Obviously if the product is dropped there is no payoff. We next calculate the EMVs for the two possible decisions to *introduce* the product after a test market (1921.5 and −93) and these are inserted at points (t) and (u) respectively. In case (t) the the value is greater than the respective value for dropping the product (p) and in case (u) it is less than the value for dropping the product (s). The higher values are carried back along the

ranches of the decision tree and inserted above the two boxes
t (v) and (w) respectively (i.e. 1921.5 and 0).

The next step is to calculate the probabilities that the test market
will be favourable or unfavourable. These we find by examining
Fig. 10. The probability that the test market will be favourable
is:

$$\text{Area EFJC} + \text{Area GHDJ} = 0.90 \times 0.60 + 0.4 \times 0.1 = 0.58$$

The probability that the test market will be unfavourable is:

$$\text{Area AKFE} + \text{Area KBHG} = 0.60 \times 0.10 + 0.40 \times 0.90 = 0.42$$

These values are inserted at (x) and (y) respectively.

Lastly we calculate the EMV of the test market:

$$0.58 \times 1921.5 + 0.42 \times 0 = 1114.47$$

and insert this value at (z).

If we compare the EMV of the test market option with that
of the no test market option, we will find that the latter has a
larger value. It would appear better, therefore, not to test market
the product.

The above decision tree is a simple one. Much more complex
decision trees can be built and a number of refinements added.
These include:

(a) incorporating discounted cashflow in to the tree;

(b) incorporating the value of marketing research i.e. enabling
the manager to estimate how much it is worth paying for marketing
research information.

(c) using *expected utility* in place of EMV.

7. Expected utility. Whilst a firm's management may be inclined
to use EMV in relatively low risk circumstances—where the risk
associated with an option is low in relationship to its total payoff
—individual managers may be less willing to do so when the risk
is higher. A middle manager may actively seek to avoid taking
a risk if he can achieve reasonable results through taking less risky
decisions. To a member of the top management team a poor
decision may prove disastrous. One of the problems with the EMV
approach is that it is based on the principle that similar decisions
are taken repeatedly over a period of time and that overall, there
will be a measurable expected pay off. Many management decisions
are however not consistently similar or are taken comparatively
infrequently. Thus there is a real probability that the actual

outcome of a particular decision may not correspond with i
expected outcome. Much depends upon the reliability of th
information upon which the decision is based.

Instead of trying to maximise expected monetary value a
executive may try to maximise his own personal expected utilit
in a given decision situation. Utility is the usefulness and suitabilit
of a particular course of action for the decision-maker. The utilit
of dropping a high risk project may be greater than going ahea
with the project and incurring the possibility of a substantial loss
The expected utility approach assumes that it is possible t
construct a *utility curve* for any individual which will reflect hi
choice between different options or indicate how much he woul
pay or accept for choosing an option. This can be made cleare
with an example.

EXAMPLE

Suppose the marketing director of a large firm is asked to con
sider whether it should invest in a risky marketing venture whic
may involve gaining or losing £1m for the company.

First, a question is put to him. "Suppose there is an even chanc
that the project will make £1m or nothing at all and that someon
makes you an offer to buy the opportunity from you. What i
the least amount of money that you would require?"

Let us assume the marketing director says that he would accep
£100,000. This figure is his *certainty equivalent* because he i
indifferent between this amount of money and this risky project
To construct a utility curve for him we must specify a scale b
which to measure utility. The upper and lower limits of the scal
may be set at any arbitrary figure. However, let us assume tha
the utility (j) for gaining £1m can be given the value of 100
therefore U (£1m) = 100. Suppose also that the utility of a gai
of zero money can be given the value 0, U (£0) = 0. We can now
work out the utility of a gain of £100,000.

$$U (£100,000) = 0.50 \ U (£1m) + 0.50 \ U (£0)$$
$$= 0.50 \ (100) + 0.50 \ (0)$$
$$= 50$$

We can now construct a utility curve which passes through th
three points U (£100,000) = 50, U (£0) = 0 and U (£1m) = 100
(*see* Fig. 11). We can check that the over-all shape of the curv
is correct by estimating other points on the curve. For example

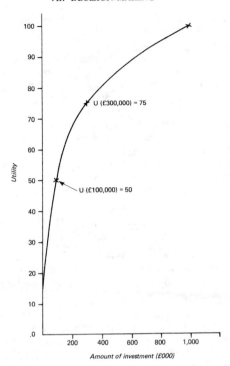

FIG. 11   *Marketing director's utility curve.*

we might ask the marketing director what he would require to forego the opportunity of making either £100,000 or £1m (assuming that each has an even chance of happening). Let us assume that his answer is £350,000, then:

$$U \,(£350,000) = 0.50 \; U \,(£100,000) + 0.50 \; U \,(£1m)$$
$$= 0.50 \; (50) + 0.50 \; (100)$$
$$= 75$$

This figure confirms the shape of the curve (*see* Fig. 11). So far we have only considered the positive part of the curve (i.e. where a loss is not expected). However, we can establish similarly the decision-maker's utility for losing £1m or nothing at all; but in this case we ask him what he is prepared to accept in order to be relieved of the risk.

The next step involves either fitting a mathematical equation to the curve or simply using the graph to obtain selected values. For the sake of simplicity we will take the latter course of action.

Suppose the marketing director has to decide in which of two new product ideas to invest. Suppose there is a 60 per cent chance that product A will yield a net cash flow of £1m and a 40 per cent chance that it will only yield £0.5m. Suppose also that there is an 80 per cent chance that product B will yield £1m and a 20 per cent chance that the project will only break even. In both cases the investment is assumed to be the same (as is the pay back period). Now the expected utility to the marketing director of each option can be calculated as follows (reading appropriate values off the graph):

Product A: 0.60 U (£1m) + 0.40 U (£0.5m) = 0.60(100) + 0.40(85) = 94
Product B: 0.80 U (£1m) + 0.20 U (£0)   = 0.80(100) + 0.20(0)   = 80

Product A thus has a higher utility value for the marketing director despite the fact that they both have the same EMV of £800,000. Under the circumstances the marketing director may well prefer product A.

8. Risk return criterion. In the case of both EMV and expected utility it is assumed that the decision-maker makes use of a single figure in reaching a decision. Many executives might well be unhappy to make a decision in the face of uncertainty unless they have information both on the expected return and on the amount of risk involved. Assuming that they have this information they would generally show a preference for a project which promised a high return and a low risk.

EXAMPLE
Suppose the same marketing director has sufficient funds to invest in a special advertising campaign and that there are two types of possible campaign. The object of the campaign is to increase customer awareness of a given product by a certain amount. Both campaigns will cost the same amount.

The marketing director should ask his four area sales managers and his marketing research manager what impact they think each of the campaigns will have on customer awareness. Assume each executive prepares three estimates showing the maximum possible, the most likely, the minimum possible effects. The marketing director then arranges the fifteen estimates in order of magnitude:

TABLE II. POSSIBLE INCREASE IN AWARENESS LEVEL (%)

Estimate	Campaign A	Campaign B
1	+10	+6
2	+ 9	+5
3	+ 8	+5
4	+ 6	+4
5	+ 5	+2
6	+ 4	+2
7	+ 3	+1
8	+ 3	+1
9	+ 2	+1
10	+ 1	+1
11	nil	+1
12	nil	+1
13	nil	nil
14	nil	nil
15	nil	nil

Next he calculates the mean and the variance for each distribution
(see Statistics, W. M. Harper, Macdonald & Evans, 1982). The
mean represents the most likely pay off for each strategy and the
variance—a value representing the spread of numbers about
the mean—represents the degree of risk. The mean is estimated by
the formula:

$$\bar{X} = \frac{\Sigma X}{n}$$

where $\bar{X}$ = the mean; Σ = the sum of all values of the .... element;
X = the values of each estimate in the distribution; and n = the
number of cases.

The variance is estimated by the formula:

$$s^2 = \frac{(X - \bar{X})^2}{n - 1}$$

where s^2 is the variance (if the sample is 30 or more, $n-1$ becomes
n). The mean of the distribution representing possible outcomes for
campaign A is calculated as 3.4 and its variance 12.25. For
campaign B, the figures are 2.0 for the mean and 4.0 for the variance
respectively.

The greater the variance the greater is the degree of risk that the actual payout will be different to the mean value. So that in this case whilst campaign A has the greatest payout potential it also has the highest degree of risk attached to it. Neither strategy may meet with the optimal criteria so the marketing director may choose according to the one which has the greater ratio of return to risk, i.e. the ratio or return to risk for the two campaigns is as follows:

$$\text{Campaign } A = \frac{3.4}{12.25} = 0.28$$

$$\text{Campaign } B = \frac{2.0}{4.0} = 0.50.$$

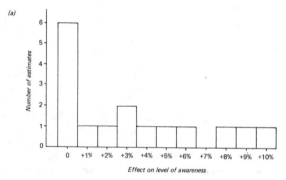

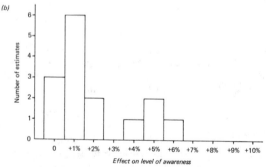

FIG. 12 *Graphical representation of predicted outcome of campaigns.*

Thus he might prefer option B, despite the fact that A has the greater mean payout. However, there may be other factors to take into account, such as whether the estimated difference in the risk to return ratios of the two options is significantly different in his view—he may still prefer A despite the fact that the ratio is lower.

Alternatively if the objective of the campaign is to increase awareness by at least 5 per cent, then he may choose neither of these two options. At a theoretical level he must also ask himself whether the mean and variance are good indicators of return and risk. We can represent the predicted outcomes for campaigns A and B graphically (*see* Fig. 12). A graphical representation indicates more clearly that campaign A is the riskier venture and that campaign B offers probably a better chance of going some way to meet the objective. However the ultimate decision will depend upon the marketing director's attitude towards risk. A conservative manager might well prefer B to A. In this case the graphical representations support the statistical calculations.

9. Minimax criterion and minimum regret criterion.

(*a*) *Minimax criterion.* The foregoing methods assume that the decision-maker can obtain a fair estimate of the odds for the contingencies surrounding his choice. However, a decision-maker may often have no idea at all of probable outcomes with research, making matters no clearer. Under these circumstances the decision-maker may prefer to abandon probability theory altogether. Returning to the example in **8** above, we can construct the following pay-off matrix:

Stragegy of adopting	Best possible outcome (%)	Worst possible outcome (%)
Campaign A	$+ 10$	nil
Campaign B	$+ 6$	nil

The best that can be expected from campaign A is an increased awareness of 10 per cent and the worst is that nothing at all could happen. Similarly in the case of campaign B the best that could happen is an increase in awareness of 6 per cent and the worst is that nothing could happen. The decision-maker's strategy is simply to minimise the maximum loss, but in this case since the maximum losses are identical (both are nil) he will be indifferent

between the two strategies. An executive who makes decisions on
this basis might therefore turn to another method, such as the
minimum regret criterion method.

(*b*) *Minimum regret criterion.* We can look at the various figures
in the pay-off matrix in **9**(*a*) above in a different way. If the marketing director knew for certain that an increase in awareness of 10
per cent would result from using campaign *A* then he would experience regret in adopting Campaign *B*. We can express the regret
in terms of loss in increase of awareness. The matrix can then be
rewritten as follows:

Strategy of adopting	Best possible outcome (%)	Worst possible outcome (%)
Campaign *A*	0	0
Campaign *B*	4	0

The regret indicated in each cell is computed in the following
manner. The best strategy in each column is assigned a zero for
zero regret and the other strategy (strategies where there are more
than two options available) is assigned a regret number which
represents the difference between its payoff and the best payoff
in the column.

The next step involves examining the most regret the marketing
director might feel with each strategy. If he were to adopt campaign
B he might experience as much as 4 per cent regret but if he were
to adopt campaign *A* he might experience zero regret. Both of
these figures represent maximum regrets and the minimum of these
figures is the zero regret. Thus the executive who wants to minimise
his maximum regret would prefer campaign *A*.

Whether or not an executive adopts the minimax criterion or
the minimum regret criterion depends upon his attitude towards
risk. The more conservative decision-maker would adopt the
minimax in preference to the minimum regret criterion.

10. Games theory. Let us consider two firms which are in competition with one another. Suppose Firm 1 has the options of
introducing a new model to its product line or modifying an existing
one instead; Firm 2 has the same options. Neither firm knows
in advance what the other intends to do. We can construct a
pay-off matrix for Firm 1 based on four possible outcomes and

the effect that the outcomes will have on Firm 1's share of the market. The figures in the cells of the matrix denote the expected change in market share from Firm 1's point of view.

		Firm 2's strategy modification New model (%)	(%)
Firm 1's strategy	new model	+1	+3
	modification	−2	−1

It can be seen that if Firm 1 makes a product modification and Firm 2 introduces a new model, Firm 1 will suffer a decrease in market share of 2 per cent.

Games theory enables the identification of the best strategy for both firms to adopt (assuming that neither knows in advance what the other intends to do). The basis of the theory is to discover the *equilibrium pair*, if there is one (an equilibrium pair will not necessarily exist in all cases). The equilibrium pair occurs in that cell which is both the maximum of its column and the minimum of its row. The minimum value in the row represents the strategy which minimises the maximum loss of market share from Firm 2's point of view. The maximum value of the column represents the maximum gain in market share that Firm 1 can attain given Firm 2 adopts the strategy which minimises its maximum loss of market share. In this particular case the equilibrium pair is in the top left hand cell (+1%). The best strategy for Firm 1 is thus to introduce a new model and that for Firm 2 is to follow suit.

The above is an example of a straightforward two-person game, known as a *zero sum game*. However, there will usually be several businesses in competition with each other with several different pay-offs for each of the participants consequent to the same events. Introducing a new model may increase Firm 1's market share by 1 per cent, for instance, but have no effect on the market share held by, say, Firm 4. These games, which involve more than two players, are known as *non-zero sum games*. Nevertheless solutions to more complex games can be found, although they tend to involve lengthy calculations. Whilst games theory

is not yet in wide general use, it has considerable development
potential.

DECISION-MAKING IN PRACTICE

The preceding paragraphs (**1–10**) outline some of the more
important theoretical approaches to decision-making, but their
practical application, described in **11–21**, is sometimes problematical.

11. Management approaches to decision-making. If managers
approach decision-making in terms of probabilities and marginal
analysis rather than of absolutes they are likely to make better
decisions. One point of view holds that in decision-making
managers do not seek to maximise the reward for endeavour—
as economic theory suggests it is possible, and mathematical techniques purport, to do. Herbert Simon (1959) supports this view.
"While economic man maximises—selects the best alternative from
among all those available to him; his cousin . . . administrative
man, satisfices—looks for a course of action that is satisfactory
or good enough." Examples of satisficing criteria that are familiar
to business men include "share of the market targets", "adequate
profit" and "fair price", etc.

EXAMPLE
A firm which manufactures a particular domestic appliance had
a monopoly of this product-market in the UK in the early 1950s.
As competitors arose the firm's market share began to fall
although unit sales began to increase, since the product-market
was expanding. In 1974 the firm's market share was around
30 per cent with unit sales increasing by some 5–10 per cent
per annum. The firm expected that its market share would
eventually fall to around 25 per cent and that actual unit sales
would decline as market saturation point was reached. The firm
considered that as long as its market share did not fall below
25 per cent in the course of the next five years, its performance
would be satisfactory. It would not consider making radical
changes to its marketing or production policies unless market
share fell below this figure.

12. Types of decision. Dale (1978) classifies decisions made in
business organisations under three separate headings:

(*a*) *Policy decisions.* Policy decisions are made by top management and include choice of product markets, key executives, choice of financial structure for the firm, volume of production output, marketing policies and the main structure of the organisation.

(*b*) *Administrative decisions.* Administrative decisions are made at a lower level in the organisation but concern the selection of a method of putting policy decisions into practice. Thus the size of the physical distribution budget would be a policy decision whereas the choice of transportation method might be an administrative decision.

(*c*) *Executive decisions.* Executive decisions are made at the point where the work is put into practice. For example the choice of vehicle by which to send a specific consignment.

13. Responsibility for decision-making. In general, the closer a decision-maker is to the point at which his decision is put into effect, the quicker a decision can be taken. Since speed is often vitally important in decision-making, it is recommended that decisions should be assigned to the lowest level in the organisation fully competent to make them. This strategy has the benefit of not overburdening top management with too many decisions. The problem is of course to determine the lowest competent level. This has been defined as "the level at which the job-holder has both access to all available information pertinent to the decision and the incentive to weigh these factors impartially" (Ernest Dale, 1978). Thus a sales manager is competent to decide how to allocate personal selling expenses between salesmen and to decide how much he feels it necessary for selling expenses in total. He is not competent to judge, however, whether sales have received a fair share of the expenses budget as compared with, say, the advertising, production or general administration departments.

14. The role of information in decision-making. Decisions can only be as good as the information on which they are taken. Sparse or inadequate information is likely to lead to poor decisions. Too much information, on the other hand, is likely to hinder, rather than help, the decision-making process; irrelevant data can only encourage confusion and obscure other, more relevant, information.

It follows, therefore, that effective decision-making is dependent on the provision of relevant and meaningful information. Information may be distorted or even lost on its way from its source to the decision-maker; it is therefore important to develop an effective management information system to overcome these problems.

The following illustrates some of the problems which can occur:

(*a*) *Lack of information.* A brand manager, contemplating a price cut on Product X has no information on how competitors will probably respond.

(*b*) *Information overload.* Top management are presented with 100 ideas for R & D projects. Each idea is backed with a fifty-page report underlining the value of the project to the company.

(*c*) *Irrelevant information.* A line manager interviewing an applicant for a position as a production foreman has information from the personnel department on the personal background and scholastic aptitude of the applicant but no references from previous employers.

(*d*) *Poor presentation of information.* Faced with the problems of setting the next year's overall sales budget, top management is presented with a wordy and unnecessarily complex forecast from the marketing department.

(*e*) *Poor management information system.* Production is held up because of a shortage of component parts, purchasing having failed to obtain them in time to keep production flowing. Production has only just received notification that a shortage exists.

15. Management information systems. It cannot be assumed that information relevant to a business organisation will flow towards it from its environment. Neither can it be assumed that such an organisation will necessarily take in that information, should it come to its attention, nor that, if it does, the information will invariably reach those who can make the best use of it. A good management information system will ensure that all this happens and in addition prevent information from being mislaid, misdirected, distorted, delayed and perhaps even suppressed. An organisation which suffers from these problems will be operating under a severe disadvantage. It is equally important that information which originates from within the organisation is similarly systematised.

A management information system need not be complex nor even computer-based. However, the advent of micro-processors has enabled many smaller firms to benefit from the advantages of a computerised management information system. A typical sophisticated computer-based management information system would have terminals and display consoles in all major departments. Any executive would, at the touch of a button, be able to ascertain (for instance):

(*a*) total ex-works despatches of all products for any given period of time at the time the information is requested, and in addition find how these figures compare with the sales plan or budget.

(*b*) stock levels (actual and planned) of all items held by the firm;

(*c*) the backlog of all items to be purchased from outside suppliers and their promised delivery dates;

(*d*) production output (actual and planned);

(*e*) materials wastage rates (actual and expected);

(*f*) lost hours due to stoppages; and

(*g*) expenses, itemised by department, both actual and budgeted, as well as other, similar, information relating to production, marketing, manpower and financial planning.

BEHAVIOURAL DIMENSIONS

16. Objectives and management beliefs and attitudes. The importance of keeping objectives in view when making decisions should be emphasised as the beliefs and attitudes of the decision-maker(s) can have an important influence on company objectives, and therefore on the type of decision that is made and the speed with which it is made and subsequently implemented. "Some decisions may never be made because they are not in accord with management's beliefs about priorities. Others may not be implemented, or their implementation long delayed, because management, although it gives lip-service to the importance of doing so, does not really believe in its value", (Rosemary Stewart, 1963). An example of this would be a small company which did not seek to expand its product market scope or size of operation beyond a particular point because it believed it had reached the optimum size compatible with the personal aims and objectives of its board of directors. The influence of beliefs and attitudes is most felt on policy and strategy decisions, but it can also influence decision-making at lower levels in the organisation.

EXAMPLE

In the early 1960s a large British engineering company undertook to develop a machine for forming metal objects by an extrusion, as opposed to casting, process. The project was handed over to one of the company's research establishments particularly interested in that field and was put under the control of a small team of five or six researchers. The executive director of the company took a keen personal interest in the project. In the first three years investment in and top management enthusiasm for the project was high, but when the executive director resigned, interest in the project at board level waned. One by one members of the R & D team either left the company or were transferred to other divisions and finally, some seven years after its inception, the highly important project was dropped.

17. Stages in decision-making. A problem must be considered in three basic stages before a solution to it can be found and an appropriate decision made.

(*a*) *Stage one.* The first and most important stage is to define the problem; a correct decision cannot be made if the problem is wrongly defined. A common error is to define a problem in terms of its symptoms, overlooking the real problem which lies behind them. Suppose a company is faced with falling sales and profits, the real reason for which is an unbalanced product mix. Its instinctive response might be to reduce its selling or production costs, thereby considerably exacerbating its problem. Thus an incorrect definition would lead management to tackle the symptoms of its problem rather than the problem itself.

(*b*) *Stage two.* The second stage is analysing the nature of the problem. Taking the example of the product-mix problem above, and assuming the problem has been correctly defined, analysis will show that different products are making substantially different contributions to profits and overheads.

(*c*) *Stage three.* The third stage involves identifying a number of possible courses of action and evaluating each in terms of its ability to solve the problem. In the example given, the correct course of action would be to decide which products to delete and what new products to introduce to the product mix.

PROGRESS TEST 7

1. What is decision-making? **(1)**
2. Upon what basis should rational decisions be made? **(2, 3)**
3. What contribution has economic theory made to the theoretical approach to decision-making? **(4)**

4. What do you understand by the term "expected pay off"? **(5)**

5. Under what circumstances might "decision trees" be a useful adjunct to decision-making? **(6)**

6. Explain the concept of "expected utility". **(7)**

7. Explain the rationale behind the "risk return" criterion. **(8)**

8. Distinguish between the "minimax criterion" and the "minimum regret" criterion. **(9)**

9. Of what use is "games theory" to management decision-making? **(10)**

10. How should one decide upon the appropriate level in an organisation at which particular decisions should be taken? **(13)**

11. What are the common problems associated with information used for organisational decision-making? **(14)**

12. How do attitudes and beliefs influence decision-making? **(16)**

13. What are the basic stages in decision-making? **(17)**

CHAPTER VIII

Control

INTRODUCTION

The control of an organisational system is directly related to its planning. Control identifies the need for revised plans and enables the effectiveness of existing ones to be monitored.

1. Definition. Control has been defined (Kast and Rosenzweig, 1974) as "that phase of the managerial process which maintains organisation activity within allowable limits as measured from expectations. These expectations may be implicit or explicitly stated in terms of objectives, plans, procedures, or rules and regulations". Broadly, then, the function of control is to make a system operate in a more reliable, convenient and economical manner. It is therefore essentially concerned with checking or verifying, so that a control must be able to measure actual performance against a standard predetermined by the planning process. Control exists in every aspect of a business, giving rise to production control, stock control, financial control, quality control, sales control, etc.

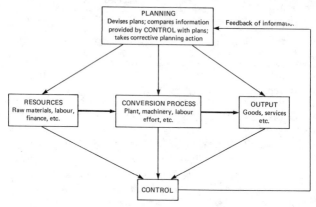

FIG. 13   *The concept of control.*

2. Elements of control. All control systems must have four basic elements in common, as follows (these are illustrated as applying to sales management, where a hypothetical company's sales force sells its product, X).

(*a*) A measurable and controllable characteristic for which standards are known; e.g. the sales manager is directed to achieve a certain volume of sales of product X, through retail outlets type Y, during a certain month.

(*b*) A means of measuring that characteristic; here the sales manager asks individual salesmen to fill in weekly sales reports for sales of product X by retail outlets type Y.

(*c*) A means of comparing actual or projected results with a known standard and evaluating any differences that arise. Here the sales manager would compare each salesman's results with individual, predetermined targets and check them against the over-all target.

(*d*) A means of making changes in the system to enable the known standard to be adjusted as necessary. Here the sales manager should be able to communicate to the sales force the need to sell more or less of product X in the following month.

3. Control phases. Control can take place before, during or after an event.

(*a*) *Precontrol.* This is essentially pre-emptive as exemplified by scheduled maintenance work on plant, machinery and vehicles etc. which prevents inconvenient and expensive breakdowns. Maintenance takes place at times when these items are required for productive purposes.

(*b*) *Concurrent control.* This form of control is exercised while an event is taking place. The partial closure of an operating plant whilst repairs are being carried out is an illustration.

(*c*) *Post control.* This, the poorest form of control, is where control is carried out after the event. It is wasteful of resources to exercise control in this way, since it inevitably means loss of production through total shutdown of operating machinery, with consequent loss of orders, cash and goodwill.

Good control corrects deviations from the planned standard at the earliest possible time. Pre-control, or "feed-forward" control, therefore, is best since it allows deviations to be corrected before they become critical.

4. Control in different departments.

(*a*) *Production control.* This involves:

(*i*) *routing*: the sequence and flow of operations and materials to be used;

(*ii*) *loading*: the advance assignment of work to a department or machine;

(*iii*) *scheduling*: determining the time at which each operation should start and finish;

(*iv*) *estimating*: assessing in advance the likely cost of producing a specific job;

(*v*) *despatching*: sending off completed jobs; and

(*vi*) *progress chasing*: following up all jobs at all stages to ensure that they are running to schedule.

(*b*) *Stock control.* This involves determining optimum stock levels and re-order quantities, ensuring that there is an adequate management information system to give an up-to-date picture of stocks of:

(*i*) raw materials;

(*ii*) work in progress; and

(*iii*) finished goods.

(*c*) *Quality control.* Quality control ensures that a firm's output conforms to its minimum standard of acceptability. The standards may be laid down by the firm itself or may be demanded by its customers. For example, in the motor engineering industry vehicle parts are machined to very fine tolerances. Quality controllers take systematic random samples of finished components and measure them to determine the proportion of the sample that is within the given tolerance. If this proportion is unduly low, corrective action will be necessary. A firm producing camshafts for sports cars, for example, may feel that five faulty camshafts out of every 10,000 tested is acceptable but that a substantial rise in that number would necessitate an investigation.

FINANCIAL CONTROL

5. Function. The purpose of financial control is to make sure that an organisation's resources are put to the most profitable use. Control is exercised primarily through accounting records which enable the financial position of an organisation to be monitored. The size and composition of a firm's working capital and the extent of its resources and commitments are critical in this respect. If its working capital is inadequate, a business may not be able to take advantage of the usual discounts for prompt settlement of accounts and may have to purchase its supplies uneconomically in small quantities. In addition, it may be forced to reduce its profit margins or even grant its customers large discounts to secure sufficient funds. It is essential, then, for a firm to know the extent of its working capital at any given moment.

6. The manager and financial control. Management is primarily concerned with the day-to-day running of a business and with the measurement and analysis of profit and loss or revenue and expenditure. Management's job is to control expenditure, i.e. to keep costs to a minimum, and to preserve working capital. For this purpose, it requires a regular and frequent supply of financial control information in order to compare actual with planned performance. Management therefore should be promptly notified of any deviations from expected performance. Expenditure analyses should break down a firm's expenditure into individual items which can be readily identified and controlled.

7. Costing. Producing these detailed analyses is a costing function which consists of classifying, recording and allocating the total expenditures of an organisation and absorbing them into the costs of its products or services. Costing serves three purposes:

(*a*) it enables control to be exercised over expenditure by providing details of every item of expense;

(*b*) it enables future costs to be estimated with reasonable precision and thus enables profitable selling prices to be calculated; and

(*c*) it indicates which of a firm's products are most profitable, enabling production to be concentrated on these to maximise profits.

8. Costing methods. The method of costing adopted varies with the area of industry in which a firm operates. In the brewing industry, a firm usually manufactures only one basic product and has standard units of production; here the *unit, or output, costing* method is adopted. On the other hand, in the shipbuilding industry, where each job or contract is carried out separately, expenses are allocated to each individual order. This is known as *job costing*. Other types of costing include: batch costing, multiple costing,

process costing and operating costing. Whatever the costing system
used, all costs must be allocated to a predetermined unit.

9. Budgetary control. Budgetary control enables an organisation's
operations to be planned in advance over a specific period. Targets
are fixed by preparing estimates of fixed and variable expenses,
sales, working capital, etc. for the forthcoming period, in the light
of previous performance and current policy. This provides a
measure by which future expectations may be judged. It involves
first preparing estimates of future sales of individual products,
based on market surveys, salesmen's estimates, etc. Next, an
estimate is made of future price levels for the products (future
revenue) together with estimates of the associated selling and distribution costs. The production department then considers the
extent to which it can satisfy such a demand and whether additional
capital will be required to expand the workforce or purchase new
equipment. Estimates of the costs of these sales plans are then
prepared and submitted to top management, who then examine
sales and production budgets and stipulate changes to produce a
more acceptable plan as necessary.

10. Standard costing. While costing enables information on
expenses which have been incurred to be obtained, standard costing
aims to monitor current costs by establishing, for each operational
process, predetermined standards against which actual costs can
be measured. This resembles the way that budgetary control establishes targets for the various activities of the organisation. *Standard
costs are what costs should be under normal conditions*; actual costs
can then be expressed as a ratio of this standard. Standard costing
monitors such variables as excess production capacity, wastage of
materials and time, etc. and brings them to the attention of management as they occur so that appropriate steps can be taken.

Detailed information about the workings of a firm is necessary
to establish a standard costing system. In particular, special attention should be given to the structure of the organisation, so that
the responsibility for variations from budgetary expectations can
be attributed to the departmental or functional managers concerned. Specifications have to be drawn up to establish a standard
for the quality, quantity and price of materials used directly in
production, together with normal rates of wastage. Standard
operation times are fixed for all the production processes (these
are ascertained from work study analyses) and standards prepared
for overhead expenses. Once such standards have been established,

the actual costs can be compared with them and the variance noted. Standard costing divides the variance into its component parts and thus enables individual variance to be traced to its source and the appropriate action to be taken.

11. Non-budgetary controls. Budgeting is not the only means of effecting control; other devices such as statistical data, special reports and analyses, charts, break-even point analyses (*see* Fig. 14) and operational audits can also be used.

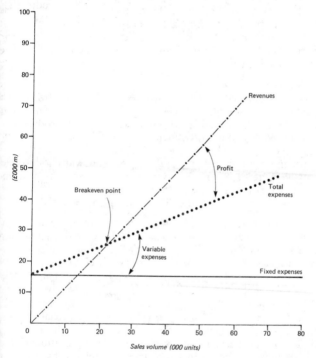

FIG. 14 *Break even analysis: Break even point is about 26,000 units. Total expenses comprise variable plus fixed costs; the former vary with the amount sold whereas the latter remain constant.*

2. Evaluating the profitability of the product mix. The price of any product (that is, the money received by the seller in exchange for the product) can be apportioned in such a way that part of it "repays" the direct costs (which can be ascertained by reference to the "cost centres" through which the product passed during production) and the remainder is a "contribution" to the indirect costs and to profits.

In the long run a firm must cover all its costs. In the short run, provided that the price of the product covers the product's direct costs and makes only a small contribution to overheads it will be worthwhile to produce it.

The concept of "contribution" is useful in showing whether the mix of products that a firm sells, plans to sell, or has sold is, or was, the best under the circumstances. It is assumed that the firm wishes to maximise the total contribution of the product mix to overheads and profit.

EXAMPLE

A firm manufactures two products, A and B. It plans to produce and sell 300 units of A and 200 units of B, each week. The selling price of A is fixed at £44 per unit and that of B at £46 per unit. Total weekly fixed costs (indirect costs, admin., etc.) amount to £3,000 per week. Variable costs (labour, raw materials, etc.) per unit of A produced amount to £35 per unit, whilst for product B the figure is £38 per unit. Given this information can we assume that the firm is maximising the contribution to profit and overheads by producing and selling in the quantities stated?

The selling price of A is £44 per unit and the variable cost amount to £35 per unit, then the contribution to profits and overheads per unit sold is £9 (£44 − 35). Per unit contribution of product B is £8 (£46 − 38). The total weekly contribution is:

$$\frac{\text{Contribution of}}{\text{product A}} + \frac{\text{contribution of}}{\text{product B}} = \frac{\text{Total}}{\text{contribution}}$$

$$(£300 \times 9) \quad + \quad (£200 \times 8) \quad = \quad (£4,300)$$

This more than covers the fixed costs (£3,000) and contribute £1,300 to profit and overheads. If there are no constraints on the firm concerning what it can produce then it ought to produce *only* product A since this is the more profitable. In practice there are constraints upon what a firm can produce, as we shall see in X where we make a number of assumptions concerning production capacity and show how it is possible to determine the optimum product mix by using a linear programming technique.

There are other constraints apart from those relating to production capacity (although these are not considered in XV). The firm
may not for instance be able to sell more of product A than 300
units per week (*this is termed demand constraint*). Fixed costs may
increase considerably if the firm attempts to sell more than 300
units per week of product A.

13. Control through return on investment. The level of return on
a company's investment can be used to measure the absolute and
relative success of a firm or one of its units. Return on investment
(ROI) is the rate of return that a company unit can earn on the
capital allocated to it. The goal of the firm, or one of its units,
is to optimise the long run rate of return on the capital which it
uses for business purposes and the measurement of its ROI helps
a company to focus managerial attention on how to make the best
possible profit with available capital. It enables the over-all
efficiency of a company to be measured as well as its major
divisions, departments and products. Management is made to think
in terms of profit relative to capital employed, which in turn is
a measure of the degree of financial success of the organisation.
Departmental managers can be made responsible for performance
in terms of profit related to the amount of capital invested in their
unit and this compels them to consider operations from the point
of view of top management.

PROGRESS TEST 8

1. Define control. **(1)**
2. What are the four basic elements of control? **(2)**
3. Differentiate between the three control phases. **(3)**
4. Indicate the types of control that may be found in a manufacturing firm. **(4)**
5. What is the purpose of financial control? **(5–10)**
6. Describe some of the non-budgetary control devices that can
be used by an organisation. **(11)**
7. What is meant by control through return on investment? **(13)**

CHAPTER IX

Organisation

1. Introduction. This chapter reviews some concepts of formal organisations. Consideration is given to ideas concerning bureaucracy and the distinction between "line" and "staff" personnel. Particular attention is paid to division of labour, scalar and functional processes, organisational structure and span of control.

2. Bureaucracy. The German social scientist and philosopher Max Weber described bureaucratic functions and characteristics as follows:

(*a*) fixed official duties are assigned to individuals and these form regular activities which are directed towards achieving organisational goals;

(*b*) all activities follow the organisational principle of "hierarchy";

(*c*) a consistent system of abstract rules enables operations to receive equal treatment; and

(*d*) officials of organisations act as "formalistic personalities" and avoid becoming emotionally involved in the work of the organisation.

3. Efficient organisation. The term "organisation" may be interpreted in at least three different ways. It can be considered as:

(*a*) the management activity which is concerned with arranging people, resources and tasks in an orderly and efficient manner;

(*b*) the outcome of organising activity; or

(*c*) a description for any business.

Efficient organisation is defined (Fulmer, 1978) as "the grouping of people and processes for the prevention of waste".

ELEMENTS OF ORGANISATION

4. Pillars of organisation. W. G. Scott (1961) identified what he considered to be the "pillars upon which classical organisation theory is built":

150

(*a*) division of labour;
(*b*) chain of command (scalar and functional processes);
(*c*) span of control; and
(*d*) structure.

5. Division of labour. This entails breaking down a task into smaller units, each of which can be performed by different individuals. This in turn leads, as a general rule, to more efficient organisation. In theory, the division of labour permits workers to improve their skills by becoming practised at a particular task. Time in passing from one job to another is also saved. The development of machinery to help with a specific operation is also encouraged. Too much division of labour can lead to an individual's job becoming highly repetitive and tedious, which can lead to inefficiency.

6. Job enlargement, job rotation and job enrichment. To overcome the problems which can result from work tedium, the following approaches have been tried.

(*a*) *Job enlargement*. This entails putting together a number of jobs, so that the worker has more different operations to perform. An operator who may previously have merely fitted wheels to cars on an assembly line may be required to fit the tyres as well.

(*b*) *Job rotation*. Here individuals are switched from one job to another on a regular basis. In a tyre and exhaust fitting business employees fit tyres and exhausts on alternate days.

(*c*) *Job enrichment*. This is where the employee is made aware of the over-all deadlines and quality standards that have to be met, but has the autonomy to determine the order in which the various tasks may be tackled to meet the objectives. A garage mechanic for example, might be given three days to complete repair work on four different cars, but have complete autonomy to decide how he is going to complete the jobs.

7. Chain of command. An organisation operates on the basis of responsibilities and the exercise of the authority necessary to carry out those responsibilities. No single organisational executive can carry out *all* the tasks for which he is responsible, so that delegation of authority becomes necessary; this in turn leads to the development of a chain of command. However, whilst authority can be delegated, ultimate responsibility cannot be delegated. Effective delegation of authority requires the delegator to be willing to:

(*a*) let other people try out their own ideas;

(b) let subordinates make decisions;
(c) let others make mistakes;
(d) trust subordinates; and
(e) employ only broad (loose) controls.

Such attitudes should lead to more efficient organisation (provided subordinates are sufficiently capable) since they enable the delegator of authority to concentrate on a smaller number of problems or decisions and to *enrich* the jobs of subordinates. An executive who is reluctant to delegate authority to subordinates runs the risk of making errors, as a result of being overburdened with work.

8. Unity of command. This can be interpreted as only one superior for each employee. The object is to avoid confusing an individual by giving him conflicting orders.

EXAMPLE
The export sales executive and the home sales manager may independently put pressure on the production superintendent to reschedule production targets to meet their individual requirements for specific customer orders. Neither the export sales executive, nor the home sales manager, can order the production superintendent to do as they wish since there is no direct chain of command (*see* Fig. 15). Instead the two marketing executives

FIG. 15   *Hierarchy.*

should approach the marketing director, who should decide upon priorities. He may then approach the production director with a specific request, who may then, in turn, issue directives to the production superintendent. In the event that the production director is unco-operative, the marketing director may appeal to the managing director.

In the above example (and in reality) the production superintendent will often agree to oblige one or other of the marketing executives on an informal basis, although he does not have to do so.

9. Span of control. Sir Ian Hamilton, commander of the British Forces at the Battle of Gallipoli in the First World War, promoted the idea that no superior should have more than half a dozen subordinates. V. A. Graicunas and Lyndall Urwick developed Hamilton's idea and Graicunas calculated that an executive who was involved in the supervision of a group of 12 subordinates could have as many as 2,000 relationships to maintain.

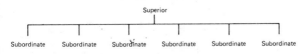

FIG. 16   *Span of control.*

Other management thinkers believe that the span of control should be unrestricted and that it should be a function of the situation. In reality, the span of control can range from 1 to over 100, but the most common appears to be between 5 and 15. In the studies reported by Joan Woodward (1965) average spans in small-batch production firms were 23; large-batch and mass production firms 49, and long-run, continuous process production, 13.

10. Structure. Employees and the tasks they perform have to be grouped into organisational sub-units to enable top management to exercise control over them. These sub-units are usually known as departments.

Initially, departments were simply numerical groupings of individuals, irrespective of their function; even factories were divided into departments on this basis. The next logical step was to create *functional* departments. Here, all workers performing similar types of tasks were grouped together. Thus, all sales staff were put into one department and all production staff into another (*see* Fig. 17 (*a*)). Creating departments in this way tends to increase the "perceptual bias" (outlook) of its members, so that salesmen may see every problem from a sales perspective and production staff from a production perspective. This difference in perceptual bias can lead to inter-departmental conflict and may in extreme cases decrease organisational efficiency.

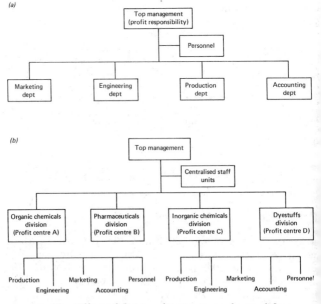

FIG. 17   *Effect of divisionalisation on a chemical firm.*

11. Other methods of creating departments. This may involve creat
ing larger units known as *divisions* which can be sub-divided int
departments. Divisions may be created on the following bases.

(*a*) *By geographical area.* This encourages local participation i
decision-making. Responsibility is placed at a low level in th
organisation and emphasis is placed on local markets and loca
problems. Regional divisions facilitate face-to-face communicatio
with local customers.

(*b*) *By product.* As an enterprise grows in size, it becomes to
unwieldy to manage on a purely functional basis. One way t
overcome this problem is to re-organise on a *product-division* basi
Such a structure enables top management to delegate authorit
to a divisional manager with respect to the manufacturing, sale
service and engineering functions relating to a particular grou
of products. It also enables top management to exact pro
responsibility from each of the divisional managers. A *function*
structure gives top management sole responsibility for profitabili

ut a divisional structure allows the responsibility to be shared
see Fig. 17 (*b*)). Each division becomes a "profit centre" and has to
work towards targets set by top management.

(*c*) *By customer.* There are occasions when departmentation by
customer is the best structure to adopt. Universities and colleges
are organised along these lines. A university is divided into a
number of faculties and within each faculty there are a number
of departments. Each department is orientated towards a particular
kind of student, e.g. a department of accounting fulfils the requirements of students wishing to study accounting subjects, and so
on.

In practice organisation structures are often combinations of
several systems and this is particularly true where holding companies are involved. The best solution is to adopt a structure which
best suits the situation.

2. Co-ordination. Organisations become more complex as they
grow in size and as they come to employ more specialists. The
employment of organisational specialists increases as a company
grows; when it becomes too difficult for an individual in a particular field to be conversant with all aspects of that field. The
problem of co-ordinating the activities of several departments at
top management level, or several sections within a department at
senior management level, or several sub-sections or individuals
at middle management level, becomes increasingly difficult as a
company gets bigger.

3. Line and staff relations. Line executives are those who make
a direct contribution to the goals of an organisation while "staff"
are those who advise and give assistance to line managers to enable
them to achieve organisational goals.

4. The need for staff departments. In large-scale organisations,
technical and other environmental developments have given rise
to the need for staff, or personnel specialists. The concept of the
personnel function as we know it today is an excellent example
of the growth of the staff function within organisations to meet
the needs of changing organisations and environments. There are
three main types of staff.

(*a*) *Personal staff.* For example, a private secretary, who may
conduct an executive's private business correspondence and
arrange appointments.

(b) *Specialised staff.* For example, personnel, accountin
engineering and research staff.

(c) *General staff.* For example, an individual having the tit
"assistant to" the managing director; or an executive committ
reporting to the chief executive; or specific groups appointed
be the eyes and ears of the chief executive.

15. Organisation charts. R. Pitfield (1978) aptly summarises t
types and uses of organisation charts. Here their purpose is simp
outlined. Organisation charts represent the structure of an orga
isation diagrammatically, in other words, they represent what
termed the *formal* organisation. Organisation charts can illustrat

    (a) the demarcation of responsibility;

    (b) the lines of authority;

    (c) the channels of communication; and

    (d) the relationship between members of the organisation.

16. The informal organisation. We must, however, distinguis
between the *formal* and the *informal* organisation. Whilst t
formal organisation, as depicted in organisation charts, represen
the physical distribution of manpower resources throughout t
organisation, it does not attempt to take account of the pow
structure which may operate within a company (its *inform
organisation*).

17. New structures. A functional structure, organised around t
primary tasks to be performed (sales, production etc.) is most sui
able for small companies, or large companies with a single produ
range and/or situations in which the business environment
relatively stable. This type of structure does not favour t
emergence of new entrepreneurial action.

(a) *Divisionalisation.* Many firms develop in size to the stag
where a functional form of structure is inappropriate for their nee
and adopt in its place a divisional structure. This form of structu
is appropriate where growth and product diversification hav
occurred and where it is reasonably easy to divide the compan
up into "profit centres". It is often adopted by companies aft
mergers and acquisitions have taken place and in situations whic
are characterised by a rapidly changing environment. Top manag
ment is able to delegate profit responsibility and thereby obtai
a better means of motivating middle management.

(b) *Intermediate structures.* Divisionalisation has been widel
successful but has been found to have certain disadvantage

Divisions can find themselves competing with one another in the same market and conflict can arise when transfer prices have to be negotiated for the purposes of internal trading. Conflict between short-term divisional objectives and long-term company objectives can result in top management imposing constraints on the divisions which restrict their freedom to operate on their own initiative. *Intermediate structures* attempt to gain the benefits of both divisional and functional structures. Divisional features are superimposed on predominantly functional structures and *vice versa*. There are three types of intermediate structure.

(*i*) *Systems structure.* Here the idea of a divisional profit centre is retained, but control over certain functional activities and resources (functional activities include purchasing, distribution etc.) rests with top management rather than divisional management. This structure has benefits where there is considerable interdependence between divisions. The pharmaceutical industry is an example of the successful employment of this type of structure. Its advantage is that it enables the best use to be made of company resources, but there is, however, more risk of making bad or poor decisions since the nature of information available to top management at the centre will be incomplete. There are also accounting and control problems and the possibility of conflict arising between profit centres and planning units.

(*ii*) *Project structures.* Here temporary project teams with decision-making powers are superimposed on an existing structure. It is an appropriate approach where problem-solving or developmental situations require the involvement of several departments; this structure is commonly found in high technology industries.

(*iii*) *Matrix structures.* Here, the line of command is divided permanently between two divisional structures (e.g. product and geographical divisions). Decision-making authority is then split according to whether the problem is one of a geographical nature or one that concerns a product (assuming that the division is based upon product and geography). Matrix structures facilitate better decision-making, since they improve the availability of expert knowledge. There is, still, the risk of potential conflict between the two lines of command and there are problems of accounting and control.

PROGRESS TEST 9

1. What is bureaucracy? **(2)**

2. What are the characteristics of an efficient organisation? **(3)**

3. What are the "four pillars" upon which classical organisation theory is built? **(4)**

4. Why is the concept of division of labour important? **(5)**

5. What has brought about the need for job enlargement or enrichment? **(6)**

6. Comment on the importance of the concept of "chain of command". **(7)**

7. What is meant by "unity of command"? **(8)**

8. How should the size of "span of control" be determined? **(9)**

9. How might one departmentalise a small manufacturing organisation? **(10)**

10. What are the different ways of creating divisionalisation within an enterprise? **(11)**

11. Why is it becoming increasingly difficult for a manager to co-ordinate the activities of a business? **(12)**

12. Differentiate between "line" and "staff" personnel in an organisation? **(13)**

13. What has given rise to the need for "staff" departments? **(14)**

14. What are the prime purposes of organisation charts? **(15)**

15. What is meant by "informal organisation"? **(16)**

16. Describe some of the newer types of organisational structure which have been developed to help combat the problems brought on by organisational growth and rapidly changing external environments. **(17)**

CHAPTER X

Motivation

INTRODUCTION

1. Introduction. This chapter examines the importance of the topic of motivation from the standpoint of management. Since management is concerned with getting others to perform tasks, a careful study of motivation is required. Various theories of motivation are described and their usefulness to managers is evaluated.

2. Motivation defined. A motive is defined as an inner state that energises, activates, or moves (hence "motivation") and directs or channels behaviour towards goals. Motivation includes drives, desires, needs, wishes and similar forces. A study of motivation theories enables us to understand people and their actions, and in a business organisation environment it enables us to understand, for example, why certain people work hard or commit themselves to organisational goals and generally work well within a team or group.

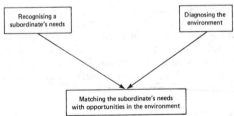

FIG. 18   *Management and motivation.*

3. Managers and motivation. Figure 18 shows how the manager has to become involved with the motivation of his subordinates. The manager's task is to recognise the needs of subordinates and to match those needs with opportunities that occur in the business environment.

   (*a*) *Recognition of subordinates' needs.* The concept of needs is not a simple one as, with the exception of the recognised innate

159

physiological needs such as hunger and thirst, they are dependent upon the individual's environment. Indeed, other "needs" such as esteem, status, power, etc. can be learned by an individual as a result of his experiences in different environments and circumstances. For example, a man who has been out of work for two years may well be motivated to work hard by the offer of a job with a very modest wage. On the other hand, a man who has enjoyed a regular income and is able to satisfy all his needs from his present income, is less likely to be motivated to work harder by additional financial inducements, particularly if higher rates of taxation are thereby incurred.

Many workers can be motivated to strive for higher performance by being offered additional financial inducements but other factors can influence their motivation.

(b) *Diagnosing the environment.* Here the manager has to search the work environment to find specific opportunities which will satisfy the needs of individual subordinates.

(c) *Matching the needs of individuals with opportunities in the environment.* An ambitious young executive may have a great need to succeed in new ventures and may become bored rapidly if the assignments with which he is presented are too easy or routine. The manager in charge of such an executive has to be alert to his subordinate's need for stimulating and difficult work and should attempt to provide the individual with it. Matching the needs of individuals with opportunities in the environment can be achieved by reassigning work within a department, for example, so that the individual's needs can be met. This is particularly possible when a new member of staff joins the department. The new member is unlikely to have precisely the same needs or the same skills as the person he or she replaces and a re-assignment or re-adjustment of jobs can be beneficial to departmental efficiency.

4. Early theories of motivation. Early theories of motivation can be categorised under three headings.

(a) *Satisfaction theories.* These adopt the standpoint that a satisfied worker is a productive worker and that management should therefore aim to find ways of satisfying workers.

(b) *Incentive theories.* These adopted the theme that individuals work harder if they are given specific reward or encouragement for good performance.

(c) *Intrinsic theories.* These suggested that man is motivated by the prospect of obtaining satisfaction from the nature of the work he performs.

5. Evidence to support the early theories. There is no conclusive evidence to support the view that a satisfied worker is a productive worker, but strong support exists for the view that satisfied workers tend to remain with an organisation. There is also strong evidence to support the validity of incentive theories. However, a number of conditions must be fulfilled if the incentive theory is to hold good.

(*a*) An individual has to consider that the incentive is worthwhile.

(*b*) It must be possible to measure the amount of effort that the individual puts into performing the task.

(*c*) The increase in performance, resulting from offering the incentive must not become accepted or recognised as the minimum standard of acceptable performance.

Evidence suggests that the intrinsic theories only work sometimes and are least effective when technology prevents an individual from exercising control over the design of his job, or when an individual does not have a strong need for self-actualisation, or prefers authoritarian leadership. Intrinsic theories are most likely to be successfully applied where individuals are engaged in, for example, "vocational" callings, self-employment, research, consultancy or teaching.

6. Rationale of the early theories. Theories of motivation evolved over a period of time and are based on contemporary assumptions about human nature. Schein (1965) outlined these assumptions.

(*a*) *Rational–economic man.* This assumed that men are ruled by self-interest, and that their motivation is based upon economic needs. It suggested that men could be motivated and controlled by others to whom they had agreed to sell their services for economic reward. It assumed that men's feelings are irrational, so that leaders have to organise individuals in such a way that these irrational feelings can be brought under control. It assumed, however, that a select band of men exists who are completely in control of their emotions and self-motivated. These individuals tend to assume responsibility for the management of others.

This view of man prevailed between the seventeenth and nineteenth centuries and it reflected the economic and social conditions of the time where the owner/manager exercised autocratic power and influence over his employees and where the landed gentry and rich middle classes exercised similar authority over their servants or farm workers. This view was fashionable at a time when the majority of the population could earn barely enough to keep themselves from starving. The workers' needs and wants barely rose above those of food, security and shelter.

(b) *Social man.* This assumed that men have social needs and gain their identity through social intercourse with others. The principle of the division of labour and job simplification had by this time stripped much of the sense of accomplishment out of work itself and as a result accentuated men's needs to gain fulfilment through the only other medium available—social interaction. The model of social man gave rise to the idea that management could only effectively motivate workers if it provided them with opportunities to participate in the kind of social relationships they required.

Industrialisation and mass production eventually led to an excessive degree of division of labour. Later mechanisation and automation reduced the status of many industrial workers to machine minders—or at least diminished the amount of work required to perform a task. Individuals had two means available in their place of work by which they could achieve satisfaction. Firstly through their work itself and secondly through their inter- actions with other workers. Whilst their ability to achieve satis- faction through the work they perform had decreased, their ability to do so through social interaction remained unimpaired. Under such conditions the interest of management researchers veered towards group behaviour and group leadership (the "human relations" approach).

(c) *Self-actualising man and complex plan.* The modern view assumes that men seek more than merely economic or social satis- faction. They look for a sense of meaning and accomplishment in their work. Men need independence and the opportunity to think for themselves; external controls threaten this independence. Men have numerous motives and these motives vary with circumstances. They learn new motives as a result of social interaction within the organisation and an individual may be prompted by a different set of motives according to the situation in which he is working at a particular time. Motives at any one time may take precedence over one another, or become hierarchical. This hierarchy is not stable and may change from situation to situation. At one period in his or her life an individual may be motivated by the prospect of higher earnings, at another by the nature of the work itself. No generalisations can be made.

MOTIVATION THEORIES

7. Hierarchy of needs. The following summarises the development of the theory of the "hierarchy of needs".

(*a*) *Maslow.* Maslow (1954) visualised human needs as taking the form of a hierarchy. He put forward the idea that once a low-level need was satisfied it ceased to become a motivator and only a higher-level need could then fulfil the same function. A common way of depicting Maslow's *hierarchy of needs* is in the form of a pyramid with the basic needs at the base of the pyramid (*see* Fig. 19).

FIG. 19   *Maslow's hierarchy of needs.*

(*b*) *Lawlor and Settle.* Lawlor and Settle (1972) tried unsuccessfully to find evidence to support Maslow's theory of the hierarchy of needs, but they noted that there appeared to be two levels of need amongst managers: *"biological"* and *"other"* needs. "Other" needs only appeared once the "biological" ones had been satisfied. In the case of the higher order (other) needs, social needs predominated in some individuals whilst in others self-actualisation needs were found to be more important.

(c) *Hall and Nougaim.* A study conducted by Hall and Nougaim (1968) found that an emphasis on an upward movement of need was related to changes in career and not to the satisfaction of lower order needs.

(d) *Porter.* Porter (1962) found that the three higher level needs on the Maslow hierarchy varied considerably according to managerial status, with lower level managers expressing less satisfaction than higher level managers.

The usefulness of Maslow's hierarchy concept and its related research to managers is threefold:

(a) it shows that individuals can and will be motivated by different sets of needs, and furthermore it identifies the basic nature of those needs;

(b) it shows that a distinction can be made between basic needs and higher order needs, and that motivation can be affected if the former are satisfied; and

(c) it shows that all individuals have needs for esteem and self-actualisation, though it may take different forms for different individuals.

8. Motivation: the hygiene theory. Herzberg (1957) identified two groups of factors which he thought would explain motivation. One of these groups contained such factors as company policy and administration, supervision, working conditions, interpersonal relations, salary, status, job security and personal life. Herzberg maintained that these factors are dissatisfiers and not motivators; whilst their existence does not motivate an individual they can lead to individuals becoming dissatisfied. In the other group of factors Herzberg uncovered what he considered to be motivators. These factors comprised achievement, recognition, challenging work, advancement and job development.

9. Expectancy theory. Vroom (1964) suggested that an individual's motivation to act is determined by whether he perceives that a particular course of action will lead to a desired outcome. The strength of a person's motivation, then, is the product of an individual's preference for an outcome and the probability that a particular course of action will achieve a desired outcome.

EXAMPLE
An individual manager is faced with the not-too-infrequency met problem of managing conflict between groups of subordinates. There are four possible lines of action. (1) Support group A and

admonish group B. (2) Support group B and admonish group A. (3) Not to interfere at all. (4) Attempt to reconcile the interest of the two groups.

The individual manager's motivation to act will depend upon whether or not he feels that it will be beneficial to reconcile the conflict. For instance, if he wishes to sustain the conflict then he has to decide which of the four possible courses of action is most likely to prolong conflict and, most important, whether undesirable side-effects will result from any of them. His motivation to adopt one or other of the strategies will depend upon his subjective estimation of which course of action will yield the most satisfactory outcome (from his point of view).

Motivation and decision-making are interrelated. Motivation leads to a particular action—that is, a decision to act. Motivation to do something may also be derived from a desire to accomplish another objective. For instance, individuals may be motivated to work hard and achieve high productivity for the prospect of greater financial reward.

Vroom's expectancy theory overcame some of the problems associated with the more simplistic approaches of Maslow and Herzberg, for it recognised the importance of the various needs and motivations of individuals. Porter and Lawler (1968) developed Vroom's ideas into a more substantial model and specifically applied it to management. According to these researchers, the strength of motivation is a function of the estimated value of the reward, together with the amount of energy the individual considers will have to be expended and the probability of actually obtaining that reward. The latter two factors are also influenced by prior experience. Figure 20 illustrates these basic ideas.

10. Needs theory of motivation. McClelland (1955) sought to establish evidence that there are three basic types of motivating need.

(a) *Need for power.* Individuals who have a high need for achieving power express great concern about exercising influence over others. Such individuals seek leadership positions, are good speakers and are forceful, outspoken, hard-headed and demanding.

(b) *Need for affiliation.* Individuals having a high need for affiliation seek acceptance by a social group. Their main concern is with maintaining pleasant social relationships and enjoying friendly interaction with others.

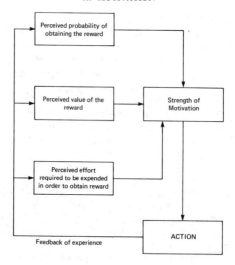

FIG. 20   *Basic components of the Porter and Lawler model.*

(c) *Need for achievement.* Individuals with a high need for achievement have an intense desire for success and conversely dread failure. They respond to challenges, set reasonably difficult goals for themselves, analyse risky problems in detail and prefer to get jobs done by themselves. Other characteristics include: need for feedback on performance, restlessness and the enjoyment of autonomy.

The needs theory holds that every individual possesses a mixture of these needs in varying degrees. Entrepreneurs tend to have a high need for achievement and a high need for power but only a low need for affiliation. Managers generally show a similar pattern but their need for power and achievement is less extreme.

11. Field theory. Elton Mayo and his associates in the celebrated Hawthorne experiments (*see* II,**8**) demonstrated that motivation is part of a complex system of human behaviour.

(a) *Kurt Lewin.* Kurt Lewin's *field theory* (1938) explained how motivations depend on organisational climate as well. His formula for human behaviour was $B = (P,E)$, where B is human behaviour, P a person and E his or her environment. In other words, human behaviour is a function of a person and his or her environment. If we relate this to motivation it implies that people can have different motivations at different times. The task of management is to identify that which will best motivate an individual or group at a specific time and in a given environment or circumstance.

(b) *Litwin and Stringer*. Litwin and Stringer's researches (1968) in this direction were extremely interesting. They found that different organisational climates gave rise to the arousal or reduction of different motivating forces. Applying McClelland's tripartite classification of major types of motivation (*see* **10**), they found that the strength of the individual's motivation was affected by organisational climate. In the case of a bureaucratically structured organisation there was considerable evidence of "power motivation" and a corresponding lack of either "achievement motivation" or "affiliation motivation". In the same way, they discovered that in an organisational setting where the feeling of "being one's own boss" was prevalent, there was evidence of both power motivation and achievement motivation, but a lack of evidence of affiliation motivation. Affiliation motivation was only in evidence in organisations where there was:

(*i*) a system of rewards for good work rather than a system of punishments for bad work;

(*ii*) a warm and friendly atmosphere;

(*iii*) a willingness for individuals to be helpful to one another; and

(*iv*) a feeling of team spirit pervading the organisation.

12. Practical implications of the field theory for management. One of the most important of these is that secondary motivation is *learned*. In interacting with different environments, individuals learn to develop values. Again, it shows that different people with different experiences have different values; what may constitute a reward to one person may not necessarily constitute a reward for another person. For instance, an individual who values freedom to do what he wishes most of the time will opt for a job or career which will afford such opportunities. (Freedom can of course mean different things to different people.) Some values are outlined in (*a*)–(*d*) below.

(*a*) *Cultural values*. Cultural traditions influence the values which people adopt. In Victorian and Edwardian times, upper middle class parents expected their sons to enter a profession (such as the law, the church, etc.) and looked down on managerial and industrial jobs. Culture plays an important part today in influencing values which form the basis of individuals' motives. An employee whose childhood was deprived of material wealth (TV, good furniture, car, etc.) could well be motivated to work hard to ensure that he can acquire the material wealth that will provide these things. But money can of course be a powerful motivator for individuals from all kinds of cultural backgrounds.

(b) *Status.* Apart from money and freedom, an individual may also value status within an organisation. Money can buy certain status symbols such as an expensive car or large house and even comparatively low organisational-status employees can acquire these things over a long period of time. But occupational status cannot be acquired in the same way. Certain occupations have high status value (doctors, lawyers, university teachers, company directors, etc.). An individual's family background may have instilled in him the notion that a high-status occupation is to be valued. Such an individual might not be willing to settle for a lesser status job even though it might provide him with all the material wealth he desires.

(c) *Value to the community.* The older married woman who goes out to work when there is not the economic necessity for her to do so is an interesting phenomenon. The reason she may give for this is that it is a source of extra money ("pin money"). Research, however, suggests that she may be motivated by other reasons. There may for instance be an underlying social need for company or a need to be of value to the community. The advent of flexible working hours has done much to make it possible for married women (and women in general), who may have other important commitments, to obtain and hold down jobs.

(d) *Environment.* In field theory the term "environment" should not be confused with the physical environment in which people work. By and large it is understood that the physical environment in which an individual works is not a "motivator" but that it can on the other hand lead to dissatisfaction. For example, an executive who has a lavish suite of offices will not necessarily be more motivated than an executive who carries an equivalent salary and responsibilities but who works under cramped conditions. However, improving the physical environment can occasionally lead to clearly increased performance. For example, operatives working in poorly ventilated work places may suffer from fatigue with a consequent high turnover in labour. Creating better working conditions could well reduce that labour turnover and thereby increase productivity, by maintaining not only a more experienced work force but also one with higher morale. The Hawthorne experiments showed clearly that the physical environment was not a prime motivator although a poor physical environment can of course create fatigue problems. While better plant layout can lead to higher productivity, and good working conditions may lead to greater satisfaction, they are unlikely to increase an individual's motivation to work.

13. The field theory and complex man. Because behaviour is a product of the interaction between the individual and his environment, there is no one best way of motivating individuals. The successful manager must be a good diagnostician who values a spirit of enquiry. In particular, if the abilities and motives of the people under him are variable (as they will generally be), he will need the sensitivity to appreciate the differences in them.

PROGRESS TEST 10

1. Define motivation. **(2)**

2. Why is it important for managers to recognise what motivates a subordinate? **(3)**

3. What are: "satisfaction theories", "incentive theories", and "intrinsic theories" of motivation? **(4)**

4. What evidence is there to support all of these theories? **(5)**

5. Explain: "rational-economic man"; "social man"; "self-actualising man" and "complex man". **(6)**

6. Outline the principles involved in Maslow's hierarchy of needs. **(7)**

7. Is Herzberg's motivation-hygiene theory substantially different from the theory proposed by Maslow? **(8)**

8. In what way is the "expectancy theory" of motivation similar to certain theoretical approaches to decision-making? **(9)**

9. Explain McClelland's need theory of motivation. **(10)**

10. Evaluate the contribution of Lewin's Field theory to our understanding of motivation. **(11, 12, 13)**

CHAPTER XI

Leadership

INTRODUCTION

1. Introduction. Management is concerned with getting people to carry out tasks, either routinely or specifically, as a result of decisions that may have been taken. Leadership is the aspect of so managing people that they will perform their assigned tasks willingly and in an efficient and effective manner. In this chapter we look at the nature and functions of leadership.

2. Definition. Leadership can be thought of as a process by which individuals are influenced so that they will be prepared to participate in the achievement of company or group goals. It is the role of the leader to obtain the commitment of individuals to achieving these goals. The leader has to co-ordinate the efforts of individuals and strive to maintain harmonious relationships between and with them to facilitate the accomplishment of company or group objectives. It is the leader's task to:

(*a*) plan and organise group activities;

(*b*) exercise control over group activities;

(*c*) admit and dismiss group members to and from group activities;

(*d*) enable all group members to perform their roles satisfactorily within the group;

(*e*) enable all group members to clarify their roles as environmental circumstances change; and

(*f*) enable all group members to understand their roles within the organisation with respect to other groups and with respect to the corporate enterprise.

3. Accomplishment. The key word is *motivation*. The leader has to motivate colleagues to commit themselves to organisational goals. Whilst a knowledge of motivation theory is important to a leader, it has to be recognised that our knowledge of the nature of motivation is incomplete.

The important point for a leader to remember is that an individual's motivation changes with time and circumstances and that it is the function of the leader to find out the appropriate motivation for individual group members in each different circumstance. Most individuals are strongly motivated by financial reward, for example, but only up to a point. Beyond that point, increasing the financial reward will not prove to be an effective motivator. One view is that the leader's task is to discover the most appropriate form of incentive to offer group members in order to obtain the fullest commitment to group objectives. Another view is that every individual has a sense of commitment and that it is the leader's task to show each person how to express their commitment.

4. Nature of leadership. Leadership is a skill which requires several specific abilities:

(*a*) to understand what motivates individual group members at different times and in different situations or circumstances;

(*b*) to inspire others; and

(*c*) to create an organisational climate which will encourage others to act on the basis of aroused motivation.

A useful first step for a leader is to make himself familiar with leadership theories. The next step, putting theory into practice, is the most difficult one. The skill lies in recognising the motivational patterns of members of the group and becoming familiar with how they think. Problems arise because the way in which leaders can acquire the skill or ability to inspire others is not clearly understood. Many managers regrettably lack the basic skills of leadership and in consequence the groups which they nominally "lead" operate either ineffectively or sluggishly or in their own way.

5. Charisma. Charisma refers to the ability of an individual to inspire great trust and devotion and admiration amongst the people with whom he or she comes into contact. Charismatic leadership exists where the personality of an individual (who naturally assumes the role of leader) is such that it causes others to seek to please him. The desire "to please the leader" can therefore lead individuals to become committed to achieving the organisational goals laid down by the leader. Individuals who are charismatic and who assume a leadership role are usually highly successful in motivating large groups of people to follow them. Many examples exist in history of religious and political leaders who have been renowned for their charisma.

Despite the apparent importance of charisma in leadership, no specific and generalisable personality traits which can be clearly associated with successful leadership have yet been identified. A number of studies have highlighted significant correlations between certain personality traits and leadership effectiveness. Intelligence, scholarship, dependability, responsibility, social participation (gregariousness) and socio-economic status have all been found to have a positive association with effective leadership, but no real indication exists of how these traits are acquired and, since they are no more than the qualities that a good manager would be expected to possess, research findings have been inconclusive.

6. The situational approach. The failure of researchers to identify generalisable personality traits which can be associated with qualities of leadership caused them to look further afield. It has been observed that individuals are likely to accept the leadership of those in whom they perceive a means of accomplishing their own personal aspirations, as instanced in such historical figures as Mussolini, Hitler and Napoleon. Researchers then switched to investigating the possibility that leaders are the product of given situations. It has been argued, for example, that had the Germany in 1920 existed in the form in which it took after the end of the Second World War, Hitler could never have risen to power. Provided that a leader has the right qualities which will enable him or her to assume the role of leader, "being in the right place at the right time" can have a very great effect on the success of his or her leadership.

7. Fiedler's theory. Fiedler's theory of leadership, the *contingency theory*, combines the situational and the personality trait approaches. Fiedler suggests that individuals adopt the role of leader not only on account of their personality traits, but also because they are able to adapt successfully to the different situations. From this it may be argued that a person who possesses leadership potential will not necessarily be an effective leader unless he is able to lead in all situations. Fiedler identified three critical dimensions of any situation that can affect the effectiveness of a leader's style.

(*a*) *Position power*; this arises from the power of the position that an individual holds in an organisation.

(*b*) *Task structure*; this is the extent to which tasks can be clearly defined and responsibility for their conduct allocated to specific individuals.

(*c*) *Leader-member relations*; this reflects the extent to which group members like and trust a leader and are prepared to follow him or her.

Fiedler recognised two styles of leadership:

(*a*) *a task-orientated approach*; here the leader seeks satisfaction in seeing jobs performed efficiently and effectively; and

(*b*) *a people-orientated approach*; here the leader seeks satisfaction by attaining a position of personal prominence.

8. Participative management. Much attention has been given to the problem of trying to determine the most effective style of leadership. However, it is evident that if leadership is *situational*, different styles can be effective in different situations. Nevertheless one writer, Rensis Likert, is a proponent of what he calls *participative management*. This approach emphasises orientation towards subordinates, with the managers having complete trust and confidence in him in all matters. Subordinates' ideas and opinions are actively solicited and used constructively and economic rewards are based upon the extent to which individuals participate in group activities. The leader and followers (manager and subordinates) agree on mutual group goals and objectives and participate in decision-making together. Here the role adopted by the leader is a supportive one, through which he or she helps individuals to identify personal objectives and the manner in which to achieve them. In his researches Likert has found that this style of leadership has been the most successful. Likert also identified three other types of leadership.

(*a*) *Exploitative-authoritative.* This style is very autocratic and little trust in subordinates is shown. There is no participation by group members in decision-making and fear or punishment are used to motivate subordinates.

(*b*) *Benevolent-authoritative.* This style is mildly autocratic and not as severe in its system of incentives as (*a*) above. Some ideas are obtained from subordinates and some decisions are delegated. This can be described as the "handing-out-of-favours" management style.

(*c*) *Consultative.* This style permits substantial trust in subordinates, makes constructive use of subordinates' ideas and opinions and motivates them with rewards and occasional punishments. Broad policy decisions are taken by the leader but specific decisions are taken by group members.

9. Showing concern for people and the task. Robert Kahn (1956) reported a study among 20,000 workers employed in producing earthmoving equipment and tractors.

EXAMPLE

The foremen with the best production records were the ones who were most skilled at and most concerned with meeting employee needs for information, support and assistance, but they were no less concerned with production ... The foremen with the best production records, in short, were both production-centred and employee-centred.

10. The managerial grid. Robert Blake and Jane Mouton (1964) devised a management training diagnostic package which enables a researcher or a consultant to identify a practising manager's current managerial style. Their work built on previous research which pointed to the need for managers to have concern for both "getting the job done" and for the needs and wants of the poeple who actually do the work. The grid (*see* Fig. 21) has been widely employed to identify different leadership styles and is also used as training tool. "Work orientation" at the bottom of the grid measures the subject's concern for the quality of policy decisions, procedures and processes, etc. "Concern for people" includes such things as wanting to maintain the self-esteem of workers and having

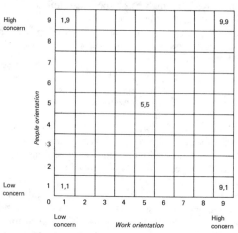

FIG. 21   *The managerial grid.*

satisfactory interpersonal relations. Four extremes of style are singled out.

(*a*) *1,1 style*. Leaders act as messengers between subordinates and their own superiors. They take little interest in their jobs or their subordinates.

(*b*) *9,9 style*. This idealised style is the complete opposite to the 1,1 style. Leaders are dedicated both to people and to production. These are the real "team managers".

(*c*) *1,9 style*. Such leaders promote a pleasing, amicable, relaxed atmosphere. This is often referred to as "country club" management. No concern is shown for working as a team towards enterprise goals.

(*d*) *9,1 style*. The autocratic style of management where the only concern shown is that for getting the job done.

(*e*) *5,5 style*. This is the "half way house" approach, where managers aim to perform adequately along both dimensions of the grid. Goals set are usually well within the reach of the organisation and the attitude of management is mildly autocratic but at the same time benevolent.

Blake and Mouton's researches using this method uncovered some interesting findings. Most managers appear to adopt a 5,5 style and these managers are moderately successful. The most successful managers adopt the 9,9 style of management but, interestingly enough, practising managers see subordinates who adopt 9,1 style of management as promotable.

11. 3-D theory of managerial effectiveness. Reddin's work parallels and develops the ideas promulgated by Blake and Mouton. Reddin developed the 3-D theory of management effectiveness. Using a "grid" in much the same fashion as Blake and Mouton he identified four basic managerial styles:

(*a*) *separated style*; low task orientation and low relationship orientation;

(*b*) *related style*; high relationships orientation only;

(*c*) *dedicated style*; high task orientation only; and

(*d*) *integrated style*; high task orientation and high relationship orientation.

These styles correspond to the styles 1,1; 1,9; 9,1; and 9,9 on the Blake and Mouton managerial grid.

Reddin next argued that any of the four basic managerial styles can be more or less effective depending on the particular circumstances in which it is used. The most effective managerial style, he suggests, must be defined with reference to the demands of the situation. The Blake and Mouton managerial grid is a two-dimensional representation; the third dimension is "managerial effectiveness", or the extent to which a manager meets or does not meet the requirements of a particular situation.

12. Flexible leadership.

(a) *Leadership continuums.* Tannenbaum and Schmidt visualise leadership styles as being along a continuum ranging from "highly boss-centred" to "highly subordinate-centred". There is no suggestion that one style is more correct than the other. Such an approach gives credence to the view that the most suitable style of management depends very much upon personalities and situations. These two writers have suggested (1973) that both the social and the organisational environments have an influence on the choice of leadership style.

(b) *Latent and aroused motivations.* Another approach has been suggested by Robert House (1971) who considers the most effective style of leadership to be where managers create situations in which both the latent and the aroused motivations of group members are responded to effectively by management. In practice, this suggests that those who help individual subordinates achieve both organisational and their own individual goals will be most successful. To facilitate this it is suggested that leaders should:

(*i*) define individuals' position and task roles clearly;

(*ii*) remove obstacles to performance;

(*iii*) have group members participate in setting goals;

(*iv*) promote co-operation and team effort;

(*v*) increase opportunities for satisfaction in terms of work performance;

(*vi*) reduce unnecessary stresses and external controls;

(*vii*) clarify reward expectations; and

(*viii*) try and meet the expectations of subordinates in all matters as far as possible.

13. Some practical considerations for management. It is quite clear that individuals at all levels in an organisation want their respective bosses to be considerate, understanding and appreciative. Whilst most managers are aware of this and want to be seen as fair, they are not always able to communicate their feelings effectively. It is inevitable that a manager will have to do and say things which

will be misperceived, disliked and considered unfair by subordinates. However, managers must reassure subordinates that the
power difference will not be misused. Leaders inspire trust through
their behaviour more than by words. In turn, the employees' sense
of security arises out of perceiving this behaviour (as distinct from
hearing it verbally), i.e. actions speak louder than words.

Robert Carlson (1969) concluded that there were two basic
dimensions in all human interaction:

(*a*) the dominant–submissive dimension; and
(*b*) the affection–hostility dimension.

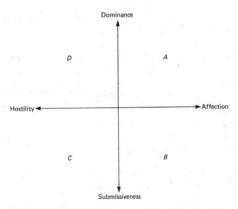

FIG. 22   *Carlson model of social interaction.*

These dimensions can be represented graphically (*see* Fig. 22).
Carlson notes that the most stable leader–follower relationship (i.e.
that which will provide an environment for subordinate motivation)
will be found in quadrant A. Dominant leaders who give modest
support to their subordinates are likely to obtain trust and respect
from them. Leaders whose actions are highly supportive are likely
to engender affection and attachment from subordinates. But if
the leader's actions fall into any other quadrant the results are likely
to lead to a relationship which may not provide an environment
for effective motivation.

COMMUNICATION

Communication is closely linked with leadership, authority and motivation. Now we have to examine the communication process and look at the different ways in which communication can take place.

14. The nature of communication. An analysis of time spent in communication shows approximately 10 per cent spent in writing, 15 per cent reading, 35 per cent speaking, and 40 per cent listening, with by far the most time spent in oral communication. Communication is not an end in itself, for its main purpose is to bring about action or to secure inaction. Communication is one of the most important keys to managerial effectiveness, since management has to make known its policies, instructions, objectives and goals to all members of the organisation. Communication also involves feedback of information from employees to management. If objectives are set for employees it must be possible for them to communicate with management if they are to achieve what is required of them. Management will need to know the nature of the problems encountered by employees in trying to put requirements into practice.

Communication is concerned with information management, i.e. it is necessary that all information presented to executives is in a form which is relevant to their particular needs. Communication may be oral, in writing or simply construed from gestures.

15. Ineffective communication. There are a number of faults which prevent effective communication and these are commonly as follows:

(*a*) assuming that because a message has been sent it will have been received;

(*b*) not transmitting the intended message;

(*c*) overselling the content of a message, so that it may raise unnecessary psychological resistance;

(*d*) failing to persist in trying to communicate a message to an audience (giving up too quickly);

(*e*) making a communication at an inappropriate time;

(*f*) failing to plan out an oral communication properly, so that its impact is insufficient;

(*g*) introducing irrelevancies into the communication and using ornate or unnecessarily complex language.

(*h*) failing to use visual aids (particularly in oral presentations);

(*i*) not having well-prepared answers available to meet anticipated objections to the purpose of the communication;

(*j*) failing to involve the other person in the communication (e.g. failing to invite a reply or discussion in written or oral communications);

(*k*) failing to listen to, or even consider, the point of view of the receiver; and

(*l*) (in an oral presentation) failing to allow sufficient time for the discussion of the points which may have been raised. (This often happens when the presenter lacks confidence in what he is saying).

16. The essence of good communication. Robert Fulmer (1978) lists five criteria for effective communication.

(*a*) *Clarity.* Is it likely to be misunderstood?

(*b*) *Completeness.* Does it impart all the intended information?

(*c*) *Conciseness.* Can the message be imparted in less words than are currently envisaged?

(*d*) *Concreteness.* Does the message contain any "woolly" words which may give rise to ambiguity?

(*e*) *Correctness.* Is the message correct?

17. Personal factors affecting the quality of communication.

(*a*) *Self concept.* A strong self-concept is necessary for healthy and satisfying interaction. A person with a poor opinion of himself may experience difficulty in communicating with others.

(*b*) *Coping with angry feelings.* Inability to deal with anger frequently results in communication breakdowns. Emotions should not be repressed but rather people should express their angry feelings constructively rather than destructively.

(*c*) *Self-disclosure.* People tend to find it difficult to talk truthfully and fully about themselves. Yet individuals cannot really communicate with one another or get to know one another unless they overcome this problem.

THE COMMUNICATIONS GAP

18. Subordinates' needs. A common problem is that companies often devote time and resources in providing employees with information which is of little interest to them.

Employees needs are for information on:

(*a*) pay;

(*b*) benefits;

(*c*) industrial relations news;

(*d*) union news;

(*e*) results of industrial relations negotiations;

(*f*) job security;

(*g*) own job performance;

(*h*) company's future plans;

(*i*) reasons for management decisions;

(*j*) job changes;

(*k*) departmental news and performance;

(*l*) changes in conditions of service.

19. Climates where communication works best. There are four basic conditions for successful communication:

(*a*) management is strong and decisive;

(*b*) management style is open trusting and honest;

(*c*) employees are talked to in terms of their own language and experiences;

(*d*) employees are consulted and their opinions sought before changes which affect their working lives are made.

20. Improving organisational communication. This can be achieved by:

(*a*) holding regular departmental meetings;

(*b*) maintaining an open, communicative management style;

(*c*) exercising strong leadership and direction;

(*d*) maintaining close contact with subordinates;

(*e*) teaching people to communicate successfully;

(*f*) increased consultation with subordinates before decisions are taken;

(*g*) greater urgency in communicating major decisions;

(*h*) improving industrial relations procedure;

(*i*) improving methods of upward communication and

(*j*) establishing a system of inter-departmental communications.

PROGRESS TEST 11

1. What do you understand by leadership? **(2)**

2. In what ways should a leader try to accomplish group objectives? **(3)**

3. Explain what is meant by "charismatic leadership". **(5)**

4. What is the importance of Fiedler's theory to our understanding of leadership?   **(7)**

5. What is "participative management"?   **(8)**

6. Explain the value of the "managerial grid".   **(10)**

7. How important do you think that the contributions of Tannenbaum, Schmidt and House have been in promoting a generalisable theory of leadership?   **(12)**

8. Of what particular use to Management is Carlson's model of Social Interaction?   **(13)**

9. What do you understand by "communication"?   **(14)**

10. Describe some common communication pitfalls.   **(15)**

11. What do you consider to be the essence of good communication?   **(16)**

12. What do you understand by the "communications gap"?   **(18)**

13. How might a manager seek to improve organisational communications?   **(20)**

CHAPTER XII

Roles and Groups

1. Introduction. Every member of an organisation is a member of a smaller group or a different number of groups and one can view an organisation as a collection of groups. Every member of the organisation plays a number of roles within both the organisation and each group to which he or she belongs. In this chapter we examine roles, groups and roles within groups and the relevance of these concepts to management.

BASIC CONCEPTS

2. The concepts of role, group and roles within groups. Any individual existing in conjunction with others occupies a role in relation to them. The nature of this role will vary with differing circumstances, i.e. according to the people with whom a relationship is held (the other members of the group), and according to the type of activity the group undertakes. Figure 23 shows how an individual can be a member of a number of different groups. Each group forms a

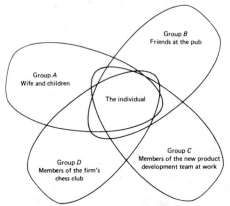

FIG. 23 *Role of the individual within different goups.*

different role set (*see* **4**) for the individual. In group A (wife and children), the individual may adopt for example the role of father, decision-maker on items of major expenditure, doer of all the physically demanding household chores, counsellor to the children, sympathetic listener to his wife etc. In group B ("friends at the pub") the individual may adopt the role of clown ("funny man"), expert gamester, raconteur, consultant on business matters and so on. In group C ("member of the new product development team at work"), the individual may adopt the role of marketing expert, statistical analyst, second-in-command, connoisseur of women, lateral thinker and so on. In group D ("member of the firm's chess club"), the individual may adopt the role of number two board on the first team, the expert on the English opening and the French defence, the man who brews the tea and so on.

3. Typologies of groups. Various attempts have been made to classify groups in order to aid understanding of group processes. Cooley (1909) distinguished between "primary" and "secondary" groups. Primary groups are small intimate groups of persons in face to face relationship, where there is a strong sense of "togetherness" and group identity—family groups are excellent examples. Secondary groups, on the other hand, tend to be much larger and relationships are cool, formal and impersonal. Argyle (1969) distinguishes between five types of small social groups:

   (*a*) the family as a small group;
   (*b*) adolescent groups;
   (*c*) work groups;
   (*d*) committees, problem-solving and creative groups; and
   (*e*) T and therapy groups.

Our main interest is in groups (*c*) and (*d*) and to a lesser extent in (*e*). We consider these below.

ROLE THEORY

4. The "focal person" and "role set". In analysing any given situation the individual who is the centre of attention is referred to as the *focal person* and the people making specific requirements of that person as the *role set*. In order to define any individual's role within a given group one has to take account of the role expectations that members of the role set will have of the focal person. For example, a department manager is the focal person for members of his department in all matters relating to the assignment of allotted tasks. From the manager's point of view, the members of his department comprise the role set; they have certain expectations of his behaviour: that is, they expect him to distribute the workload fairly so that no one person has too much or too little work to perform. They also expect that in overseeing the assignment of work he will try to take into account their own personal preferences for types of assignments. Here the expectations of the role set define the manager's role as one of ensuring that individuals are treated fairly.

5. Role signs. Role signs are necessary to establish and define the role of an individual within a group and thus to help him carry out his role effectively. Role signs can take many different forms, but within the context of the organisation are broadly of two types.

(*a*) *Uniform.* The clothes that an individual wears (his "uniform") can define his role clearly. Uniforms are divided into two kinds as follows:

(*i*) *Formal.* A security man's or a doorman's uniform is an example of a formal uniform.

(*ii*) *Informal.* The "City gent's" bowler hat and "executive-style" pin-stripe suit is an example of an informal uniform. However, recent trends are for more informal dress at work, and this is particularly true of younger employees, so that it is no longer as easy as it once was to define an individual's seniority within an organisation by his age and dress.

(*b*) *Office.* The size and location of an individual's office, together with furnishings, can often be interpreted as role signs. The executive with a large office, or one situated in a prominent position, is thought to have higher status than an executive who has a smaller office which is placed in a less prominent position. Office furnishings and fittings may also reflect the status of an individual.

6. Role problems.

(*a*) *Role ambiguity.* This occurs when there is ambiguity or uncertainty in the minds of either the focal person or members of his role set as to precisely what is the nature of his role at any given time. There could be ambiguity about how an individual evaluates his prospects for advancement in his work, or about what other people expect him to do in terms of performance on the job. There may also be ambiguity about the amount of responsibility and authority an individual possesses. Role ambiguity is thus a potential source of friction amongst organisational members.

(b) *Role incompatibility.* This can arise in the following ways:

(*i*) where the expectations of members of the role set are clearly known but are incompatible a manager may wish to exercise authority and leadership in a particular manner but his subordinates may feel that they would prefer a different management style.

(*ii*) where there is conflict between the individual's self-concept and the role he is expected to play in the organisation. For example, an individual who is highly self-centred may experience role incompatibility when, as a member of the middle management team, he is expected to be totally organisation-centred.

(c) *Role conflict.* This exists when an individual is expected to carry on two or more roles at the same time. If and when the demands of the two roles conflict with one another, then the individual is said to be experiencing role conflict: for example, when one individual in an organisation is promoted there may be conflict between his new found status and his role as a friend to others who are now his subordinates.

(d) *Role overload.* Most people can handle role conflict to some extent. However, once the number of roles that a person has to handle becomes considerable the possibility of *role overload* arises. This often happens when an executive takes on managerial responsibilities for the first time. Not only is role overload a function of the *number* of roles that an individual has to perform, but it may also be a function of the *variety* of roles which have to be adopted. Unlike work overload, no amount of overtime will alleviate the problem.

(e) *Role underload.* This occurs when an individual in an organisation is prevented from carrying out the roles for which he feels he is best suited. Under such circumstances, the roles which the individual has to adopt do not fit in with his self-concept. This often arises where an individual is given a job to perform which is well below his capabilities. Whether or not the job is well below an individual's capabilities is of no consequence it is the fact that the individual believes it to be so that is important.

7. Role stress. The above mentioned problems can give rise to what is known as *role stress*. Stress can sometimes be good but more often it is harmful. Before people can work hard and give of their best, a certain degree of stress or anxiety has to be present; individuals have to be anxious that they will complete a job satisfactorily. If, however, there is too much anxiety or if that anxiety is misdirected, the results can be quite damaging. Social scientists differentiate between:

(*a*) *role pressure*, meaning the beneficial type of role stress; and
(*b*) *role strain*, meaning harmful role stress.

An individual suffering from role strain exhibits tension, tends to be occupied with trivial and unimportant matters, is over meticulous in his work or actions, looks at things as "black or white extremes", and shows himself to be responsive to rumours and group pressures. Other symptoms include low morale where the individual is expressing low confidence in the organisation and a general dissatisfaction with his job. He may also experience communication difficulties. In the latter case, the individual may attempt to break off communication entirely, become silent and withdrawn, and tend towards absenteeism.

8. Dealing with role stress. Individuals try to cope with the problems of role stress in a number of different ways.

(*a*) An individual may simply refuse to admit that the problem does in fact exist and may try to laugh it off as unimportant.

(*b*) He may withdraw completely from the organisation, either by creating an artificial psychological barrier between himself and other members or by quitting the organisation altogether.

(*c*) He may rationalise the situation, coming to the conclusion that conflict is inevitable and that he must live with it.

Role problems and role stress are a feature of the task of managing. They can result from situations where an individual has responsibility for the work of others, or is engaged in innovative activities or even acting in a co-ordinative or "link man" role. If the nature of the job demand it, organisations should pay attention to the need to select individuals who are able to tolerate role stress.

People who are capable of tolerating stress are thought to have the following characteristics.

(*a*) *Sociability*. They are prepared to share the problems that exist with others and to resolve them through a consensus of independent views.

(*b*) *Emotional sensitivity*. They have neither too much nor too little emotional sensitivity.

(*c*) *Flexibility/rigidity*. They exhibit a degree of steadfastness in their opinions.

Where individuals do experience role problems, they will need help to resolve their difficulties.

9. Role identification. Our interactions with other people are affected to a large extent by *interpersonal perception*: the things we say and what we do to each other. Our perceptions are also affected by our respective roles and our mutual view of each other's roles. Most people, when they meet someone new, will try to assign that person some kind of role. Role identification therefore enables people to form a basis for communication with another individual through identifying that individual's characteristics. If it is difficult to identify roles immediately, individuals will seek for clues.

(*a*) What is the other's role?

(*b*) How does he perceive his role?

(*c*) What are the other's goals?

(*d*) What does he expect to gain from the interaction?

(*e*) What are his immediate intentions?

(*f*) How is he going to behave towards me?

GROUPS

10. Roles in groups. Each individual in a group adopts a role. Wallen (1963) suggested that there are three important roles which must be filled if a group is to survive:

(*a*) logical thinker;

(*b*) friend and helper;

(*c*) strong fighter.

Many other suggestions have been made about the number and type of roles that individuals may play in a group. Amongst the better known ones are the following.

(*a*) *The comedian.* He enables tension to be relaxed. Unfortunately, many people who try to achieve popularity through this role are overlooked because they appear frivolous.

(*b*) *The organiser.* He likes to take on the arranging of social activities for the group and willingly takes on administrative jobs.

(*c*) *The deviant.* He who disagrees with all group consensuses in order to attract attention. Unfortunately, he too seldom receives serious attention.

EXAMPLE

A six-man group is assigned the task of integrating their efforts and sharing their workload. Previously all six individuals have worked independently, each going about his own work separately. The six men and their respective roles are: Howard—the politician/logical thinker/organiser. Martin—the deviant/

cynic. Robert—the strong fighter/logical thinker. Henry—the organiser/salesman. Alec—the organiser/bully/commentator/organiser. Doug—the quiet man.

A number of observations can be made about the six man group:

(a) most individuals have more than one role;

(b) there are three organisers, two logical thinkers and two strong fighters;

(c) there is no "friend and helper";

(d) Alec and Howard probably suffer from role overload;

(e) Martin and Doug probably suffer from role underload and Martin is a threat to group cohesiveness.

The group finds it difficult to integrate its ideas and objectives as there is considerable conflict amongst its members. Howard and Robert are the "ideas" men, but they seldom agree with each other. In addition Howard, Henry and Alec all want to organise activities and Alec tries to bully everyone around to his way of thinking. Doug finds the whole thing too much for him and withdraws. Martin plays the deviant and cynic: "It'll never work", he says, "the boss has got it all wrong trying to get us to share each other's jobs. He should never have got his job in the first place".

11. Groups and their purposes. It is necessary to distinguish between a random collection of individuals and a group. A group is a set of individuals who perceive themselves as having a collective identity. Groups in organisations serve many useful purposes and some of these are listed as follows:

(a) to facilitate work allocation—bringing a set of skills etc. to bear on a specific task;

(b) to enable work to be effectively controlled and managed by one individual;

(c) to facilitate decision-making and problem-solving—bringing a set of skills to bear on a particular problem;

(d) to enable information to be passed on to appropriate people for action;

(e) to gather together ideas and information;

(f) for testing out and ratifying decisions;

(g) to enable co-ordination and liaison between different organisational factions to take place;

(h) to promote increased involvement and participation in organisational planning and work;

(i) to enable negotiations to take place and conflict to be resolved, and (*j*) to promote inquiry into what has happened in the past.

Individuals may make use of group situations for the following reasons:

(*a*) to enable them to satisfy their need for affiliation;

(*b*) to enable them to test their own realities and self-concepts through relationships with others; and

(*c*) to enable individuals to gain support to carry out objectives which may or may not conflict with organisational goals.

12. The Hawthorne studies and group behaviour. The Hawthorne studies (*see* II,**8**) threw light on the subject of group behaviour at work and the pressure exerted by the group on its constituent members. The research showed that individuals can aspire to membership of work groups and, once they have joined, the norms and objectives of the group will strongly influence the norms and objectives of the individual. This refers specifically to the observation made of Western Electric workers in the company's "bank wiring room". The group as a whole had "norms" (i.e. a consensus of ideas) of what was a fair day's output. Another norm was that an individual should not attempt to work at a rate which was significantly slower or faster than that of the other members of the group. Deviance in either direction resulted in social pressures being exerted by the group on the individual concerned which forced him "back into line". Failure to respond to milder forms of social pressure could have led to social ostracism.

13. Group effectiveness. Every organisation is made up of a network of social and work groups. Each group contributes towards the overall effectiveness of the organisation; factors which influence individual group effectiveness are:

(*a*) the compatibility of the group members, the tasks which they are to perform and the environment in which they operate;

(*b*) the type of leadership, the processes and procedures adopted to guide group activities, and the extent to which individuals are motivated to work.

14. Group effectiveness and group size. Group size can have important implications for the level of participation of individual group members. This in turn can have implications for group effectiveness. Studies have shown that those who participate most actively in a group are seen as having the most influence. As a group gets larger, the influence pattern is such that those with low thresholds of participation tend to participate even less. The distribution of influence in a group may not therefore be in accordance with th distribution of knowledge and experience, hence the "neglected" participant (the retiring expert) whose views are never heard o never noticed, because his participation level is so low, is a common feature of groups, particularly larger ones.

A group size of between five and seven appears to offer the bes opportunity for participation by all members. Where tasks per formed by group members are complex group compatibility i critical to good group performance. An assertive leader with dependent followers constitutes a compatible group; a group in which all members are on very friendly terms may also be com patible. Where tasks to be performed are relatively simple, group compatibility is much less critical.

15. Group effectiveness and individual's objectives. Another in fluence on group effectiveness is the individual objectiveness o each member of the group. If these happen to coincide with group or organisational goals and objectives, no difficulties arise. How ever, individuals within a group may separately pursue uncon structive, personal objectives such as impressing the boss at any cost or "scoring off an opponent". This clearly will have a detri mental effect on the group's performance.

16. Cohesion in the face of adversity. It has been shown that when a group or organisation faces a common threat from outside it tends to cohere. This tendency frequently is strong enough to counteract any difficulties arising from the conflict of objectives either between individuals in the group, or between the individua and the organisation.

EXAMPLE

XYZ Ltd is a small firm which manufactures electrical compo nents. In recent years the firm has been experiencing problems in labour relations. A series of wild-cat strikes over a twelve month period has reduced the firm's profitability to the point where it is actually making a loss and productivity is so low that the owners are actively thinking of selling the business, if they can. The chairman of the firm receives an indication from a much larger organisation that it is interested in acquiring XYZ Ltd but that its interest is merely in the firms fixed assets. The chairman discusses the matter with his board of directors and a meeting of shop stewards is called to which the local union representatives are also to be invited. At the meeting, the chairman puts forward the firm's position and indicates that if the firm were to sell out, most of the employees would probably lose their jobs. After lengthy discussion and argument the shop stewards agree to do all they can to prevent further strikes, if the management is prepared not to sell out.

FORMAL GROUPS

17. Committees. These are groups which work entirely through verbal communication and are concerned with solving problems and taking decisions in a way that will be acceptable to the majority of committee members. A committee normally comprises between three and twenty members, and is always headed by a chairman who has the power to control the discussion and to influence decisions. The chairman's role in encouraging the committee to come to a decision is therefore critical. There is also a secretary or clerk, who keeps the minutes of meetings. All meetings follow a formal pre-arranged agenda and must abide by certain rules of procedure. An individual's status within a committee often reflects his status outside the committee and this is particularly true of committees set up within an organisation and composed of members of it. This is an extremely important point, since the "external" power structure affects the social interaction within the committee group and, more importantly, the solution arrived at. High status committee members are likely to have more attention paid to their ideas than are low status members and they will accordingly carry the greater weight in decision-making. But this does not mean that the decisions thus reached will automatically be the best or reflect the opinions of those with the greatest expertise. It is extremely important therefore to have a good chairman whose perception and judgment are keen.

Maier and Solem (1952) suggested that the role of the chairman is to:

(*a*) identify the problem, consider the available facts and ask each member for his views about the important factors;

(*b*) focus on disagreements in the group and try to arrive at a creative solution;

(*c*) evaluate different solutions in relation to criteria, if these can be agreed upon;

(*d*) ask stimulating questions to make the group question its approach or consider other aspects;

(*e*) divide a problem into sub-problems, which are taken in turn; and

(*f*) get the group to consider two possible solutions.

18. Effectiveness of committees. Argyle (1969) suggests that the main conditions under which committees are most effective in arriving at accurate or qualitatively good decisions are:

(*a*) when the group comprises very able members and they all have individual skills which will contribute to the solving of the problem;

(*b*) when the degree of co-operation between group members is high;

(*c*) when the skills of the leader or chairman are considerable. He should:

(*i*) restrain the operation of the informal status hierarchy and allow the expression of minority opinions;

(*ii*) reduce the inhibiting effects of differences in formal status; and

(*iii*) prevent conformity pressures which lead to premature decisions.

PROGRESS TEST 12

1. Use the concept of role to explain why people's behaviour varies from one situation to another **(2)**

2. Explain the essence of "role theory". **(4)**

3. What are the basic "role problems"? **(6)**

4. Explain "role stress". What is its significance? **(7, 8)**

5. Why are roles important in social interaction? **(9)**

6. To what extent does the survival and proper functioning of a group depend upon certain roles within the group being played? **(10)**

7. How do groups serve the interests of individuals and organisations? **(11)**

8. What factors affect group effectiveness? **(13)**

9. What factors can lead to group cohesion when otherwise there would be none? **(16)**

10. What are the purposes of committees? **(17)**

11. How can committees be made as effective as possible? **(18)**

CHAPTER XIII

Staffing

1. Introduction. Staffing is the fitting of people to jobs. It is concerned with:

(*a*) *recruitment*, i.e. obtaining applicants for job vacancies as they arise,

(*b*) *the selection* of the best qualified people from amongst those who make applications,

(*c*) *transfers and promotions* within the organisation, and

(*d*) *training* those who need further instruction in order that they can perform their work competently or so that they may subsequently qualify for promotion.

2. Recruitment. Recruitment in an organisation is a continuous process. It may mean recruiting hundreds of employees for a major expansion or recruiting for vacancies as and when they arise.

(*a*) *Lower grade workers.* Here the individual department makes out a job requisition outlining its requirements. Job requisitions should list such matters as the amount of education and experience needed to perform the job satisfactorily. Sources of candidates for this type of appointment may include:

(*i*) the files which the firm's personnel department holds of people writing in for jobs;

(*ii*) respondents to an advertisement placed in a local newspaper;

(*iii*) contact with local employment agencies/job centres; and

(*iv*) recruiting employees direct from colleges, universities and schools (when apprentices and trainees are required).

(*b*) *High grade workers.* Different techniques are usually adopted when high-ranking executive positions are to be filled. It may be possible to obtain respondents:

(*i*) directly by advertising in "quality" newspapers such as the *Sunday Times* or the *Daily Telegraph*;

(*ii*) through employment agencies which specialise in high level jobs;

(*iii*) through a firm of management consultants which special-
ises in obtaining and vetting candidates for managerial positions.

(*iv*) personal contacts; the firm's directors or top executives
may simply approach contacts in other firms to see if they can
recommend anyone for a particular job.

SELECTION

3. Selection. In practice many individuals are selected for jobs on
the basis of the subjective judgment exercised by one individual.
People tend to believe that they can judge intuitively, in the course
of an interview with a candidate, his or her suitability for a particular job.

Despite this tendency for management to rely upon subjective
judgment, a large number of more objective methods have been
developed to help in assessing a candidate's suitability for a particular post. Such methods include examining the candidate's past
work record, tests of actual performance, and various psychological tests. Although these methods can also prove to be fallible
they can to some extent reduce the risk of making errors.

4. Examination of past records.

(*a*) *Application forms.* These forms enable information about a
person's past experiences and qualifications to be elicited. They
should, however, only be regarded as a starting point and at most
as a means of screening out unsuitable candidates at the beginning
of the selection procedure. Unfortunately, application forms and
letters of application do not allow the personality of the applicant
to be evaluated so that a number of good and suitable applicants
may inevitably be overlooked when a short list of interview candidates is eventually drawn up.

Past records can be useful in evaluating prospective candidates
but it is important to bear in mind that individuals may change
substantially over a period of time. Furthermore, it is comparatively difficult to substantiate an individual's record of his or
her past experience, especially in the case of someone whose
work record may stretch back over twenty years. Moreover, it
should also be borne in mind that applicants do tend to orientate
their claimed experiences to suit the job for which they are applying.

(*b*) *Academic credentials.* These can be checked very easily with
the university, college or school concerned. It is worth checking

his information out, since people are apt to blur their quali-
ications if their academic record is less than good.

(c) *References.* References can provide a good guide to a candidate's previous experiences, qualifications and personal qualities.
The problem for the prospective employer is one of assessing the
objectivity of a referee's report. A poor reference from a current
employer for instance, could reflect the current employer's reluc-
tance to part with the individual. Alternatively, it could reflect a
degree of animosity arising from interpersonal conflict. It could
also, of course, be an honest one. References can therefore provide
invaluable assistance in evaluating a candidate's suitability for a
post, but they may not always be entirely objective.

5. Interviewing. Candidates for a particular post are traditionally
selected by interview. It is generally thought this method provides
ample opportunities to find out what a person is really like and
whether he or she will be suitable for a particular post. Unfortunately, in many instances, the interview is far too short to enable
an impression of the individual to be gained. Indeed many would-
be candidates for jobs develop an interview technique which
enables them to hide any characteristics which they consider the
interviewer(s) might consider unfavourable. On the other hand,
less "slick" but potentially better candidates may fail totally to
create a favourable impression at an interview.

To summarise, it seems unlikely that the conventional twenty-
minute interview is an entirely satisfactory method of accurately
assessing a candidate's personality.

Much attention has been directed towards finding better ways
of finding out about someone during an interview. There are a
number of ways in which this can be done:

(a) by allowing a candidate to interact with members of the interview panel individually (where the interview is conducted by more
than one person).

(b) by extending the length of the interview session;

(c) by varying the surroundings or circumstances under which
the interview is conducted.

EXAMPLE
A firm wishes to appoint a new engineer. Application forms are
sent out by the personnel officer to twenty-two applicants who
return them; a short list of four is drawn up by the chief engineer
in consultation with the personnel officer. Candidates are invited
to the factory individually for interview and on separate days.

Each candidate is interviewed by the chief engineer and the personnel officer together, and separately by the three other engineers with whom he will have to work if he is selected. The itinerary is as follows:

(1) 10.00a.m. Interview with the chief engineer and the personnel officer.
(2) 10.30a.m. Introduced to Engineer A, who takes him for coffee and has a general chat with him about the job.
(3) 11.00a.m. Introduced to Engineer B who takes the candidate for an informal tour of the works.
(4) 11.30a.m. Introduced to Engineer C who chats informally to the candidate in his office.
(5) 12.00p.m. Lunch with Engineers A, B and C in the staff canteen or social club.
(6) 2.00p.m. Joined by the chief engineer for about half an hour.
(7) 2.30p.m. Candidate departs.

It can be seen that each candidate is interviewed by different people in different settings continuously from 10.00 a.m. onwards. Most of the time the setting is fairly informal so that the candidate can be interviewed unobtrusively. Indeed the candidate will in all likelihood only look on the first half hour, with the head of department and the personnel officer, as being the interview. In the less formal discussions with the other engineers and finally with the chief engineer, conversation may switch to topics not directly related to the job. In this way a better insight can be gained into an individual's attitudes and his personality, thus allowing the final selection to be made on the basis of better information.

6. Testing. A number of different psychological tests can be applied to aid in the selection of candidates for jobs.

(*a*) *Intelligence tests.* These tests attempt to measure a person's IQ (intelligence quotient). This refers to the innate intelligence of an individual and his or her ability to learn. But it should be noted that comparatively recent research has shown that such factors as education and family background can have an important influence on the score that an individual obtains on such tests.

"Innate intelligence" and "ability to learn" are debatable concepts and intelligence tests may in fact merely reflect the level of educational attainment achieved by the subject. They can, however,

e a useful indicator when used in conjunction with other more
pecific tests of ability and specific skills.

Occasionally a manager may interview a candidate for a job who
as a comparatively low level of educational attainment but who
ppears to be much "brighter" than his educational record sug-
ests. Under such circumstances an intelligence test can provide
bjective evidence to support the interviewers subjective impres-
ion.

Some personnel managers adopt the view that it is unwise to
mploy people with high IQs for routine jobs, since it is reasoned
hat they will become bored quickly and quit their job, or, if they
tay, become dissatisfied and create problems for the organisation.
By and large most businesses hire an individual to occupy a par-
icular vacancy rather than *create* a job for an individual who has
ust been hired. In such circumstances, it could well be unwise to
ire a person with a high IQ to do a routine job.

(b) *Performance tests*. Very few jobs are such that it is possible
o fully test an applicant's skill in carrying out the work which
he candidate will be expected to do before he or she is appointed.
Though a typist may be asked to type a couple of pages or an
dvertising copywriter be required to submit copy for a particular
product, for most jobs it is not possible. Attempts have been made
o devise tests which will actually simulate the tasks to be per-
ormed. For example, management "in-basket" exercises are often
iven to prospective management trainees. Here the candidate is
iven a bundle of papers, letters, memoranda, etc. and is asked
ow he would deal with the points raised in the documents and
he order in which he would deal with them. Many of the facts
presented in the material may be related to one another and it will
ot be possible to satisfy the demands of each situation. The onus
s therefore upon the candidate to allocate priorities by weighing
he degree of importance of each problem and the effects that the
various courses of action will have on the various departments concerned. These tests are designed to assess the candidate's judg-
mental ability.

(c) *Trade tests*. Trade tests have been devised to separate those
who cannot do a particular skilled job from those who can. They
do not necessarily show the selectors which of the individuals who
complete the task successfully will be the best one to employ. These
ests are of the "pencil and paper" or oral type in which skilled
workers have to answer questions relating to the particular trade
or task in which they profess to have a skill.

(*d*) *Aptitude tests.* Aptitude tests are different from trade tests in that they are designed to show that an individual has the capacity to learn a new job rather than exercise a current skill. They include manual dexterity tests in which the individual may be required to perform delicate manual tests, but they may also be of the pencil and paper variety. For example, a person's aptitude to become a computer programmer may be tested by assessing the ability to understand or construct flow charts.

(*e*) *Personality tests.* Difficulties arising from personality differences are one of the largest contributors to problems at work. There are no satisfactory paper and pencil tests which enable a selector to determine the suitability of a candidate's personality for a particular job. Tests do exist, but they are relatively unsatisfactory. Even tests consisting of questions which require straightforward answers can easily give a distorted result if they are answered in a way which the candidate hopes will create the right impression. It has been suggested that projective tests might prove to be more satisfactory, but it is difficult to construct a suitable test. Moreover, even if it were possible to measure personality characteristics in people with relative ease, a further test would be required to determine whether a particular individual would be automatically a suitable occupant of a particular organisational position.

STAFF APPRAISAL

7. Transfers and promotions. The difference between a transfer and a promotion is that a transfer is a lateral move while a promotion is an upwards move, both within the organisational hierarchy. Promotions are necessary in order to fill vacancies in the organisational hierarchy as and when they occur so that employees can see their career developing in a logical progression. Transfers, however, perform a separate function. They may be made at the request of the individual himself because he or she feels a change is required and there may be better prospects in doing something different. They can also be appropriate if there are personality differences within a department. Management may also itself transfer an individual from one post to another to give him or her wider experience as a step towards promotion. Transfers may also be effected to solve management succession problems.

8. Making appraisements. Generally it is advisable to promote individuals from within the organisation. Sometimes however it is necessary to recruit from outside; non-internal promotions can bring new approaches and ideas. Whether for the purposes of promotion or annual review of salary, a manager must appraise his subordinates as to:

(*a*) their efficiency at performing their current task; and

(*b*) their potential, or "promotability".

9. Merit rating. One method of appraisement widely used is known as *merit rating*. Superiors are asked to rate their subordinates matters as to:

(*a*) the quality and quantity of the work they perform;

(*b*) their attitudes towards the company; and

(*c*) their attitudes towards fellow employees.

This method is often employed at the lower levels in the organisational hierarchy. There is often strong trade union resistance to merit rating schemes; the attitude of lower paid employees and their representatives towards merit rating is commonly that "merit" increases in earnings should be strictly related to seniority —length of service with the organisation.

10. Executive merit rating. A number of different executive merit rating schemes have been tried. One method used now, but somewhat less widely than at one time, is *trait rating*. Here the personnel department draws up a list of traits which it believes might be valuable to an efficient and effective manager, for example:

(*a*) ability to delegate authority;

(*b*) ability to sell ideas to subordinates, superiors and other members of the organisation;

(*c*) ability to analyse problems;

(*d*) attitude towards company and colleagues; and

(*e*) capacity to supervise.

Superiors are then expected to rate their subordinates as "good" "fair" or "poor" on each trait. One problem with this approach is that it is difficult to determine exactly what traits are essential for the successful performance of a particular job. An alternative approach is to rate the individual in terms of how well he performs in his present job, considering, for example, whether he meets the production or service requirements of the job.

However no method will be entirely satisfactory. The most difficult problem concerns the way in which different raters will interpret the same question, as each rater will attribute different values to each quality under consideration according to his different experiences and expectations. Two individuals with exactly the same academic credentials and of the same age may be at totally different levels in an organisation's hierarchy. Nevertheless, in rating an individual, they will compare the individual to themselves and what they have accomplished. They may very well rate the same individual in such a way that a third party would not recognise the individual concerned.

EDUCATION AND TRAINING

11. Industrial training legislation.

(a) *The Industrial Training Act 1964*. This followed from the 1962 White Paper on industrial training. The Act made provision for a series of Industrial Training Boards (ITBs), one for each industry, which were to be responsible for the training of all young people throughout their particular industries. The Boards place a mandatory levy on all firms in their industry and those firms which make satisfactory provision for training receive a grant in return. The remainder of the levy money is used to provide new training facilities. The Board also lays down standards for in-company training schemes.

Altogether twenty-eight were set up between 1964 and 1970. An ITB consists of an independent chairman, members representing employees and employers within the industry and members from the education service. It also has a permanent staff of administrators and advisers.

(b) *The Employment and Training Act 1973*. This was passed to standardise the levy-grant system. This was necessary because not all ITBs interpreted the system envisaged in the 1964 Act in the same way. In 1973 the Act laid down that the maximum levy should not exceed one per cent of payroll and that a company should be exempted entirely if it could show that its training was adequate for its needs. In addition, the Act also set up the Training Services Agency (TSA) to manage the work of the ITBs and to encourage training in industries not covered by the ITBs. Another aspect of the TSAs work is to administer TOPS (Training Opportunities Scheme) a service for people wishing to acquire a new skill.

12. Industrial training schemes. Many companies run their own training schools or arrange specific courses which their employees can attend. There are several different kinds of training that an employee can be given and some are reviewed below.

(*a*) *Orientation training.* This aims to give new employees an over-all view of the company. It may involve talks, lectures, film shows, guided tours of the factory and offices, or even, in some cases, spending of a day in each of the firm's various departments as an observer. Where a new employee is required to perform a skilled manual or clerical job, orientation will include supervisory instruction by a more experienced person over the first month or so of employment.

(*b*) *Apprenticeship training.* This is a formal system whereby practical on-the-job training is combined with classroom study. The former involves working alongside a skilled tradesman from whom the apprentice learns practical job skills, while college studies cover theoretical aspects together with basic education in associated areas, such as mathematics, for example.

In the UK in the early 1960s there was a chronic shortage of well trained junior and middle managers. This gave impetus to the idea of developing commercial apprenticeship schemes. Firms operating such schemes rotate their apprentices through the various departments of the firm (three months in each department, for example) whilst allowing them one day off a week to attend a Business Education Council (BEC) National or Higher Course at a local college. Other firms operate graduate recruitment and training schemes and here training is often given within the firm.

(*c*) *Training of supervisors.* First line supervisors are often promoted to such positions because they are extremely competent at their work and appear to have the necessary qualities to make good managers. But, since they will have no previous management experience, they will need some training to help them handle their subordinates successfully. Their course could include briefings on company policies, how their department fits into the overall organisation structure, cost reduction and work scheduling, etc. Local Colleges of Further Education offer a variety of courses in supervisory studies.

3. Management development. The need to train and develop employees for management positions became evident in the 1960s. In the 1920s and 1930s jobs of all kinds were scarce and individuals who could secure managerial posts tended not to leave them until retirement. There was consequently little opportunity for rapid advancement and little emphasis on replacing existing executives. But one of the effects of the Second World War was to create

shortages of both practising and potential managers. The rapi
industrial expansion of the 1950s, coupled with a mass exodus c
senior managers as they all simultaneously reached retirement age
created a gap at the senior and junior middle management leve
in most firms. A distinct shortage of people to fill junior and middl
management positions thus became apparent in the 1960s.

Management development programmes blossomed in the 1960
and 1970s. Many large commercial concerns such as the majc
banks, ICI, Shell, etc., run their own schools. In the USA th
General Electric Company founded a staff college in New Yor
as early as 1955, while most universities and colleges now offe
management courses.

14. Management development programmes. Robert Fulmer (1978
lists a number of popular approaches to management training.

(*a*) *Planned progression.* Here the young manager is given
definite career progression and promotion route in the firr
(assuming that he performs satisfactorily). It is mapped out fo
him so that he can tell exactly how far he has progressed alon
the route at any one time. Planning out a route enables th
"trainers" to systematically put into perspective the kinds of experi
ences that the young manager will require on his way to the to
and the sequence in which they will occur.

(*b*) *Job rotation.* There are several variations of the job rotatio
plan. Rotation may involve non-supervisory work slots, puttin
supervisors into higher management positions, or middle manager
into "assistant" positions, rotations for observation only, or fo
unspecified times and purposes.

(*c*) *"Assistant to" positions.* Trainees of any age can be assigne
to positions of "assistant to" a senior executive. The senior execu
tive serves as a teacher and trainees may learn to emulate thei
teachers. Much depends on the executive's ability to adopt such
role and this system may be far from ideal, especially where th
"senior" is too authoritarian or a poor communicator. It is axio
matic that a talented trainee who is placed in the position of assis
tant to a poor manager usually goes down or out but rarely up

(*d*) *Serving on committees.* A younger manager who is put t
serve on a committee along with seasoned executives will quickl
become familiar with numerous problems and different points o
view.

(*e*) *Junior boards.* This training device is frequently used t
provide young managers with simulated board-of-director experi

nce. At meetings junior managers consider problems which they
ave encountered. Changes and ideas that emerge are submitted
o regular managerial boards for further consideration. Such meet-
ngs give young executives the opportunity to develop skills of
ebate and the preparation of reports and proposals.

   (*f*) *Outside experience.* This usually takes the form of attendance
t conferences or on short courses run by management consultants,
olleges, or business schools.

5. Advantages of management training. Management training has
he following advantages:

   (*a*) management skills are developed or increased;

   (*b*) it enables executives to gain a broad appreciation of the
ompany's over-all background, operations and objectives;

   (*c*) it becomes possible to achieve a greater delegation of
uthority as lower ranking executives become more competent;

   (*d*) it enables management succession to be achieved by internal
romotions (which are good for morale) more easily. It can also
nake it possible to create more promoted positions if the demand
rises;

   (*e*) it makes selection procedures for promotion easier, and

   (*f*) it reduces the delay and disruption that occurs when an
xecutive resigns or retires since the position can be filled
mmediately by a trained individual.

6. Organisational development. Organisational development is
oncerned with changing the structure of an organisation to
ncrease its flexibility. Programmes of this kind focus attention on
he organisation and its weaknesses. Seminars, group meetings and
vorkshops explore the concept of flexible organisations and topics
uch as problem-solving and conflict management figure high on
he list for discussion. Discussions follow the course of structuring
nd analysing problems and group communication techniques are
mployed to solve the problems. Some development programmes
ttempt to change attitudes, motives and values of individuals to
ncourage them to adopt more participative behaviour; these
hanged values are then used as the basis for restructuring the
rganisation.

PROGRESS TEST 13

1. Indicate the main sources for recruiting employees.   **(2)**

2. What do you consider to be the best method of checking on a person's previous record of achievements? **(4)**

3. Indicate the problems that are encountered in the formal interview. Suggest means of circumventing the problems. **(5)**

4. Describe some of the different forms of objective tests which have been developed to aid in selection. **(6)**

5. Differentiate between a promotion and a transfer. **(7)**

6. What criteria should a manager employ to appraise a subordinate? **(8)**

7. Describe some of the different kinds of training methods which a firm may employ. **(12)**

8. What do you understand by "management development"? **(13)**

9. Outline the different kinds of management development programmes. **(14)**

10. What are the advantages of management training? **(15)**

11. Explain "organisational development". **(16)**

CHAPTER XIV

CHAPTER XIV

Employee Relations

INTRODUCTION

1. Introduction. This chapter examines the employee–management interface. The need for trade unions is discussed together with their role in negotiating conditions of service for their members. Attention is also given to legislation relating to working conditions. Good industrial relations are the joint responsibility of both management and employees and the trade unions representing them. The primary responsibility for the promotion of good industrial relations remains with management and it should therefore take the initiative in creating and developing them.

2. Conditions of service. Conditions of service include such matters as:

(*a*) rates of pay;
(*b*) hours of work;
(*c*) duties to be performed;
(*d*) holidays;
(*e*) leave of absence;
(*f*) pension rights;

(*g*) sickness pay;
(*h*) termination of employment;
(*i*) dismissal;
(*j*) retirement;
(*k*) redundancy procedures; and
(*l*) safety policy.

3. Trade unions. Trade unions evolved in the nineteenth century in response to a need to protect the interests of employees against unscrupulous employers. In particular, agreements as to what constituted reasonable working hours, pay, job security and conditions of work were in need of negotiation. During the present century, the trade union movement has grown in importance until today when it has become a very powerful force in the economy of the UK.

Some of the traditional roles of the trade unions have since been taken over by the social security and welfare systems provided by the State, but their collective bargaining function continues, whereby they continually seek to achieve higher wages and better working conditions for their members. Indeed the Trades Union Congress (the body which represents all trade unions) has not infrequently had a considerable part to play, along with its management equivalent the Confederation of British Industry, in formulating the government's national wages, and even economic, policy.

4. Employers' Associations. Employers in similar industries customarily form associations. An important function of such an association is to establish a mechanism by which industrial relations matters for the industry can be negotiated. It can play an important role in dispute procedures if a matter cannot be resolved within the individual firm itself (*see* **10** below). The Confederation of British Industry is the body which collectively represents the views of British Industry.

5. Trade union–management interface. Historically, each craft had its own trade union (originally known as guilds). In modern times many amalgamations have taken place between different trade unions but there is still a relatively large number. Management may therefore find that it may have to bargain with several different unions within a single factory unit. An agreement negotiated successfully with one union may not be equally acceptable to another union which may represent a different set of individuals within the same factory. Both unions may have different ideas on pay differentials and may not agree on the appropriate rate of pay for a particular job. An additional hazard is that union officials may not always be able to prevent its members coming out on unofficial or "wild-cat" strikes; these are particularly difficult to settle since they do not have the support of the appropriate trade union.

6. Industrial action. Industrial action can result from the non-settlement of employees' grievances. The failure of management to interpret conditions of service fairly in the eyes of employees or failure to agree to, or implement, a new wage demand, can give rise to grievances. Industrial action can take several different forms.

(*a*) *Work to rule.* Here employees work strictly according to their contracts of employment and job descriptions. No extra duties are performed.

(*b*) *Sit-in.* Here employees peacefully occupy their employer's premises and prevent management from carrying out its tasks.

(*c*) *Strike.* Here employees refuse to turn up for work.

7. Legal rights of employers in industrial actions.

(*a*) *Dismissal.* All employees taking part in a strike can be dismissed by their employer since they are in breach of their contract.

As long as the employer refuses to re-engage any of them, they cannot claim unfair dismissal.

(b) *Secondary action.* It is illegal for any person to induce a breach of contract of employment with an employer not in dispute, unless the main purpose is directly to prevent or disrupt supplies between an employer or an associated employer in dispute and his supplier or customer.

(c) *Picketing.* No legal right exists to picket, but it is not illegal for an individual or group of individuals in a public place to peacefully persuade others to adopt a certain course of action. Nevertheless, such individuals are subject to the ordinary laws of obstruction, trespass and nuisance.

(d) *Sit-ins.* Employees who occupy industrial premises as part of a "sit-in" cannot be evicted by the police unless violence or damage to property is threatened. Employees can only be evicted as a result of a civil action.

8. Joint consultation. Industrial action may be averted by joint consultation between management and workers. Here, problems of mutual concern are examined and discussed and mutually acceptable solutions, through a genuine exchange of views and information, are sought. In establishing consultative arrangements, management should make sure that:

(a) opportunities are provided for employees to express their views on proposed changes which will affect them;

(b) employees' representatives are provided with enough information to enable them to participate effectively in discussions;

(c) senior managers take an active part in consultation;

(d) a means of reporting back the results of discussion to employees exists.

Joint consultation can do much to further goodwill and co-operation.

9. Productivity bargaining. Collective bargaining can establish a good framework of relations between management and employees, provided that a reasonable and constructive approach to negotiation is taken by both parties. It may take place at various levels ranging from a whole industry, or part of one, to a group of employees within an establishment. Negotiations for the same group of employees may be conducted at different levels about different subjects. Productivity bargaining (a form of collective bargaining) is at the centre of many joint consultation sessions: it

works on the principle that management is better able and more
inclined to increase workers' pay if they can produce more. This
differs somewhat from traditional collective bargaining, which
increases labour costs without benefiting the employer directly.

Productivity bargaining is frequently most in evidence where
there is labour inefficiency and friction—demarcation disputes,
go-slows and too much overtime. Under circumstances where productivity is low there is clearly more scope for productivity bargaining. It also occurs where mechanisation will lead to a need for fewer
employees and where therefore some special form of motivation
is required to facilitate the acceptance of the new working arrangements.

10. Grievances and disputes procedures. It is management's responsibility to make arrangements with employee representatives or
trade unions through which employees can raise grievances and
have them settled fairly and promptly.

(*a*) *Individual grievance procedures.* Such procedures should be
written down and made provision for:

(*i*) the grievance to be discussed in the first place between the
employee and his immediate superior;

(*ii*) the employee to be accompanied at the next stage of discussion with management by his employee-representative, if he
so wishes;

(*iii*) there to be a right of appeal.

(*b*) *Collective dispute procedures.* Such procedures should be in
writing and:

(*i*) state the level at which an issue should be raised in the
first instance;

(*ii*) define time limitations for each stage in the procedure,
making provision for extension by agreement;

(*iii*) preclude the taking of industrial action until such time
as all stages of the procedure have been exhausted and failure to
reach an agreement has been formally recorded.

The stages involved in grievance procedure should allow un-
settled disputes to be referred to progressively higher levels of
authority within an establishment and eventually to national
representatives of the relevant employer's association.

EXAMPLE

(1) The shop steward discusses the grievance with middle
management in the organisation. If a settlement is not achieved:

(2) a district official of the relevant trade union raises the grievance with senior management in the organisation where there is a dispute. If a settlement is not achieved: (3) union officials raise the matter with the regional committee of the employers' association. If a settlement is not achieved: (4) national officials of the trade union raise the matter with national officials of the employers' association. If a settlement is not achieved: (5) provided that both parties agree, an independent arbitrator may be called in to give advice or make a decision. Such a decision is not, however, legally binding.

11. Arbitration. Where joint consultations fail to find a remedy for a particular problem, a dispute can be taken to arbitration. There are three main bodies which arbitrate in industrial disputes.

(a) *The Employment Appeal Tribunal.* Established in 1975, it is composed of both judges and lay members with special knowledge of industrial relations.

(b) *The Central Arbitration Committee.* Established in 1975 the CAC replaced the Industrial Arbitration Board which had in turn replaced the Industrial Court, established in 1919.

(c) *Industrial tribunals.* Established in 1964, their jurisdiction has expanded considerably since then.

12. Industrial tribunals. The best policy is to prevent industrial disputes from arising in the first place, or to settle them quickly once they have occurred. Should joint consultations or arbitration fail to help settle a dispute, employers and unions may seek redress before an industrial tribunal. This is an independent judicial body. It has a legally-qualified chairman, appointed by the Lord Chancellor in England and Wales, and in Scotland by the Lord President. Two other members are appointed by the Secretary of State for Employment—one after consultation with employee's organisations and the other after consultation with employer's organisations. Applications to a Tribunal are sent direct to the Secretary of a Tribunal. Forms are available from local employment offices, Job Centres and unemployment benefit offices. The Secretary of a Tribunal sends a copy of the application to the person or firm against whom the application is made and requests particulars of the grounds upon which the latter might contest the case. A case can be settled at this stage without a hearing taking place. Copies of all relevant documents are usually sent to a conciliation officer of the Advisory Conciliation and Arbitration Service (ACAS). This does not impede or delay the hearing taking place. In England

and Wales, awards made by industrial tribunals are enforceable by an application to the county court.

13. Scope of industrial tribunals. Industrial tribunals may consider the following matters:

(*a*) matters relating to health and safety at work (Health and Safety at Work etc. Act 1974);

(*b*) matters relating to equal pay and conditions for men and women alike (Equal Pay Act 1970);

(*c*) matters relating to discrimination in aspects of employment on grounds of colour, race or ethnic origin (Race Relations Act 1976);

(*d*) matters relating to discrimination in aspects of employment, training and related fields on the grounds of sex or marriage (Sex Discrimination Act 1975);

(*e*) matters relating to disputes concerning redundancies (Employment Act 1980);

(*f*) matters relating to disputes concerning redundancy payments; suspension on medical grounds; time off to find other work in the face of impending redundancy; time off for trade union duties; union membership and the closed shop; rights on termination of contract, and the right to receive itemised pay statements (Employment Act 1980);

(*g*) matters relating to disputes concerning rights for the expectant mother; unfair dismissal; rights to receive guaranteed pay during lay-offs (Employment Act 1980).

HEALTH AND SAFETY

14. Health and safety law. There is a legal obligation on management to look after the well-being of their employees. The following legislation is relevant.

(*a*) *The Factories Act 1961 and the Offices, Shops and Railway Premises Act 1963*. These Acts lay down the minimum requirements relating to provisions for safety and health at work. Heating, lighting, ventilation, toilet facilities, guarding of machinery etc. all come within the scope of these Acts.

(*b*) *The Health and Safety at Work etc. Act 1974*. This important and wide-ranging Act lays down broad principles on health and safety at work but does not replace the laws previously in existence.

15. Health and Safety Commission. This is the top body for all health and safety matters. Its main functions are to:

(*a*) promote health and safety at work;

(*b*) recommend new regulations or update existing ones;

(*c*) prepare codes of practice on particular health and safety issues;

(*d*) issue guidance notes on health and safety;

(*e*) encourage research into issues and to publish the results; and

(*f*) liaise with the Training Boards to provide safety education and training.

The Health and Safety Executive is the operating and enforcement arm of the Commission. This is effected through its inspectorate.

16. Duties of Employers. Any breach of employers' duties set out in the Health and Safety at Work etc. Act could render an employer liable to criminal prosecution. Section 2 of the Act states that an employer must ensure, so far as is reasonably practicable, the health, safety and welfare at work of all his employees. This duty also extends to all visitors to the premises.

An employer must produce and periodically revise a written statement of his general policy with respect to the health and safety of his employees at work.

DISCIPLINARY PROCEDURES

17. Disciplinary procedures. These should be agreed with employee representatives or trade unions. Employees should be informed by management about:

(*a*) disciplinary rules and agreed procedure;

(*b*) circumstances which lead to suspension or dismissal.

The written procedures should:

(*a*) indicate who has authority to take disciplinary action (making sure that the individual supervisors must refer a dismissal case to more senior management);

(*b*) enable the employee to state his own case and be accompanied by his employee representative;

(*c*) make provision for a right of appeal to a higher authority in the establishment; and

(*d*) make provision for independent arbitration to be sought if both parties agree to it.

18. Disciplinary action. The following procedures should be observed when taking disciplinary action.

(*a*) an oral warning should be given in the first instance, unless there is evidence of serious misconduct, in which case it should be in writing;

(*b*) only in the case of gross misconduct should an employee be dismissed for a first breach of discipline;

(*c*) final warnings or suspensions without pay or dismissal should be recorded in writing;

(*d*) details of disciplinary action should be made in writing to the employee;

(*e*) disciplinary actions against shop stewards should not be taken until the case has been discussed with a full-time official of the union.

PROGRESS TEST 14

1. What are the main functions of the trade unions? **(3)**

2. Can an employer dismiss all employees taking part in some form of industrial action? **(7)**

3. What is meant by secondary action? **(7)**

4. Do pickets have any legal rights? **(7)**

5. Under what circumstances can management evict persons who are taking part in a "sit-in"? **(7)**

6. What are joint consultative committees? **(8)**

7. What is productivity bargaining? **(9)**

8. What steps should management take when joint consultation fails? **(11, 12)**

9. What matters can be referred to industrial tribunals? **(13)**

10. What is the function of the Health and Safety Commission? **(15)**

CHAPTER XV

Management Services

1. Introduction. Management services assists management in its task of organising, planning and controlling the activities of an organisation. In this book we consider management services to be the following activities:

(a) work study;
(b) organisation and methods; and
(c) operational research (including short term forecasting).

WORK STUDY

2. Definition. Work study is a technique of management involving analytical study of a job for the following purposes:

(a) to determine what exactly has to be done; what are the optimum conditions—methods, layout, batch size and equipment; and to eliminate causes of ineffective work;

(b) to measure the work content of a job for use in planning, costing, wage payment (incentive) and control activities;

3. Method study. The first stage of work study is method study. Relying upon systematic observation and analysis, method study aims to establish the best way of performing a task. Method study can be applied in all kinds of organisational settings ranging from the factory floor to the typing pool. There are four stages to method study:

(a) observing the performance of a task; establishing all the relevant facts and recording the information;

(b) analysing all the data obtained and assessing how the method of doing a job can be improved;

(c) establishing the procedures in a new method;

(d) installing a new method.

4. Process charts. Process charts (*see* Fig. 24) assist in the recording of the various elements of a task. A number of symbols have been developed to help record actions carried out by a worker. Though

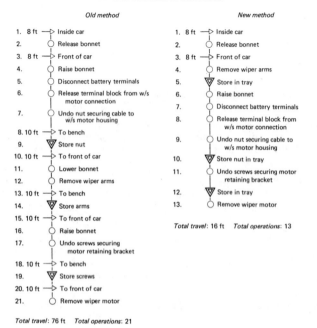

FIG. 24   *Removal of windscreen wiper motor.*

there may be slight variations in practice, the following symbols
are commonly used:

○	operation
⟶	transport (movement)
▽	permanent storage
▼	temporary storage
☐	inspection
◉	delay or idle time

A process chart portrays the sequence in which operations and
other activities take place. The way in which a worker performs
a task is first recorded and the method study expert then examines

the chart to see if there are better ways of performing the task. Unnecessary transport or movement activities need to be eliminated or curtailed. Delays and idle time should also be minimised. The sequence in which elements of the task are performed may be changed. In the example illustrated in Figure 24 the provision of a "temporary" mobile storage tray eliminates unnecessary travelling to and from the bench. In addition, by removing the wiper arms at the beginning of the task the number of operations is reduced.

5. String diagrams. Much time can sometimes be saved by rearranging the objects with which a person has to come into contact in performing a job. Unnecessary movement takes up valuable time and it is a foremost aim of method study to eliminate all unnecessary movements. String diagrams show the actual movement of operators, material and equipment. Coloured pieces of string, indicating different persons, material or equipment are stretched around pins which are pressed into a scale drawing of the layout of the place where the job is performed. The length of string is a scale measure of the distance travelled.

6. Work measurement. The notion of Taylor's fair day's work eventually led to the development of a systematic means of measuring the work content of a particular task or job. An added impetus to find a means to measure the work content of a job was provided by the need to plan production programmes. Orders have to be delivered to customers by a given date which means that products have to be produced within a specific period of time. If the work content of a job cannot be estimated reasonably accurately it is difficult to plan production to any degree.

7. Steps in the process of work measurement/time study. Efforts have been directed towards producing a standard work unit which can be used for planning, costing, measurement of individual performance and so on. A. W. Fields (1963) defined this unit as follows:

> The amount of work performed in one minute at a standard rate of working, including time for relaxation. This unit involves a definition of a standard rate of working. A standard rate of working is taken to mean the normal or moderate rate which can be kept up without undue fatigue by an average qualified operator working well within his or her capacity.

A person working at a standard rate can produce 60 work units per hour and this can be used as a measure by which to "rate" a job. On this basis a job which it is estimated will consume 150 work units should take 2½ hours to complete. Similarly a job which should take 40 minutes to complete has a value of 40 work units. This method of rating is known as the Bedaux 60/80 points system but there are two other performance rating systems in operation. These are: the British Institute rating (BSI) and the International Labour Organisation system (ILO). The following table enables a comparison between the scales to be made.

TABLE III. WORK UNITS PER HOUR RATING

Bedaux	BSI	ILO	Description
120	150	200	exceptionally quick
100	125	166.67	very quick
80	100	133.33	brisk
60	75	100	average
40	50	66.66	slow
20	25	33.33	very slow

Time study divides work up into discrete measurable parts called *elements*. Each element is then separately timed and the timing for all the elements are added to give an "observed time" for the job. As is noted above, values are adjusted to take into account the "rate" at which the observed operator is performing the job. This then becomes the "basic time" for the job. Allowances for fatigue and personal needs are then added to the basic time to form the "standard time" for the job.

Management and the union representative should agree on the selection of a qualified worker for the purpose of the study. He must neither be exceptionally skilled nor a poor worker and all aspects of the job should be as near normal as possible. The performance of each element is observed a number of times and an average value is taken to be representative of the value of that element.

8. Estimating. The key to successful work measurement lies in good estimating. Consider for a moment the different job types that can be measured. Here are a few examples:

(*a*) attaching the wheels to a car, on a production line;

(*b*) stripping, cleaning, reassembling and testing an electric motor;

(*c*) operating a photocopying machine.

It has to be remembered that the time that individuals spend on a particular job can be allocated to three types of activity:

(*a*) actually working at what they have been allotted to do;

(*b*) relaxing in order to compensate for fatigue;

(*c*) doing things which do not contribute to the actual completion of the work.

A competent work study officer should have little difficulty in identifying the different types of activities with respect to job types (*a*) and (*c*) above but in the case of (*b*) more specialised knowledge may be required. Where knowledge of the job requires knowledge of a specific skill that the work study officer does not possess it is common practice to employ an estimator. An estimator is usually a skilled operator who possesses the necessary knowledge.

9. Job evaluation. Job evaluation is the comparison of jobs to determine the relative position of one job to another in a wage or salary hierarchy. There are four main types of evaluation method practised.

(*a*) *Ranking.* This involves drawing up a list of jobs and then converting the list into a "league table" which reflects the degree of importance of each job. It is suggested that the pay for the job should be commensurate with its position on the league table. The higher up the league table then the more pay there should be for that particular job. It is a simple method to understand and is easy to establish. However, it pays little attention to the amount of effort or responsibility attached to a job and is difficult to operate where there are many jobs of different kinds.

(*b*) *Job classification.* Firstly, all the specifications for a number of different grades of jobs are listed. The lowest grade jobs are those which require little skill and are closely supervised. At each successive higher grade skills, knowledge and responsibility increase. This represents a framework into which jobs in the firm can be slotted. Every job in the firm is matched against the specifications listed and given an appropriate grading. This method is often applied in the case of clerical jobs. It does not however involve analysing a job in depth and in consequence is vulnerable to workers' claims that their job has been misclassified.

(c) *Factor comparison.* This is similar to *job classification* above and involves analysing a job according to the following factors:

(i) mental requirements;
(ii) physical requirements;
(iii) responsibility; and
(iv) working conditions.

Firstly a number of key jobs are selected and ranked according to these factors. Next one has to discern how the wages paid for each job can be allocated between the various factors. This enables a relationship to be established between: money paid, each factor and ranking. It provides a frame of reference against which to evaluate other jobs.

It is a difficult method to put into practice and is not widely used.

(d) *Points rating.* This method is widely used in practice and is accepted by trade unions as a systematic method for evaluating jobs. There are some variations in practice but the method shown here is typical of them. In implementing a scheme, every job is first broken down into factors and sub-factors and a range of points is assigned to each:

Factor	Sub-factor	Range of points	Sub-total
Skill	education	0–10	
	training	0– 8	
	initiative	0– 7	25
Effort	physical	0–10	
	mental	0– 8	
	visual	0– 7	25
Responsibility	for other's work	0–10	
	for the product	0– 9	
	for safety	0– 6	25
Conditions	working conditions	0–15	
	hazards	0–10	25

The total points allocated to various jobs are then plotted against the hourly wage scale for the job on a scatter diagram (*see* Fig. 25):

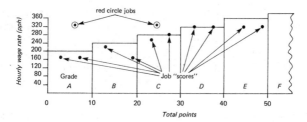

FIG. 25   *An example of a scatter diagram (adapted from J. Powell,* Work Study, *Arrow,* 1976).

Job grades are assessed on the basis of the points system independently and then a rate worked out for each grade. These are then superimposed on the diagram. Some jobs, known as "red circle jobs", will be found to be paid at a higher rate than is appropriate for the grade. Holders of such jobs may retain their special grading on a personal basis. Other jobs will be below what is "the grade" for the job and should be paid more accordingly.

Job evaluation should not be conducted by a single individual since this may lead to a biased judgment. Usually a committee—comprising the personnel officer work study officer and the O & M officer together with members drawn from line management personnel—consider job specifications and apply the chosen evaluation method.

ORGANISATION AND METHODS

10. Definition and purpose. Organisation and methods (O & M) is the application of systematic, action-orientated research to organisational problems and procedures. It aims to maximise organisational efficiency, subject to a cost constraint and it borrows many of the techniques of work study.

11. Characteristics of the O & M department. The size of the O & M department will vary according to the size and the nature of the organisation. Factories or works in which there are few clerical staff and managers will probably not have O & M personnel at all. Local government offices and insurances companies may very well have a considerable number of O & M staff. There are, however, no hard and fast rules and one finds O & M personnel in all kinds of organisations.

The O & M function is purely advisory to management and

carries with it no line authority. An O & M officer cannot instruct a clerk or a progress chaser on what he is to do. He can only advise management in a particular department on the most appropriate way of doing a particular task or solving a particular problem. He may on occasion be requested to implement and control the procedures which he recommends. Of necessity this may require temporary delegation of authority.

12. The activities that an O & M officer may perform. Problems may arise which require a solution to be found. A new clerical procedure which has previously been updated or amended may be causing problems and the O & M officer has to sort it out. Alternatively, a system which has been in operation for many years may have difficulty in coping with the ever increasing workload put upon it as the business expands.

13. Clerical methods and work study. O & M studies aim to find more cost efficient methods of performing tasks. In every organisation there is "organisational slack". This develops in times when there are plenty of funds available to expand the activities of an organisation and staff are taken on to cope with additional work. The amount of work going through a particular sub-system within an organisation fluctuates over a number of years with the result that periodically many sections and departments become over-manned. Moreover, a change in one sub-system—production control—may have implications for another sub-system—stock control. Clerical method study can involve designing new paper work systems and documents. This in turn can result in the reduction of the workload of certain clerks and by combining one or more jobs together staff savings can be made. In both instances the same level of efficiency can be maintained but with fewer staff.

14. An illustration of an O & M assignment. A large insurance company decides to open a new district office in Cumbernauld new town, Scotland. Three potential suites of offices are available and all are at a similar cost. An O & M Officer from the London head office is assigned the task of:

(*a*) recommending which of the suites of offices is the most suitable for use as a district office;

(*b*) recommending the grades and numbers of employees which will be required to staff the district office;

(*c*) designing the layout of the office and the different types of equipment, fittings and furniture which will be required;

(*d*) advising on the appointment of clerical staff;

(*e*) designing the paperwork information system to be used at the district office so that it fits in with the current practice in the rest of the company;

(*f*) designing any additional forms or procedures that are required;

(*g*) preparing job descriptions for the staff at the office; and

(*h*) ensuring that the setting up of the office is a smooth operation and ironing out any problems that arise during this phase.

OPERATIONAL RESEARCH

15. Nature. Operational Research (OR) may be defined as the scientific approach to the analysis and solution of management problems to provide a quantitative basis for management decision-making. Its distinctive approach is to develop a scientific model of the system and incorporate into it measures which reflect chance and risk. The model can then be used to predict and to compare the outcomes of different decisions, strategies or controls.

At the basis of OR is the attempt to quantify all the variables in a given problem situation and to formulate a mathematical model that will show the final effect of any proposed change. In effect this has much in common with the early scientists' attempts to formulate "laws" such as Boyle's Law, expressed as the formula $PV = RT$, where P is pressure, V is volume, R is a constant and T is temperature of a gas. An equivalent example in the business field might be a simple equation for a profit model such as: $P = pq - (vq + f + x)$, where P is profit, p is unit price, v is variable unit cost, f is fixed costs, x is promotional expenditure per unit sold and q is units sold per period of time. Of course, much more complex models may be constructed.

16. Applications of OR. Since OR is an approach to solving problems it is appropriate to consider it in the light of the different problems that it can help to solve. Ackoff and Rivett (1964) suggest that management scientists tend to view problems in terms of structure rather than content. The different types of structure they identify are:

(*a*) allocation;
(*b*) queuing;
(*c*) inventory;
(*d*) sequencing;

(*e*) routing;
(*f*) replacement;
(*g*) competition;
(*h*) search.

17. Allocation of resources. Successful allocation of resources is achieved when available resources are deployed to maximum effect. Management's problem is therefore to ensure that resources are allocated as successfully as possible. Typical examples of allocation problems in a business context are as follows:

(a) assigning salesmen to territories to maximise sales generated;

(b) determining how much of given products to ship from each factory to each warehouse so as to maximise the availability of products;

(c) demining how to allocate advertising expenditure between different media so as to maximise the chances of attaining a specific number of objectives; and

(d) determining how much to produce of a given set of products so as to maximise the overall contribution to fixed overheads.

Linear and mathematical programming techniques can be applied to deal with such problems (*see* Stafford, *Business Mathematics*).

A simple graphical illustration of the application of linear programming to solving a management problem is shown below. More complex problems require a mathematical solution, employing the *simplex* method (*see* Stafford, *Business Mathematics*).

EXAMPLE

A firm manufactures two products (Product A and Product B). Each product requires different machining, painting and assembly times. In addition each product makes a different contribution towards overheads. The firm has limited capacity available for each of the manufacturing operations and these are summarised below:

Operation	Product A hours required per unit	Product B hours required per unit	Capacity available hours per week
Machining	5	4	2,400
Painting	3	3	1,500
Assembly	1	2	800

The contribution towards overheads per unit is £9 per unit for Product A and £8 per unit for Product B. Maximise contri-

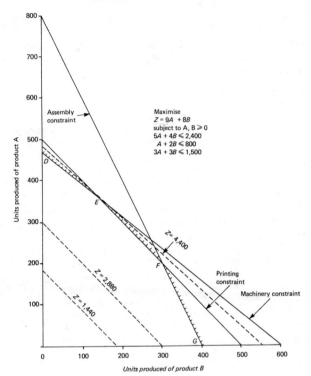

FIG. 26 *Graphical representation of an exercise in linear programming.*

bution to overhead subject to satisfying a production capacity constraint (*see* Fig. 26).

The first step is to draw up the graph axes as in Fig. 26. The next step is to draw in the line which represents the machining capacity constraint. Mathematically this line takes the form of the equation:

$$5A + 4B = 2,400$$

The position of the line on the graph is identified as follows. The maximum amount of Product A that can be produced, assuming zero work on product B, is $\dfrac{2,400}{5} = 480$ units, i.e. total capacity available (in hours), divided by the number of hours required to machine one unit of product A. Similarly it will be found that the maximum number of units of product B that can be produced, assuming zero work on product A is $\dfrac{2,400}{4} = 600$ units. Next we draw in the line, starting at 480 units of A on the vertical axis to 600 units of B on the horizontal axis. The lines representing "assembly constraint" ($1A + 2B \leqslant 800$) and "painting constraint" ($3A + 3B \leqslant 1,500$) are inserted in a similar manner.

The objective is to maximise the contribution to overheads (maximise $Z = 9A + 8B$). We first select an arbitrary value for Z, say 1,440 and using the same method as before, i.e. letting A and B equal zero in turn, we draw in the arbitrary line $9A + 8B = 1,440$. This is shown as the dotted line on the graph in Fig. 26. Now production constraints (indicated by the line $DEFG$) define the area of the graph within which the maximum contributions to overheads will be made. Furthermore, this will be at one of the points D, E, F, or G. By moving the contribution to overheads line to the right and keeping it parallel with the line $Z = 1,440$ we eventually find that the very last point at which the line remains within the bounded area ($DEFG$) is at point E. It is here that contribution to overhead will be maximised. Reading off values on the vertical and horizontal axes shows that this will be achieved by producing 400 units of product A and 100 units of product B. This gives the maximum contribution of £4,400.

18. Queuing and inventory problems. Queuing problems are of the kind where one has to determine the level of facilities to provide in order to cope with the demands of users. Problems in this category include determining the optimum number of:

    (*a*) checkout points to have in a supermarket;
    (*b*) barmaids needed to staff a bar;
    (*c*) telephone operators to employ on a switchboard;
    (*d*) typists to employ in a typing pool; and also
    (*e*) whether a taxi firm should use its own repair shop or contract the work out (*see* Stafford, *Business Mathematics*).

This kind of problem is in many ways similar to one of stock control or inventory. However, in the case of a queuing model the following factors have to be taken into account:

(*a*) *the queue discipline*; whether there are any rules which govern priorities;

(*b*) *the arrival pattern*; whether it is regular (probabilistic), cyclical or random; and

(*c*) *the service time*; whether it is constant or variable.

Stafford (*Business Mathematics*) gives some simple illustrations of how queuing and inventory models are constructed.

19. Sequencing problems. Sequencing problems involve finding a serial order of items which minimise some cost associated with their processing. Examples include:

(*a*) planning the sequence of events leading to the introduction of a new product;

(*b*) sequencing the events by which to dismantle and reassemble plant and equipment for servicing or repair.

Critical path techniques (critical path analysis, network analysis and programme evaluation and review technique or PERT) can be used to solve such problems.

20. Routing problems. Here the problem is one of trying to find the best path to follow amongst a variety of locations so as to minimise some measure—time spent, distance travelled etc. Examples include:

(*a*) routing a travelling salesman;

(*b*) supermarket flow problems, i.e. how to route customers through a supermarket; and

(*c*) production flow problems.

The basic data required for a solution is a matrix showing the distances (or travel cost or time) between all pairs of customers. Many techniques have been applied to this matrix including linear programming, integer programming, dynamic programming, heuristic programming and branch and bound techniques (*see also* W. M. Harper, *Operational Research*).

21. Replacement problems. This type of problem can be sub-divided into two categories:

(*a*) where items are involved whose efficiency decreases with use over time;

(*b*) where items are involved whose failure occurs without previous deterioration (the "light bulb" problem).

The nature of the problem is to determine the time for replacing the item such that the sum of the operating costs and investment outlays are minimised. Examples include determining:

(*a*) when to introduce new products or product modifications;
(*b*) the length of an advertising campaign;
(*c*) the servicing schedule for machinery; and
(*d*) job rotation policies involving repetitive work.

Replacement problems can be examined using probability theory and statistical analysis (*see* W. M. Harper, *Operational Research*).

22. Search problems. These are of the type where there is a need to decide between "extensive" and "intensive" investigation of a process, when the resources for investigation are fixed. The nature of the problem requires a plan of action to be designed that minimises the risk of making errors. Errors may be associated with "too intensive" or "too extensive" a search procedure. Examples include:

(*a*) deciding the nature that a marketing research study should take;
(*b*) establishing quality control procedures; and
(*c*) information retrieval procedures.

SIMULATION

23. Simulation. Simulation enables a manager to study how a system which he controls works. It involves the building of a physical model to represent the object of the study and performing experiments with the model under conditions similar to those which the model would operate. Examples include "wind tunnels" in aircraft engineering in which models of projected aircraft designs are tested. This enables deductions to be made about the likely aerodynamic behaviour of a new aircraft before it is actually produced. Other examples include models of dams and reservoirs or tidal flows which provide the source of power for electricity generating stations. A simulation model, however, need not be mechanical and can be represented mathematically on a computer.

In computer simulation, a computer program which will simulate the logical structure of the situation to be studied is prepared. Here "experience" is generated synthetically by the computer which processes the information that has been fed into it.

24. Applications of simulation. The following are some of the areas of management where simulation can be applied:

(*a*) *risk analysis*—considering the impact of various differing factors (selling, market growth rate, etc.) upon parameter such as reorder levels etc.;

(*b*) *inventory control*—analysing the effects of different inventory policies on costs/profits;

(*c*) *network models*—tracing the behaviour of a PERT network under a variety of suppositions;

(*d*) *job scheduling*—tracing the effect of different routing, sequencing, etc. on job completion times, and maximising the effective utilisation of equipment etc.;

(*e*) *marketing decisions*—evaluating the effect on sales/profits of different decisions, e.g. introducing a new product into the product mix.

25. Advantages of simulation. The advantages of simulation are that it:

(*a*) permits the study of problems too complex to be represented by a mathematical algorithm;

(*b*) allows the exploration of many more strategies than is possible by means of intuitive thinking;

(*c*) enables variables to be identified to which the system is more sensitive; and

(*d*) enables experiments to be conducted where the actual system would not otherwise permit this or where it would otherwise be very expensive to conduct an experiment.

SHORT-TERM FORECASTING

26. Introduction. Where a firm has many products, packages and different types of material to manufacture or process, planning and control is an onerous task. A reasonably reliable and simple method of forecasting short-term demand is extremely helpful therefore. A computer-based system has obvious advantages in being able to cope with the vast amount of data which will be generated. There are a number of simple mathematical methods which lend themselves to be used in making forecasts of this kind. Generally speaking short term forecasts are for up to six months ahead. An examination of the periodic demand for a product will reveal four components:

(*a*) an underlying trend;

(*b*) a seasonal variation;

(*c*) a cyclical variation; and

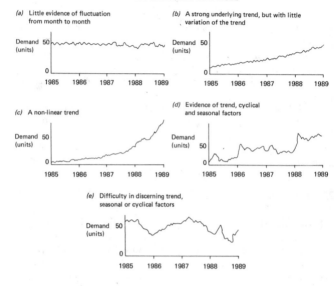

FIG. 27   *Patterns of historical data.*

(*d*) a residual random variation.

In trying to devise a suitable short-term system the first step is to examine past and current data. Forecasting data is best represented in graphical form so that its underlying patterns can be identified more easily. Examination of the data may reveal any one of a number of patterns.

(*a*) A pattern in which there is little fluctuation from month to month and which reveals no underlying trend in the series (*see* Fig. 27(*a*)). If this is the case then "moving averages" and "exponential smoothing" are appropriate techniques (*see also* **27–29**).

(*b*) A pattern in which there is a strong underlying trend (upwards or downwards) but where there is little variation about the trend (*see* Fig. 27(*b*)). Applicable techniques in this case include double exponential smoothing and time series regression (*see* **30**).

(*c*) A pattern in which the trend is non-linear (*see* Fig. 27(*c*)), as for example the sales of a new product where initial sales are slow but grow at an ever increasing rate thereafter. Under these circumstances a mathematical expression may be formulated to represent the growth curve and this can be used as a basis for forecasting—provided there are no seasonal variations in demand for the product.

(d) A pattern which reveals cyclical and seasonal factors influencing demand (see Fig. 27(d)). Under these circumstances "the classical decomposition of time series" technique is the simplest (see 32).

(e) A pattern in which there is evidence of strong fluctuations but in which it is difficult to discern seasonal or cyclical demand trends (see Fig. 27(e)). Here "adaptive techniques" are best employed.

A detailed illustration of all these techniques is beyond scope of this book. Readers are referred instead to Appendix III: Further Reading. Some of the simpler techniques are, however, illustrated (see 27–32).

27. Moving averages. Moving averages may be used most successfully where there is little variation in data and where there is no discernible underlying trend. The moving average technique involves adding together data for a number of weeks or months and dividing this sum by the number of months or weeks, as appropriate, to obtain a "moving average". For example, the forecast for April in Table IV below is calculated by adding sales figures for the preceding three months (6500 + 6400 + 6200) and dividing by three to give the moving average (6367). The moving average itself then becomes the forecast for the next month in the series,

TABLE IV. CALCULATION OF MOVING AVERAGES

Month	Sales	Forecast	(3 months moving average)
Jan	6500		
Feb	6400		
Mar	6200		
Apr	5800	6367	(6500 + 6400 + 6200)/3
May	6150	6133	
Jun	6250	6050	
Jul	6350	6067	
Aug	6000	6250	
Sep	6400	6200	

and so on. The choice of the number of months to include is arbitrary: one has to find by trial and error the number of months that gives the most accurate prediction.

It is a principle of the moving average that equal weight is given to each period in calculating the average.

28. Weighted moving average. Here each period is allocated a predetermined "weight" which is related to the demand for that period (the "weights" must all sum to unity). The weighted moving average is then calculated by multiplying demand by weight (*see* Table V).

TABLE V. CALCULATION OF WEIGHTED MOVING AVERAGE

Period	Demand (000 units)	Weight	Weight × demand
1	16.6	0.002	0.0332
2	16.6	0.004	0.0664
3	16.8	0.008	0.1344
4	17.4	0.016	0.2784
5	16.9	0.032	0.5408
6	17.3	0.063	1.0899
7	17.8	0.125	2.2250
8	18.2	0.250	4.5500
9	17.9	0.500	8.9500
		1.000	17.8681

The demand forecast for Period 10 is 17,868 units.

The weighted moving average can also be calculated by the formula:

$$\text{Next period forecast} = (0.5 \times \text{latest demand figure}) + (0.5 \times \text{forecast for the previous period}).$$

In Table V suppose the demand for period 10 was actually 18,026. The forecast for period 11 would therefore be:

$$(0.5 \times 18,026) + 0.5 \times 17,868 = 17,947 \text{ units.}$$

29. Exponential smoothing. This is a statistical technique which makes use of the idea of the weighted moving average. The formula is:

$$\text{Next period forecast} = (\text{this period's forecast}) + a (\text{actual demand in this period minus this period's forecast})$$

i.e. the old forecast plus *a* times the error in the old forecast. The weight *a* represents a fractional constant which is ascertained by inspecting the data (in the same way as in calculating the weighted moving average in **28**). The constant takes a value between zero and 1 and in practice is usually between zero and 0.2. (this range has been found to give the most satisfactory results). Remember, however, that for the first period no earlier forecast is available. Instead, the actual sales should be used in its place, i.e. we assume no error in the forecast. Assuming $a = 0.2$, forecasts can be made as in the following table.

Month	Actual demand (Units)	Forecast
Jan	1,500	(1500)*
Feb	1,700	1500
Mar	1,650	1540
Apr	1,600	1562
May	1,725	1569.6
Jun	1,680	1600.68
July	. . . . .	1616.544

* Actual demand since there is no forecast.

For example the forecast for March is calculated as $1500 + 0.2 (1700 - 1500)$, i.e. 1540.

If an *a* value of greater than 0.2 gives the "best" fit to the dates, it suggests that the data contains a "trend" factor. In this case a more suitable forecasting method is required. By trying out different values for *a* we can eventually find the value which gives the best prediction. This figure can then be used for forecasting purposes.

30. Trend analysis. Simple moving averages and simple exponential smoothing are much less useful where there is an underlying trend in the data. When there is evidence of a trend in the data "double moving averages" or "double exponential smoothing" might be employed. The trend has, however, to be of the nature where a roughly similar amount is added to or deducted from the previous value of the variable. Double moving averages are not widely used in practice since they do not give the accuracy of double exponential smoothing. This being the case, only double exponential smoothing is mentioned here.

31. Double exponential smoothing. The method of double exponential smoothing involves first computing the exponentially smoothed values for a series of data as in **29** above. Next we would use the predicted values (or "exponentially smoothed" values a they are usually called) as data to calculate another series o exponentially smoothed values. Adjustments are then made to this latter figure in order to obtain the forecast.

32. Seasonal data. The traditional method of forecasting used where there is evidence of seasonal variation and cyclical influences is *time series decomposition*. The simplest model to work with is:

$$D_t = (T_t \times S_t \times Ck + I_t)$$

Where D_t = demand in period t; T = trend factor; S = seasonal factor; C = cyclical factor; and I = irregular or random element in the series. The procedure is as follows.

(*a*) *Calculate the seasonal factor* (*see* **33**). This involves finding the "average ratio" of the actual demand (D) to the centre moving monthly average.

(*b*) *Calculate the trend factor* (*see* **34**). This can be computed in several ways and the simplest method involves conducting a *linear regression analysis* of the centred moving averages with respect to time. (For a full understanding of regression analysis *see* Firth 1977). Another method which can often be applied is the method of *semi-averages*. In the example shown below it is this latter method which is employed.

(*c*) *Calculate the cyclical factor* (*see* **35**).

(*d*) *Make a forecast* (*see* **36**). This is achieved by substituting values for T, S, and C into the equation shown above. We cannot forecast the irregular fluctuations (I). It is possible, however, to gain some idea of the likely magnitude of I by comparing forecast values, using the above equation, with actual values. In the example shown below we have included only four years' data though in practice, we would prefer many more—up to twenty. However, for the sake of simplicity we have included only four years' data in the following example (*see* Table VI).

The table of data (*see* Table VI) shows the demand for a hypothetical product for the years 1974 through to 1977 inclusive (*see* column 1).

33. Calculating the seasonal factor. We first calculate the twelve months' total (column 2) for each set of twelve-monthly figures (i.e. January 1974 to December 1974, February 1974 to January

TABLE VI. DEMAND FOR HYPOTHETICAL PRODUCT, 1974–77

Year/month	Demand (000)	12 month total	Centred moving total	12 months moving monthly average (centred)	Ratio of actual to centred moving mon. average	Trend factor	Cyclical factor
	(1)	(2)	(3)	(4)	(5)	(6)	(7)
'74 Jan.	58						
Feb.	59						
Mar.	57						
Apr.	54						
May	52						
Jun.	51	710					
Jul.	57	724	717	59.75	0.954	59.75	1.000
Aug.	59	739	731.5	60.96	0.968	61.02	0.999
Sep.	62	753	746	62.17	0.997	62.29	0.998
Oct.	64	767	760	63.33	1.011	63.56	0.996
Nov.	68	784	775.5	64.63	1.052	64.83	0.997
Dec.	69	801	792.5	66.04	1.045	66.10	0.999
'75 Jan.	72	818	809.5	67.46	1.067	67.37	1.001
Feb.	74	835	826.5	68.88	1.074	68.64	1.003
Mar.	71	852	843.5	70.29	1.010	69.91	1.005
Apr.	68	870	861	71.75	0.948	71.18	1.008
May	69	886	878	73.17	0.943	72.45	1.010
Jun.	68	900	893	74.42	0.914	73.72	1.009
Jul.	74	915	907.5	75.63	0.978	74.99	1.009
Aug.	76	927	921	76.75	0.990	76.26	1.006
Sep.	79	943	935	77.92	1.014	77.53	1.005
Oct.	82	958	950.5	79.21	1.035	78.80	1.005
Nov.	84	971	964.5	80.38	1.045	80.07	1.004
Dec.	83	983	977	81.42	1.019	81.34	1.001
'76 Jan.	87	997	990	82.50	1.055	82.61	0.999
Feb.	86	1013	1005	83.75	1.027	83.88	0.998
Mar.	87	1030	1021.5	85.13	1.022	85.15	1.000
Apr.	83	1046	1038	86.50	0.960	86.42	1.001
May	82	1062	1054	87.83	0.934	87.69	1.002
Jun.	80	1079	1070.5	89.21	0.897	88.96	1.003
Jul.	88	1095	1087	90.58	0.972	90.23	1.004
Aug.	92	1109	1102	91.83	1.002	91.50	1.004
Sep.	96	1124	1116.5	93.04	1.032	92.77	1.003
Oct.	98	1142	1133	94.42	1.038	94.04	1.004
Nov.	100	1158	1150	95.83	1.044	95.31	1.005
Dec.	100	1174	1166	97.17	1.029	96.58	1.006
'77 Jan.	103	1190	1182	98.50	1.046	97.85	1.007
Feb.	100	1204	1197	99.75	1.003	99.12	1.006
Mar.	102	1219	1211.5	100.96	1.010	100.39	1.006
Apr.	101	1230	1224.5	102.04	0.990	101.66	1.004
May	98	1245	1237.5	103.13	0.950	102.93	1.002
Jun.	96	1259	1252	104.33	0.920	104.20	1.001
Jul.	104						
Aug.	106						
Sep.	111						
Oct.	109						
Nov.	115						
Dec.	114						

1975 etc.) The figure for January 1974 to December 1974 (710) is recorded in the row opposite June, the figure for February 1974 to January 1975 (724) is recorded opposite July, and so on. The next step is to calculate the *centred moving total* (column 3). The first of these values is written in opposite the seventh month of the first twelve-month period. The figure (717) is obtained by taking an average of the June and July figures (for that year), of the *moving total* in column 2. The general formula is therefore

Centred moving total $t =$

$$\frac{(12 \text{ months' moving total } t) + (12 \text{ months' total } t - 1)}{2}$$

The figures in column 4 represent the centred moving monthly average. This is obtained by dividing each of the figures in column 3 in turn by 12. This enables us to calculate the ratio of the actual demand to the centred monthly moving average. This forms the basis of the estimate of the seasonal factor. The ratio (column 5) is calculated simply by dividing the value in column 1 by the figure in column 4.

Next we take the figures in column 5 and average them out for each month. For example, January = (1.067 + 1.055 + 1.046)/3 = 1.056. The values obtained for each month are shown below and each of these represents the seasonal factor for that particular month.

January	1.056	July	0.968
February	1.035	August	0.987
March	1.014	September	1.014
April	0.966	October	1.028
May	0.942	November	1.047
June	0.910	December	1.031

34. Calculating the trend. There are several ways of calculating the trend. One way which gives good results is to use *linear regression analysis* (*see* Firth 1977). Another method which can be used when the trend is approximately linear, as is the case in the preceding example, is the method of *semi-averages*. The procedure is as follows: first we divide into two equal parts the list of twelve-month centred moving averages (column 4) for the whole period. Next we calculate the mean for each half of the data. The figures July 1974 to December 1975 (inclusive) yield a mean of 70.79, whilst the figures January 1976 to June 1977 yield a mean 93.69. Subtracting the lesser of these values from the larger one gives a figure of 22.90 which represents an average per month of $\frac{22.90}{18}$ or 1.27.

This now enables us to calculate a trend value for each month in which we have a centred moving monthly average. To estimate the value for each of these months we use the formula: Trend value for period t = (value of the first centred moving average in the series) + (1.27 × where p is the number of periods since the first centred moving monthly average. The trend value for August 1974 therefore equals 59.75 + 1.27 × 1, or 61.02. The values for each period are recorded in column 6.

35. Calculation of the cyclical factor. Cyclical influences are the most difficult to detect. However, we can attempt to identify the cyclical influence in the following manner. First we divide each figure in column 4 of Table VI by the corresponding figure in column 6. The resulting figure is then recorded in column 7. We then average out the cyclical variation for each year. For example taking the figures in column 7:

1974 (6 month period)
$$\frac{1.000 + 0.999 + 0.998 + 0.996 + 0.997 + 0.999}{6} = 0.998$$

1975 (12 month period)   = 1.006
1976 (12 month period)   = 1.002
1977 (6 month period)   = 1.004

In this particular case it is difficult to identify a cyclical value for each year since there is too little variation in the above figures. We will therefore assume that the cyclical factor (C) is the same in every year, i.e. 1.000. If a pattern had been noted, for example a "high" one year followed by a "low" the next year, in making a forecast we would multiply by the appropriate cyclical factor according to whether the year in question was one which coincided with a "high" in the cycle or a "low" in the cycle.

36. Forecasting. We would forecast the demand for January 1978 as follows:

$$D_{42} = (T)\,(S)\,(C) + I$$
$$= (59.75 + 42 \times 1.27)\,(1.058)\,(1.000) + I$$
$$= 119.65 + I$$

January 1978 is the forty-second period since the first centred moving monthly average.

NOTE: We cannot forecast *"I"* since it is a randomly distributed variable. The error in our forecast will always be equal to *I*.

37. Adaptive methods. Such methods adapt themselves to the pattern of the data with which they are dealing. Unlike the techniques discussed so far the weightings used in this particular technique adjust as new data is obtained. Methods include:

(*a*) *Adaptive filtering*—this uses moving averages in which the specific data points have their own weights;

(*b*) *Trigg and Leach's method* (*1967*)—this is akin to exponential smoothing but instead of incorporating an *a* value, the value of Trigg's tracking signal is used. This changes according to the volatility of the data. For further details of these techniques *see* Firth 1977.

PROGRESS TEST 15

1. What is work study? **(2)**
2. What are the basic stages of method study? **(3)**
3. Evaluate the usefulness of process charts. **(4)**
4. How can "string diagrams" be used in method study? **(5)**
5. Define "work measurement". **(6)**
6. How is the "standard unit of work" established? **(7)**
7. What are the functions of an estimator? **(8)**
8. What are the various methods of job evaluation? **(9)**
9. Define O & M. **(10)**
10. What kind of activities might an O & M officer perform? **(12)**
11. Explain the basic aims of OR. **(15)**
12. What kind of problems can linear programming help to solve? **(17)**
13. Distinguish between queueing and sequencing problems, give examples of each. **(18–20)**
14. What are search problems? **(22)**
15. What use are computer simulators to management decision making? **(23, 24)**
16. Explain how the simple moving average works. Make a forecast for period 10 using a three period moving average for the following data:

Period	Sales (000 units)	
1	163.58	
2	159.72	
3	191.6	
4	188.74	
5	201.65	
6	231.79	
7	188.65	
8	201.74	
9	204.99	(27)

17. Explain the term "exponential smoothing". **(29)**
18. Prepare a forecast for January 1979 based on the following data. **(32–36)**

Sales (000 units)

	J	F	M	A	M	J	J	A	S	O	N	D
1974	64	56	56	50	46	43	45	49	54	60	65	69
1975	68	62	60	54	50	47	48	52	58	64	68	73
1976	73	66	64	57	54	50	52	57	62	69	73	79
1977	78	70	68	62	58	55	56	61	66	73	78	83
1978	84	76	74	67	63	59	61	66	71	79	84	90

Management in a Changing Environment

INTRODUCTION

1. Introduction. Management's greatest task is to keep pace with change. Here we consider the nature of change and the influence that bring about change. One of the hardest jobs that management consultants encounter is effecting change and reducing management's resistance to it. Psychologists have paid considerable attention to the way in which change can be effected and we discuss this process in the chapter.

2. The phenomenon of change. Organisations are constantly changing their structure, their aims, objectives and goals and consequently what they produce and sell. New machinery and processes replace old ones; new buildings are put up and older ones pulled down; new salary scales and terms of employment are negotiated with employees; new contracts are negotiated with new suppliers of raw materials and new customers are found. Indeed the way in which organisations undergo change are too numerous to list. Organisations change because their environments change and they need to meet environmental needs. Effective management is therefore concerned with *managing change*.

3. The nature of change. Changes in an organisation come about as a result of changes in the environment.

EXAMPLES

(1) A major customer decides not to obtain any more products from firm X. Other customers of firm X follow suit and in a short time sales of the firm's products are reduced by fifty per cent. Firm X has to seek to change its products to remedy the situation. (2) A firm recruits a number of university graduates in Business Studies into its ranks as management trainees. Over a period of ten years some leave, but a few stay and work their way up in the hierarchy of the organisation. In whatever jobs they do they bring some element of change into the tasks performed. (3) Government legislation on safety protection for

agricultural workers forced tractor manufacturers to introduce changes into their product design. In particular, safety cabs became a standard fitting.

4. Organisational resistance to change. Employees often resist impending change in an organisation for several reasons.

(*a*) *Economic.* People may individually or collectively resist change because they fear it will affect their livelihood. Workers resist automation and takeovers/mergers because they fear redundancy. Board directors may resist takeovers because they fear they will lose their status and income as directors. Family firms may resist "going public" for similar reasons.

(*b*) *Inconvenience.* Unless individuals can see some benefit or reward coming to themselves as a result of pursuing a particular line of action which involves making changes they will resist. It is difficult to persuade people that breaking with their customary way of doing things is desirable, since change does involve spending more effort and learning new ways of doing things. In O & M work or in Work Study assignments, resistance is often encountered from individuals who will be expected to change their routine because of the implementation of a new system or procedure. Unless an individual perceives some reward—usually in the form of some increased pay—he will resist the inconvenience of change.

(*c*) *Uncertainty.* Even if an individual is offered incentives he may still resist because he is uncertain as to whether the proposed change is really desirable from his point of view. Individuals may turn down jobs which carry promotion at work because they are uncertain in their own minds about whether they want the accompanying responsibility attached to the promotion. Such a change may mean both breaking and re-creating social relationships, which they may not wish to do.

(*d*) *Resentment of control.* Individuals resent being directly manipulated by others in organisations. They do, however, accept that it has to take place through the medium of the superior–subordinate relationship. Any attempt to strengthen the amount of control that they have customarily come to expect is, however, viewed with extreme suspicion and resistance will be felt.

5. Overcoming resistance to change. Where one party has more power than another, the former will overcome the latter and will be able to enforce change. However, this is, perhaps, the less desirable way of creating change since it will create a high degree of

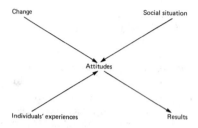

FIG. 28   *Roethlisberger's X chart.*

resentment in the repressed party. It is much better to try to lessen the resistance to change rather than to try to enforce change. Roethlisberger's famous "X chart" (Fig. 28) shows that psychological and sociological dimensions of a situation contribute towards the eventual end-result. Individuals interpret a situation which involves change according to their attitudes towards it. Attitudes themselves reflect previous experience.

The best way in which to try to effect change involves overcoming prejudiced attitudes. Kurt Lewin (1951) developed the idea of "Force Field Analysis", which suggests that in the face of resistance to change, the situation should be analysed to find out what factors are accounting for this resistance together with the relative strength of the resistance. Overcoming the resistance involves changing individuals' attitudes to the identified factors or changing the nature of the identified factors themselves.

EXAMPLE

Management decided to remove the canteen section from a warehouse so that the warehouse could be extended. At break time the workers would have to go to the main canteen some 250 metres away. Opposition to the move was encountered from the workforce. Workers felt that they would be inconvenienced by having to walk further and would get wet when it rained (or unduly cold in the bad weather). Management felt that it could easily overcome the inconvenience factor by allowing individuals an extra ten minutes at break-times but it felt that the "bad weather" problem was a more difficult one to solve. Then management hit upon the idea of running a competition amongst the workers to see if anyone could come up with a solution—a small reward of £10 was offered to the winner. A panel of workers was asked to review the ideas and to choose the best idea put forward. In the event one suggestion received unanimous support from the panel and backing from the workers: management should provide weatherproof clothing to employees for bad weather protection. The degree of commitment from all groups helped to make the agreed solution work.

6. Effecting change. Individuals and groups react psychologically rather than logically to proposed changes. Unless an individual is considered to be the "appropriate" expert on matters relating to the proposed change, persuasion and rational argument may not be accepted. To affect change the following steps are recommended.

(a) Create an awareness of the need for change by exposing people to the facts of the situation.

(b) Choose an appropriate individual, or group of individuals, who are held in esteem by other members of the work group and who will be accepted as a credible source of information. Convince this group that "change" is warranted.

(c) Allow the workers to adapt the final strategy for themselves—or at least to play a participative role in the planning of it.

(d) Allow the workforce the credit for effecting the change themselves.

(e) Be prepared to accept a less than optimal strategy—since some change is better than none at all.

SOURCES OF CHANGE

7. Purchase behaviour of consumer markets. Consumers affect the firm through the nature of the goods they demand. Over the last fifty years there has been a considerable change in the characteristics of consumers and in the nature of their purchase behaviour. A major change has been the increase in income per family unit. A contributory factor to this has been the increase in the number of working wives. Other changes have included the development of a vast new teenage market and also, mainly as a result of lower working hours and better pay, a growing demand for leisure products. In the former case, products are now being made specifically for teenagers—even very young teenagers. Cosmetic manufacturers now produce and market a range of products which are aimed at the 11–13 years old girl. All such products are fully supported by advertising programmes which are tailor-made to fit the dreams and aspirations of the young teenager. The impact of this trend on the management structure of the organisation has been quite considerable—senior executives concerned with this type of business are customarily under thirty years of age.

Alongside the growth in incomes per family unit and per head of the population has developed an increased demand for convenience shopping. This has resulted in a widespread demand for convenience products and convenient ways of obtaining and paying for them, etc. In the last twenty-five years the packaging of goods, their distribution and the way in which their purchase is financed have all been revolutionised. Demand for conveniently and attractively packaged goods has led to a vast increase in the demand for packaging machinery and export package designers. This has also led to a much greater emphasis upon establishing brand names in the market place and increased the emphasis on advertising as well. As a result of these factors the importance of the marketing function has escalated, resulting in changes in distribution needs. Supermarkets and shopping centres have blossomed everywhere. More people today depend on credit to finance their purchases than ever before and this too has led to an increase in many subsidiary services—e.g. hire purchase companies.

8. Increasing competition. The classical economists believe that competition is good for the consumer since it leads to an increase in the quality of goods and services which are marketed. There have been three major developments in the past thirty years or so which have had, and will continue to have in the future, a major impact on the strategy and structure of British industry.

From 1946–1960 USA-owned companies began to set up or acquire subsidiary companies in Western Europe and, in particular, in Britain. The American companies brought with them not only expertise of a technical nature and a huge financial backing, but also a dynamic approach to marketing products which had a considerable impact on Western European economies. Companies such as IBM have gobbled up the computer market, General Foods and Kelloggs have made their presence felt in the convenience food markets. In all, they introduced a new element of competition into post-war Britain and Europe.

The nature of the American "invasion" was such that it created a new type of firm—the "multinational". As a result, larger British and European firms were forced to think in terms of expanding their size in order to acquire the resources to combat the challenge.

n many cases this involved restructuring companies along multi-ivisional lines and introducing many managerial changes.

The 1960s saw the rebirth of Japan as a formidable competitor n world markets. The first impact of their onslaught was felt in he motor cycle industries of Western Europe. British manufac-urers, in particular, "went to the wall" as a direct result of their nability to meet the competition from Japan. Japanese com-•etition has also been felt in other areas—for example Japanese amera manufacturers have eroded the West German producers' •ositions in the world markets.

•. Government policy. In the public sector of industry, commerce nd education, Government policy has an overriding influence on ¹ow organisations are managed. Planned change brought about •y direct government control can have spectacular results and •ring about widespread upheaval and change in management tructure. Following on from the Robbins Report in 1963, a large ¹umber of Polytechnic Institutes were formed in the Higher ³ducation Sector along with a number of new "technological" ¹niversities. In the last dozen years or so these institutions have ¡rown at a considerable rate, usually from the base of a technical :ollege or a college of advanced technology. The management tructure of such institutions and the types of courses offered have :hanged rapidly in a short period of time.

Government policy can also affect private industry. Alterations o VAT charges and hire purchase regulations can have consider-ble repercussions in terms of short term demand for products. ⁻irms operating in industries which are sensitive to such changes ¹ave often tried to diversify their product-market interests to •vercome such problems. This, in turn, has led to managerial •roblems. The Equal Opportunities Act, giving equal employment erms to women has had its effects on all firms. Various other Acts elating to safety and health at work have also caused firms to ntroduce changes.

¹0. Computers and automation. Computers and automation have heir greatest impact on manual and clerical jobs. Unfortunately, ᵥhilst automation undoubtedly leads to greater efficiency in terms ᵢf output it also leads to unemployment and has caused embittered ⁻esistance from trade unions. Automated processes, which are :omputer controlled, can replace hundreds of skilled and unskilled ᵯanual workers at a stroke. Resistance to change of this nature ᵢnd from this direction receives greatest attention in the media and can form the subject of extremely long power struggles between management and unions. Certain industries have been decimated with the advent of micro-electronics. The Swiss watch industry has suffered considerably in this respect, with the result that seventeen firms went out of business, incurring the loss of a considerable number of jobs. Certain occupations are likely to suffer more than others. It has been estimated that as many as two million German clerical staff could be made redundant over the period 1980-85. Word processors will have a considerable impact on the need for typists.

LOOKING AHEAD

11. The post-industrial society. "Futurists" maintain that we are now on the verge of a new life style. They suggest that this will take the form of a society of a kind that the world has not seen before. The term "post-industrial" suggests a relative decline of industry as a prime force in our society. Robert Fulmer (1978) notes:

> It seems likely that in the future the secondary industries' share of both employment and GNP will continue to be a steadily declining one. In their place will rise the tertiary sector (which supplies goods and services to primary and secondary organisations) and the quarternary sector which supplies service to organisations and individuals and to society as a whole. Profit-making institutions will decrease in their proportion of the national effort and power structure.

In the immediate future it is envisaged that there will be a glut of qualified workers at both ends of the occupational hierarchy. It is thought that jobs which are normally filled by college graduates and those which are filled by school leavers will not expand fast enough to keep pace with the projected need. Already in this country we have seen government-sponsored "work experience" programmes to alleviate the unemployment problem among the younger people. It is expected that in the future, as a result of automation and computerisation, there will be substantially less demand for people to perform jobs of a highly routine nature.

12. Attitudes towards work. As might be anticipated, rising educational attainment amongst employees will affect their attitudes towards work. Individuals will come to expect more from their jobs and will be less willing to engage in jobs which require considerable manual effort. It is hard to foresee what the likely outcome of these attitudes will be. However, it is not foreseen that people's willingness and ability to work will change significantly in the next decade or so. It is, however, expected that the average hours worked per week (on the whole) will continue to fall—probably to around 33 hours by 1990.

3. The challenges of the 1980s. Neil Jacoby (1976) suggests that managers are likely to face six major challenges in the 1980s:

(a) *Conditions of change.* A great deal of political turbulence and uncertainty resulting from:

(i) inflation, unemployment, energy shortages, environmental improvement, consumerism and minority rights;

(ii) competing claims for special economic treatment by different groups in the economy;

(iii) an excess of graduate labour seeking a scarcity of suitable jobs;

(iv) more confrontations between unions, management and government.

(b) *Slow economic growth.* Growth will be small in most industrial sectors of the economy and in some cases management will be faced with the problem of managing declining or stagnating industries. Moreover, considerable capital investment is required to develop new sources of energy and it is likely that much effort will be put in this direction.

(c) *Expensive money.* Captial and credit is likely to be expensive. Capital is likely to be in relatively short supply and interest rates are likely to be high.

(d) *Labour relations.* There will be a weakening of industrial discipline and support for the work ethic. It is anticipated that there will be significant changes in worker attitudes towards authority. Criticisms of working conditions in business, on the theme that they are both monotonous and dehumanising, are likely to undermine the authority of business managers. Moreover, it is likely to lead to increased pressure on the behalf of employees to participate in decisions that affect their future well-being.

(e) *Increase in legislation.* There will be a rising public demand for governmental regulations. The pressure put on governments by a variety of pressure groups—e.g. environmentalists—will cause governments to introduce more and more legislation and regulations. These in turn will complicate the problem of "managing".

(f) *The private sector of industry.* There will be a challenge to the whole system of private enterprise. Most people appear to have only a relatively small understanding of the system of private enter prise. This lack of understanding is accompanied by a degree of hostility and suspicion. It is possible that over-regulation and taxation may, through ignorance, begin to stifle private enterprise.

14. The manager of the 1980s. The role of the manager in the 1980s will be that of a *contingency co-ordinator*. Contingency co-ordinators recognise that every situation is somewhat unique. He/she will not attempt to apply hard and fast rules but will seek to anticipate developments and be able to draw from past education and experience to keep things moving toward pre-determined objectives. The contingency co-ordinator anticipates the uncertain and unpredictable nature of the future. While vision into the future is seldom crystal-clear, this manager has a healthy concern for what is about to happen.

PROGRESS TEST 16

1. What do you understand by the term "change"? **(2, 3)**
2. Enumerate the reasons why organisations may resist change. **(4)**
3. What do you consider to be the key factor in effecting organisational change? **(5)**
4. How should one try to effect change? **(6)**
5. Explain how the purchase behaviour of consumers can lead to organisational change. **(7)**
6. What effect has competition had on organisational structure in Western Europe? **(8)**
7. In what ways can government policy influence organisational development? **(9)**
8. Why does the prospect of automation in a factory lead to trade union resistance to the idea. **(10)**
9. What are the likely features of a post-industrial society? **(11)**
10. In what ways do you expect attitudes towards work to change in the future? **(12)**
11. What do you consider to be the main challenges that businesses will face in the 1980s? **(13)**
12. What is a "contingency co-ordinator"? **(14)**

APPENDIX I

Specimen Questions

Institute of Practitioners in Work Study and Organisation and Methods.

1. Explain why some people continue to work when it is no longer financially necessary. (*IPWSOM Motivation and Communication*)

2. (*a*) Outline three methods of job evaluation; and (*b*) describe one such method explaining its application to a manufacturing organisation. (*IPWSOM Motivation and Communication*)

Institute of Cost and Management Accountants

3. Discuss the factors likely to influence the extent to which a manager allows his subordinates to participate in decision-making. (*ICMA Organisation and Marketing Management*)

4. Identify the external factors that can influence and change the organisation of a business and indicate, for each factor, the likely effects of that influence. (*ICMA Organisation and Marketing Management*)

5. A manufacturer of leather wishes to research the United Kingdom market for footwear. In particular, he wishes to establish the type and frequency of purchase of footwear and the purchasing habits of different members of households. (*a*) In this situation, what sampling procedures are available? (*b*) What sort of sample should ideally be used and how might the cost of the sampling procedure be reduced in practice? (*ICMA Organisation and Marketing Management*)

6. The term "marketing mix" was first used in 1952. Discuss the principal elements of the "mix" and identify those particularly relevant to: (*a*) a manufacturer of domestic washing machines; and (*b*) a manufacturer of heavy commercial vehicles. (*ICMA Organisation and Marketing Management*)

7. Discuss the evidence which suggests that in order to be effective, a manager can and should be flexible in the choice of his managerial style. (*ICMA Organisation and Marketing Management*)

8. (*a*) What is advertising? (*b*) What range of objectives migh be set for an advertising campaign? (*c*) How might this success be evaluated? (*ICMA Organisation and Marketing Management*)

9. What do you understand by the term "alienation"? Wha steps can be taken to reduce alienation in an organisation? (*ICMA Organisation and Marketing Management*)

Institute of Personnel Management.

10. What are the main sources of outside finance available to a public company in the UK? What are the advantages and disadvantages of each in the present business climate? (*IPM Management Systems*)

11. Describe both the self-actualising model and the expectancy model of motivation and indicate the extent to which they can be recognised as scientific theories. (*IPM Management Systems*)

Institute of Administrative Management.

12. How would you try to ensure management succession in an organisation? (*IAM People, Organisations and Change*)

13. Discuss the influence of technology and environment on an organisation's structure, illustrating your answer with examples from published research. (*IAM People, Organisations and Change*)

14. Describe the main purposes and characteristics of a Management by Objectives scheme. Are there shortcomings to this scheme? (*IAM People, Organisations and Change*)

15. What are the main advantages/difficulties of involving employees in the decision-making process? (*IAM People, Organisations and Change*)

16. Conflict within an organisation may be regarded as avoidable or inherent, functional or dysfunctional. What are your views on conflict, and what would be the implications of these views for management policies? (*IAM People, Organisations and Change*)

17. Your organisation produces two types of product, Super and Deluxe. Super provides a contribution of £3 per unit, whilst Deluxe has a contribution of £2 per unit. Two processes are involved in production, process A and process B; however each process has only 500 hours of capacity available per period. Each unit of Super uses two hours of process A and 1.25 hours of process B, whilst Deluxe uses 1 hour of A and 2 hours of B. What would be the optimum production plan of Super and Deluxe per period? (*IAM Management Information and Control: Administration*)

18. Giving examples, both from published research and from

our own experience, discuss how primary working groups exert influence over the successful functioning of an organisation. (*IAM People, Organisations and Change*)

Institute of Works Managers.

19. Speculate on the changes that may take place in the next decade or so as a result of changes in technology and social attitudes. (You may discuss this generally or in relation to your own organisation.) (*IWM Organisational Analysis*)

20. "Managers must have power *with* not power *over*." "A manager's job is to manage." "Management is the leadership of an organisation, large or small, towards an objective." To what extent, if at all can these statements be reconciled? (*IWM Organisational Analysis*)

21. What do you understand by delegation? Compare the problems and requirements of delegation in: (*a*) an organisation subject to the pressures of change and fluctuation; and (*b*) a fairly stable organisation. (*IWM Organisational Analysis*)

22. You are about to take over a new department. You are used to the processes involved and feel able to deal with most technical problems. However, you know none of the supervisors concerned and have heard that the relationship between them and the previous manager was not good. He has left the company. How might you set about examining the situation in order to discover a successful leadership style? (*IWM Organisational Analysis*)

23. Comment on the following statement from the point of view of a works manager. "Authority emanates from the office or position that a person holds and not from the person himself." What particular problems does this situation pose? (*IWM Organisational Analysis*)

24. How far is it possible to design a profitable industrial organisation so as to increase employee motivation and satisfaction in work? (*IWM Organisational Analysis*)

Institute of Chartered Secretaries and Administrators.

25. Should managers make a scientific approach to decision-making or should they also rely on intuition and experience? State your reasons. (*ICSA Management: Principles and Policy*)

26. Discuss the contribution to management theory and practice of any two of the following: (*a*) H. Fayol; (*b*) D. McGregor; (*c*) P. Drucker; (*d*) I. Ansoff. (*ICSA Management: Principles and Policy*)

27. "The classical theory of organisation tends to ignore or at

least to minimise the importance of the human factor, treats th worker primarily as an economic animal, is obsessed with th scientific measurement of a fair day's work and pays little or n heed to the human aspect of work." (From *Is scientific managemer possible?* Joe Kelly, 1968.) Discuss. (*ICSA Management: Principle and Policy*)

28. What major factors would you consider when developing five-year corporate plan for one of the following organisations: (*a* a food manufacturing organisation; (*b*) a college or university; (*c* a building society; (*d*) a national charity? (*ICSA Managemen Principles and Policy*)

29. Describe the main results of the "Hawthorne" experiment concentrating on the practical application of the findings b management. (*ICSA Management: Principles and Policy*)

30. The manager of a small factory manufacturing toys i considering the introduction of new machines. What advice woul you give him on the employee-relations aspect of such a projecte change? In particular discuss why the employees might resist thi change. (*ICSA Management: Principles and Policy*)

31. Describe what you understand by the phrase "matri management". (*ICSA Management: Principles and Policy*)

32. Discuss the contribution to management theory and practic of any two of the following: (*a*) F. Herzberg; (*b*) Joan Woodwarc (*c*) Elliot Jaques; (*d*) H. A. Simon. (*ICSA Management: Principle and Policy*)

33. Describe what you understand by the phrase "managemen information system". In particular, you should explain how th effective provision of information can assist management decision making. (*ICSA Management Principles and Policy*)

34. In highly labour-intensive organisations the major scope fo improvements in efficiency and effectiveness must come throug more effective use of human resources. Discuss. (*ICSA Manage ment: Principles and Policy*)

35. What do you understand by the phrase "matrix organisation"? In what kinds of organisations and situations would you expec matrix organisation to apply? Give reasons for your answer. (*ICS Management: Principles and Policy*)

36. How many organisations provide for the systematic develop ment and application of strategy? (*ICSA Management: Principle and Policy*)

37. Motivation of subordinates is an important aspect of manager's job. (*a*) What do you think motivates a person to d

ell? (b) What steps can a manager take to motivate his sub-rdinates? (*ICSA Management: Principles and Policy*)

38. What are the main functions of a bureaucratic organisation? Iow effectively do bureaucratic organisations respond to changing ircumstances in the environment? (*ICSA Management: Principles nd Policy*)

39. Describe how you would apply a "management by objec-ves" scheme in one of the following departments: (a) a marketing epartment; (b) a computer department; (c) a personnel depart-1ent; (d) a production department. (*ICSA Management: Principles nd Policy*)

40. What in your opinion are the essential qualities, apart from cademic and professional qualifications, required by a person in rder that he or she may become an effective departmental 1anager? In your answer, discuss the extent to which training an develop these qualities. (*ICSA Management: Principles and °olicy*)

nstitute of Supervisory Management.

41. Provide a definition, in psychological terms, of the word motivation". (*ISM Certificate*)

42. Compare and contrast the main features of a primary group /ith those of a secondary group. (*ISM Certificate*)

43. Recommend a procedure for the adoption by management, he use of which will facilitate the effective selection of persons or jobs in your organisation. (*ISM Certificate*)

44. Define the term "delegation" as used in the organisational ense. (*ISM Certificate*)

45. What is the difference between authority and responsibility? *ISM Certificate*)

46. Discuss the following statement: "Effective communications re the lifeblood of any industrial or commercial organisation." *ISM Certificate*)

47. Prepare a report for the attention of your Board of Directors vhich sets out the arguments for and against the introduction of oint consultation into your organisation which employs 1,200 vorkers, all on one site. (*ISM Certificate*)

48. Describe the purpose and function of a Production Planning nd Control Department in a manufacturing enterprise. (*ISM ertificate*)

49. How may the application of work study techniques improve roductivity achievement? (*ISM Certificate*)

50. How may research and development aid the effectivene of a business? (*ISM Certificate*)

51. Explain the main features of the following systems of pr duction: (*a*) unit/jobbing; (*b*) small batch; (*c*) flow. Provide example to illustrate each type. Discuss the advantages and d advantages of each system. (*ISM Certificate*)

52. List and describe in detail each step in the procedure method study. (*ISM Certificate*)

53. What is the purpose of job evaluation? Describe in det four methods of evaluating jobs and provide appropriate examp of the application of each. (*ISM Certificate*)

54. Give five factors which must be covered in a job descriptio (*ISM Certificate*)

55. How can an employer ensure the physical safety of his worker (*ISM Certificate*)

56. What are the basic procedures to be used in decision-maki and problem-solving? (*ISM Certificate*)

Institute of Industrial Managers.

57. Explain the terms "authority", "power", "responsibilit and "delegation of authority". Discuss the steps a manger mu take and the attitude he must adopt for delegation to be effectiv (*IIM Organisational Analysis*)

58. Outline the basic process of control and discuss the essenti requirements a manager should keep in mind when designing h control systems. (*IIM Organisational Analysis*)

59. Discuss the relationship between managerial style ar effectiveness, referring to research findings. (*IIM Organisation Analysis*)

60. What are the advantages of (*a*) verbal and (*b*) written con munication? Give two examples each of circumstances where (and (*b*) would be the best method of communication. (*IIM Orga isational Analysis*)

Examination Technique

Practice in writing out examination type questions and having the opportunity to check out whether the answers are correct is the best way of developing an examination technique. It is the *doing* and the *feedback* which are important. The progress tests in this book enable a student to check to see if he/she can retain the main points in his or her memory after reading the chapter. Specimen examination questions are given to allow the student the opportunity to try out actual questions under the guidance of a tutor.

Perhaps the biggest pitfall that students fall into when taking examinations is that they do not attempt to answer the question that has been set. The "kitchen sink" approach, in which the student writes down all he/she knows about a topic featured in a question will not score high marks. If the word "motivation" appears in a question students are apt to block out every other word in the question and simply write down all that they know about motivation. It is absolutely essential that one should avoid this pitfall. If you know enough about a topic, you should be able to answer the actual question which has been set.

Questions on an examination paper should be scanned in the first instance, with the object in mind of discounting all those questions which you feel you cannot answer. Be careful at this stage—the wording of a question may be difficult, at first glance, but you may be able to answer it well. Only attempt those questions which you know you can answer well—unless you cannot avoid answering questions which you cannot do well. It is a good idea to spend a few minutes jotting down a few notes on the questions you have decided to attempt. You will soon find out whether you know enough to be able to do them successfully.

The time allotted for the examination should be equally divided up amongst the questions. A common fault is for students to spend *far too long attempting one or more questions*. It is better to do four questions fairly well than three questions very well.

Some other points to bear in mind are:

(*a*) Poor handwriting, spelling and grammar irritate an examiner and create a bad impression of the candidate.

(*b*) Questions set are seldom entirely expecting a descriptive answer. A comparison requires a number of things to be compared. A comment requires you to exercise a qualitative assessment. A discussion involves assessing the advantages for and against a topic.

(*c*) Do not overlook a second or subsequent part to a question.

(*d*) Always allow yourself enough time to re-read your written answer. You will find this extremely beneficial and may be quite shocked at what you read.

Further Reading

Only the most up to date edition available of each book should be used.

CHAPTER I

Church, R. A. *The Great Victorian Boom 1850–1873*, Macmillan, 1975

Coleman, D. C. *Industry in Tudor and Stuart England*, Macmillan, 1975

Mant, A. *The Rise and Fall of the British Manager*, Pan, 1977

Payne, P. L. *British Entrepreneurship in the Nineteenth Century*, Macmillan, 1974

Pollard, S. *The Genesis of Modern Management*, Penguin, 1968

CHAPTER II

Ansoff, H. I. *Strategic Management*, Macmillan, 1979

Fayol, H. *General and Industrial Management*, Pitman, 1967

George, C. S. *The History of Management Thought*, Prentice Hall, New Jersey, 1968

Handy, C. B. *Understanding Organisations*, Penguin, 1976

Mooney, J. D. *The Principle of Organisation*, Harper and Row, New York, 1947

Pugh, D. S. (ed.) *Organisation Theory*, Penguin, 1971

Pugh, D. S. *Writers on Organisations*, Penguin, 1971

Rose, M. *Industrial Behaviour: Theoretical Developments since Taylor*, Penguin, 1978

Taylor, F. W. *Principles of Scientific Management*, Harper and Row, New York, 1911

Wren, D. *The Evolution of Management Thought*, Ronald Press, New York, 1972

CHAPTER III

Allen, G. C. *Structure of Industry in Britain*, Longmans, 1970

Barker, P. J. *et al. Case Studies in the Competitive Process*, Heinemann, 1976

Barret, B. *et al. Industrial Relations and the Wider Society*, Collier Macmillan, 1975

Blois, K. *et al. Case Studies in Competition Policy*, Heinemann, 1975

Bruner, J. *Relevance of Education*, Penguin, 1974

Child, J. *The Business Enterprise in Modern Industrial Society*, Collier Macmillan, 1969

Farquhar, J. D. *The National Economy*, Philip Allan, 1975

Friedman, W. *Law in a Changing Society*, Penguin, 1972

Grove, J. W. *Government and Industry in Britain*, Longmans, 1962

Hardern, G. *Business Organisation and Management*, Philip Allan, 1978

Hirsch, F. *Social Limits to Growth*, Routledge and Kegan Paul, 1977

Mackintosh, J. P. *The Government and Politics of Britain*, Hutchinson, 1974

Rise, A. K. *The Enterprise and its Environment*, Tavistock, 1963

Rose, R. *Politics in England Today*, Faber, 1974

Smith, B. *et al. Renewing the Management Structure*, British Institute of Management, 1972

CHAPTER IV

Ackoff, R. L. *A Concept of Corporate Planning*, Wiley-Interscience, New York, 1970

Ansoff, H. I. *Strategic Management*, Macmillan, 1979

Ansoff, H. I. (ed.) *Business Strategy*, Penguin, 1969

Argenti, J. *Corporate Planning*, Allen and Unwin, 1968

Channon, D. F. *Strategy and Structure of British Enterprise*, Macmillan, 1973

Copeman, G. *The Role of the Managing Director*, Business Publications, 1960

Drucker, P. F. *The Practice of Management*, Pan, 1968

Gilbert, M. (ed.) *The Modern Business Enterprise*, Penguin, 1972

Institute of Directors *Directors' Guide to Management Techniques*, Gower Press, 1974

Mann, R. *The Arts of Top Management: a McKinsey Anthology*, McGraw Hill, 1970

Read, A. *The Company Director, his Functions, Powers and Duties*, Jordan, 1971

Sheffield, B. *Company Boards: their Responsibilities to Shareholders, Employees and the Community*, Allen and Unwin, 1971

CHAPTER V

Production
Buffa, E. S. *Modern Production Management*, Wiley, 1969
Lockyer, K. G. *Factory and Production Management*, Pitman, 1974
Radford, L. J. D. and Richardson, D. B. *The Management of Production*, Macmillan, 1972
Wild, R. *The Techniques of Production Management*, Holt, Rinehart and Winston, 1971

Finance
Batty, J. *Accountancy for Managers*, Heinemann, 1970
Bierman, H. and Drebin, A. R. *Managerial Accounting*, Collier Macmillan, 1972
Bull, R. J. *Accounting in Business*, Butterworth, 1976
Goff, W. S. *Finance for Managers*, Macdonald and Evans, 1975
Sizer, J. *Insight into Management Accounting*, Penguin, 1970

Personnel
French, W. *The Personnel Management Process*, Houghton Mifflin, 1974
Institute of Personnel Management *A Textbook of Personnel Management*, 1976
Institute of Personnel Management *Training in Industry and Commerce*, 1977
Pitors, P. and Myers, C. A. *Personnel Administration*, McGraw Hill, 1977
Wright, M. *Labour Law*, Macdonald and Evans, 1979

Research and Development
McLeod, T. S. *Management of Research, Development and Design in Industry*, Gower Press, 1969

Marketing
McCarthy, E. J. *Basic Marketing*, Irwin, Illinois, 1978
Chisnall, P. M. *Marketing: a Behavioural Analysis*, McGraw Hill, 1975
Tarpey, L. X. *et al. A Preface to Marketing Management*, Business Publications Inc., Dallas, 1979
Woodruff, R. B. *et al. Marketing Management Perspectives and Applications*, Irwin, Illinois, 1976

Marketing research

Chisnall, P. M. *Marketing Research*, McGraw Hill, 1973

Kinnear, T. C. and Taylor, J. R. *Marketing Research: an Applied Approach*, McGraw Hill, 1979

Tull, D. S. and Hawkins, D. I. *Marketing Research*, Macmillan, 1977

Worcester, R. M. and Downham, J. *Consumer Market Research Handbook*, Van Nostrand Reinhold, 1978

CHAPTER VI

Anthony, R. N. *Planning and Control Systems: A Framework for Analysis*, Harvard Business School, Boston, 1965

Argenti, J. *Systematic Corporate Planning*, Nelson, 1974

Battersby, A. *Sales Forecasting*, Pelican, 1970

Firth, M. *Forecasting Methods in Business and Management*, Arnold, 1977

Humble, J. W. *Improving Business Results*, Pan, 1972

Hussey, D. E. *Corporate Planning: Theory and Practice*, Pergamon, 1974

Koontz, H. and O'Donnell, C. *Management: A Systems and Contingency Analysis of the Managerial Functions* (Ch. 6–11), McGraw Hill, Tokyo, 1976

Lockyer, K. G. *Introduction to Critical Path Analysis*, Pitman, 1977

Moskowitz, H. and Wright, G. P. *Operational Research Techniques for Management* (Ch. 18), Prentice-Hall, 1979

Wheelwright, S. C. and Makridakis, S. *Forecasting Methods for Management*, John Wiley, New York, 1977

CHAPTER VII

Alexis, M. and Wilson, C. Z. (eds) *Organisational Decision-Making*, Prentice-Hall, 1967

Argenti, J. *Management Techniques*, Allen and Unwin, 1969

Barker, P. J. and Button, K. J. *Case Studies in Cost Benefit Analysis*, Heinemann, 1975

Battersby, A. *Mathematics in Management*, Penguin, 1970

Bauma, W. J. *Economic Theory and Operations Analysis*, Prentice-Hall, 1965

Couts, B. D. *et al. Management Decision-making*, Pan, 1969

Coyle, R. G. *Mathematics for Business Decisions*, Nelson, 1961

Cyert, R. and Welsch, L. *Management Decision-making*, Penguin, 1970

Kotler, P. *Marketing Decision-Making*, Holt Reinhart Winston, New York, 1970

Moore, P. G. *The Anatomy of Decisions*, Penguin, 1976

Shone, K. J. *Problem Solving for Managers*, Collins, 1974

Simon, H. A. *The New Science of Decision-making*, Prentice-Hall, New Jersey, 1977

Starr, M. K. *Management: a Modern Approach*, Harcourt Brace Jovanovich, New York, 1971

Thomas, H. *Decision Theory and the Manager*, Pitman, 1972

Turban, E. and Loomba, N. P. *Readings in Management Science*, Business Publications Inc., Dallas, 1975

Wagner, H. M. *Principles of Management Science*, Prentice-Hall, New Jersey, 1975

CHAPTER VIII

Argyris, C. *The Impact of Budgets on People*, The School of Business and Public Administration, Cornell University, 1952

Brech, E. F. L. *The Principles and Practice of Management*, Longman, 1963

Edey, H. C. *Business Budgets and Accounts*, Hutchinson, 1966

Houghton, C. T. *Accounting for Managerial Control*, Prentice-Hall, 1974

Koontz, H. and O'Donnell, C. *Management: A Systems and Contingency Analysis of the Managerial Functions* (Ch. 27–30), McGraw Hill, Tokyo, 1976

Tannenbaum, A. *Control in Organisations*, McGraw Hill, New York, 1968

Vaughan, D. E., Norgaard, R. L. and Bennett, H. *Financial Planning and Management*, Goodyear Publishing Co., California, 1972

Whitmore, D. *Management Science* (p. 254 ff.), Teach Yourself Books, 1979

CHAPTER IX

Barnes, M. C. *et al. Company Organisation, Theory and Practice*, Allen and Unwin, 1970

Brown, W. *Organisation*, Heinemann, 1971

Hall, R. *Organisation, Structure and Process*, Prentice-Hall, 1972

Koontz, H. and O'Donnell, C. *Management: A Systems and Contingency Analysis of the Managerial Functions* (Ch. 12–18), McGraw Hill, Tokyo, 1976

Litterer, J. A. *Organisation: Structure and Behaviour*, John Wiley, 1970

O'Shaughnessy, J. *Business Organisation*, Allen and Unwin, London, 1972

CHAPTER X

Brown, J. A. C. *The Social Psychology of Industry*, Penguin, 1970

Handy, C. B. *Understanding Organisations* (Ch. 2), Penguin, 1976

Lupton, T. *Management and the Social Services*, Penguin, 1971

Nord, W. *Concepts and Controversies in Organisational Behaviour* (pp. 44–118), Goodyear Publishing Co., California, 1972

Schein, E. *Organisational Psychology* (pp. 43–75), Prentice-Hall, New Jersey, 1965

Vroom, H. and Deci, L. (eds) *Management and Motivation*, Penguin, 1970

Willsmore, A. W. *Managing Modern Man*, Pitman, 1973

CHAPTER XI

Fiedler, F. E. *A Theory of Leadership Effectiveness*, McGraw Hill, 1967

Fulmer, R. M. *The New Management* (Ch. 14), Macmillan, New York, 1978

Gibb, C. A. (ed.) *Leadership*, Penguin, 1969

Handy, C. B. *Understanding Organisations* (Ch. 4), Penguin, 1976

Irvine, A. S. *Improving Industrial Communication*, Gower Press, 1973

Leyton, A. C. *The Art of Communication*, Pitman, 1968

Little, F. *Communication in Business*, Longman, 1970

Nord, W. (ed.) *Concepts and Controversies in Organisational Behaviour* (pp. 512–91), Goodyear Publishing Co., California, 1972

Parkinson, C. N. and Rowe, N. *Communicate*, Pan, 1977

Parsons, C. J. *Communications for Business Studies*, Arnold, 1978

Porter, L. W. and Roberts, K. H. *Communications in Organisations*, Penguin, 1977

Ross, M. and Hendry, C. E. *New Understandings of Leadership*, Association Press, 1957

Sayles, L. R. *Leadership*, McGraw Hill, New York, 1979

CHAPTER XII

Argyris, C. *Integrating the Individual and the Organisation*, John Wiley, New York, 1964

Berne, E. *Games People Play*, Andre Deutsch, 1964

Biddle, B. J. and Thomas, E. J. (eds) *Role Theory: Concepts and Research*, John Wiley, New York, 1966

Cartwright, D. and Zander, A. (eds) *Group Dynamics: Research and Theory*, Harper and Row, New York, 1960

Davis, J. H. *Group Performance*, Addison Wesley, Massachussetts, 1969

Goffman, E. *Encounters*, Penguin, 1962

Houlton, Bob, *The Activist's Handbook*, Arrow, 1975

Smith, P. B. (ed.) *Group Processes*, Penguin, 1970

Sprott, W. J. H. *Human Groups*, Pelican, 1958

CHAPTER XIII

Argyle, M. *The Social Psychology of Work*, Penguin, 1972

Holdsworth, R. F. *Personnel Selection and Training*, British Institute of Management, 1972

Lupton, Tom and Gowler, Don *Selecting a Wage Payment System*, Kogan Page, 1969

Munro Fraser, J. *Employment Interviewing*, Macdonald and Evans, 1978

Singer, E. J. *Training in Industry and Commerce*, Institute of Personnel Management, 1977

Stammers, R. and Patrick, J. *The Psychology of Training*, Methuen, 1975

Ungerson, B. (ed.) *Recruitment Handbook*, Gower Press, 1970

CHAPTER XIV

Her Majesty's Stationery Office *Industrial Relations Code of Practice*

Torrington, D. P. *Handbook of Industrial Relations*, Gower Press, 1972

CHAPTER XV

General
Stafford, L. W. T. *Business Mathematics*, Macdonald & Evans, 1979

Work study

Currie, R. M. *Work Study*, Pitman, 1959

Larkin, J. A. *Work Study: Theory and Practice*, McGraw Hill, 1969

Whitmore, D. A. *Work Measurement*, Heinemann, 1975

Whitmore, D. A. *Work Study and Related Management Services*, Heinemann, 1976

Organisation and methods

Anderson, R. G. *Organisation and Methods*, Macdonald and Evans, 1980

Cemach, H. P. *Work Study in the Office*, "Office" magazine, London, 1958

Denyer, J. C. *O&M and Management Services*, Macdonald and Evans, 1976

Harmer, L. C. *Clerical Work Measurement*, Occasional Paper No 9, HMSO, 1968

Milward, G. E. *Organisation and Methods*, Macmillan, 1967

Thomas, H. A. *Automation for Management*, Gower Press, 1969

Operational research

Ackoff R. L. and Rivett, P. *A Manager's Guide to Operational Research*, John Wiley, New York, 1963

Duckworth, E. *A Guide to Operational Research*, University Paperbacks, London, 1965

Eddison, R. T. *et al. Operational Research in Management*, English Universities Press, 1962

Harper, W. M. *Operational Research*, Macdonald and Evans, 1982

Littlechild, S. C. (ed.) *Operational Research for Managers*, Philip Allan, 1977

Loomba, N. P. *Management: a Quantitative Perspective*, Collier Macmillan, 1978

Mackower, M. S. and Williamson, E. *Operational Research*, Teach Yourself Books, 1967

Moskowitz, H. and Wright, G. P. *Operational Research Techniques for Management*, Prentice-Hill, 1979

Forecasting

Firth, M. *Forecasting Methods in Business and Management*, Arnold, 1977

CHAPTER XVI

Bell, D. *The Coming of the Post-industrial Society*, Penguin, 1976

Bennis, W. G. *Changing Organisations*, McGraw Hill, New York, 1966

Burns, T. and Stalker, G. M. *The Management of Innovation*, Tavistock, 1966

Galbraith, J. R. *Matrix Organisation Designs*, "Business Horizons", Feb. 1971

Kahn, H. and Bruce-Briggs, B. *Things to Come: Thinking about the Seventies and Eighties*, Macmillan, New York, 1972

Mack, R. P. *Management 2000*, American Foundation for Management Research, New York, 1968

Miller, E. J. and Rice, A. K. *Systems of Organisation*, Tavistock, 1967

Toffler, A. *Future Shock*, Random House, New York, 1970

Woodward, Joan *Industrial Organisation: Theory and Practice*, Oxford University Press, 1965

Bibliography

Ackoff, R. L. and Rivett, R. *A Manager's Guide to Operational Research*, John Wiley, New York, 1963

Ammer, D. S. *Manufacturing Management and Control*, Appleton, Century, Crofts, 1968

Ansoff, H. I. *Corporate Strategy*, Penguin, 1965

Ansoff, H. I. *Strategic Management*, Macmillan, 1979

Argyle, M. *Social Interaction*, Methuen, 1969

Argyris, C. *Management and Organisational Development*, McGraw Hill, New York, 1971

Argyris, C. *Integrating the Individual and the Organisation*, John Wiley, New York, 1964

Barnard, C. I. *The Functions of the Executive*, Harvard University Press, Massachussetts, 1938

Barnett, C. *The Human Factor in British Industrial Design* (pamphlet: Working Together campaign), 1975

Baumler, J. V. "Defined criteria of performance in organisational control", *Administrative Science Quarterly*, September 1971

Bellman, R. "Control Theory", p. 186 *Scientific American*, September 1964

Bennis, W. "Towards a 'truly' scientific management: the concept of organisational health", *General Systems Yearbook*, 1962

Berelson, B. and Steiner, G. A. *Human Behaviour: an Inventory of Scientific Findings*, Harcourt Brace and World, 1964

Bierstadt, R. "An analysis of social power", p. 733 *American Sociological Review*, December 1950

Blake, R. R. and Mouton, J. S. *The Managerial Grid*, Gulf Publishing, Houston, 1964

Brech, E. F. L. *The Principles and Practice of Management*, Longman, 1963

Burns, T. and Stalker, G. M. *The Management of Innovation*, Tavistock, 1966

Carlson, R. *Interaction Concepts in Personality*, Aldine, Chicago, 1969

Channon, D. F. *Strategy and Structure of British Enterprise*, Macmillan, 1973

Churchman, C. W. *et al. Introduction to Operational Research*, John Wiley, New York, 1957

Cleland, D. and King, W. R. *Systems Analysis and Project Management* (p. 239), McGraw Hill, New York, 1968

Cooley, C. H. *Social Organisation*, Scribner, New York, 1909

Cyert, R. M. and March, J. G. *A Behavioural Theory of the Firm*, Prentice-Hall, 1963

Dale, E. *Management: Theory and Practice*, McGraw Hill, Tokyo, 1978

Dale, E. and Michelon, L. C. *Modern Management Methods*, Penguin, 1966

Denyer, J. C. *O&M and Management Services*, Macdonald & Evans, 1976

Drucker, P. F. *The Practice of Management*, Pan, 1968

Drucker, P. F. *The New Markets and Other Essays*, Pan, 1971

Drucker, P. F. *Management Tasks, Responsibilities, Processes*, Harper & Row, New York, 1974

Drucker, P. F. "The rise of production sharing", *The Wall St. Journal*, 17th March 1977

Eldred, S. H. and Price, D. B. "Linguistic evaluation of feeling states in psychotherapy", *Psychiatry* 21, 1958

Emery, F. E. and Trist, E. L. "The causal texture of organisational environments", *Human Relations*, February 1965

Etzioni, A. *Modern Organisations*, Prentice-Hall, New Jersey, 1964

Fiedler, F. E. *A Theory of Leadership Effectiveness*, McGraw Hill, New York, 1967

Field, A. C. *see* Brech, E. F. L.

Firth, M. *Forecasting Methods in Business and Management*, Arnold, 1977

Follett, M. P. "Constructive conflict", from H. C. Metcalf and L. Urwick (eds) *Dynamic Administration: the Collected Papers of M. P. Follett*, Pitman, New York, 1941

Fulmer, R. N. *The New Management*, Macmillan, New York, 1978

General Foods *The Food Makers: A History of General Foods Ltd.*, General Foods Press, 1972

Georgopoulos, B. S. and Mann, F. C. *Hospital Administration* (pp. 57–58), Fall, 1962

Goff, W. S. *Finance for Managers*, Macdonald & Evans, 1975

Grant, W. P. and Marsh, D. "The politics of the CBI: 1974 and after", *Government and Opposition* xci, 1975

Gretton, J. and Jackson, M. *William Tyndale: Collapse of a Schoo* *or a System?*, George Allen and Unwin, 1976

Gulick, L. and Urwick, L. "Notes on the science of administration" (p. 13), *Papers on the Science of Administration*, Institute of Public Administration, New York, 1937

Hall, D. T. and Nougaim, K. "An examination of Maslow's need hierarchy in an organisational setting" (pp. 12–35), *Organisational Behaviour and Human Performance*, February 1968

Handy, C. B. *Understanding Organisations*, Penguin, 1976

Hanson, D. G. *Service Banking*, Institute of Bankers, 1979

Herzberg, F. *Job Attitudes: Review of Research and Opinion*, Pittsburg Psychological Services, 1957

Herzberg, F. *et al. The Motivation to Work*, John Wiley & Sons, New York, 1959

Holt, C. G. *et al. Planning Production, Inventories and Work Force*, Prentice-Hall, New Jersey, 1960

Homans, G. C. *The Human Group*, Harcourt Brace and Fields, New York, 1950

Houlton, Bob *The Activists' Handbook*, Arrow, 1975

House, R. "A path goal theory of leadership effectiveness" (pp. 331–338), *Administrative Science Quarterly*, vol. 3, 16, 1971

Jacoby, N. "Six big challenges businesses will face in the next decade" (pp. 36–40), *Nation's Budget*, August 1976

Kahn, R. L. "The prediction of productivity" (pp. 41–49), *Journal of Social Issues*, 12, 1956

Kahn, H. and Wiener, N. *Toward the Year 2000: a Framework for Speculation*, Macmillan, New York, 1967

Kast, F. E. and Rosenzweig, J. E. *Organisation and Management: a Systems Approach*, McGraw Hill, Tokyo, 1974

Karger, D. W. and Murdick, R. G. *New Product Venture Management*, Gordon and Breach, New York, 1972

Katz, D. and Kahn, R. L. *Social Psychology of Organisations*, John Wiley, New York, 1966

Koontz, H. and O'Donnell, C. *Management: A System and Contingency Analysis of the Managerial Functions*, McGraw Hill, New York, 1976

Kotler, P. *Marketing Management: Planning, Analysis and Control*, Prentice-Hall, New Jersey, 1976

Lawlor, E. and Settle, J. "A causal correlation of the need-hierarchy concept" (pp. 265–287), *Organisational Behaviour and Human Performance*, April 1972

Leavitt, H. J. "Applied organisational change in industry: structural, technical and human approaches", W. W. Cooper, H. J. Leavitt and M. W. Shelley (eds) *New Perspectives in Organisational Research*, John Wiley, New York, 1964

Leavitt, H. J. and Whisler, T. L. "Management in the 1980s", *Management Systems*, ed. P. Schoderbok, John Wiley, New York, 1967

Lewin, K. *The Conceptual Representation and the Measure of Psychological Forces*, Duke University Press, North Carolina, 1938

Lewin, K. and Cartwright, N. D. (eds) *Field Theory in Social Sciences*, Harper & Row, New York, 1951

Likert, R. *New Patterns of Management*, McGraw Hill, New York, 1961

Litwin, G. H. and Stringer, R. A. *Motivation and Organisational Climate*, Harvard Graduate School of Business Administration, Boston, 1968

McClelland, D. *Studies in Motivation*, Appleton, Century, Crofts, New York, 1955

McClelland, D. *The Achieving Society*, Van Nostrand, New Jersey, 1961

McGregor, D. *The Human Side of Enterprise*, McGraw Hill, New York, 1960

Maier, R. F. and Solem, A. R. "The contribution of a discussion leader to the quality of group thinking: the effective use of minority opinions" (pp. 277–288), *Human Relations* 5, 1952

March, J. G. with Simon, H. A. *Organisations*, John Wiley, New York, 1958

March, J. G. with Cyert, R. M. *A Behavioural Theory of the Firm*, Prentice-Hall, New Jersey, 1963

Maslow, A. *Motivation and Personality*, Harper & Row, New York, 1954

Mehrabian, A. "The interference of attitudes from the posture, orientation and distance of a communication", *Journal of Consultant Psychology* 32, 1968

Merret, A. J. and Sykes, A. *The Finance and Analysis of Capital Projects*, Longman, 1965

Merton, R. K. *Social Theory and Social Structure*, The Free Press of Glencoe, New York, 1957

Newbould, G. D. *Management and Merger Activity*, Guthshead, Liverpool, 1970

O'Meara, T. "Selecting profitable products", *Harvard Business Review*, January, February 1961

Pareto, V. (ed. Arthur Livingstone) *The Mind and Society*, Harcourt Brace and World, New York, 1935

Parker, G. G. and Segura, E. L. "How to get a better forecast" (pp. 99–109), *Harvard Business Review*, March/April 1971

Pitfield, R. *Business Organisation*, Macdonald & Evans, 1978

Porter, L. W. "Job attitudes in management. Perceived differences in need fulfilment as a function of job level" (pp. 375–387), *Journal of Applied Psychology*, December 1962

Porter, L. W. and Lawler, E. L. *Managerial Attitudes and Performance*, Irwin, Illinois, 1968

Reddin, W. J. *Managerial Effectiveness*, McGraw Hill, 1970

Riley, G. "Banks and advertising", *Journal of the Institute of Bankers*, August 1959

Roethlisberger, J. *Manpower and Morale*, Harvard University Press, Massachussetts, 1941

Sayles, L. R. *Leadership*, McGraw Hill, New York, 1979

Schein, E. H. "Management development as a process of influence", *Industrial Management Review*, May 1961

Schein, E. H. *Organisational Psychology*, Prentice-Hall, 1965

Scott, W. G. *Organisation Theory*, Irwin, 1961

Selznick, P. *Leadership in Administration*, Harper & Row, New York, 1957

Shaw, M. *Developing Communication Skills*, Educational Systems and Design Inc., Connecticut, 1968

Sherif, M. and Sherif, C. A. *Social Psychology* (Ch. 11), Harper & Row, New York, 1969

Simon, H. A. *Administrative Behaviour*, MacMillan, New York, 1959

Simon, H. A. and Newell, A. "Heuristic problem solving", *Operations Research*, vol. 6, January 1958

Stewart, R. *The Reality of Management*, Heinemann, 1963

Tannenbaum, A. *Control in Organisation*, McGraw Hill, New York, 1968

Tannenbaum, A. and Schmidt, W. H. "How to choose a leadership pattern", *Harvard Business Review*, vol. 36, no. 2, March/April 1958

Thibaut, J. W. and Kelley, H. H. *The Social Psychology of Groups*, John Wiley, New York, 1959

Trigg, D. W. and Leach, A. G. "Exponential smoothing with adaptive response rate", *Operational Research Quarterly*, 1, 18, 1967

Trist, E. L. and Bamforth, K. W. "Some social and psychological consequences of the Longwall method of coal getting" (pp. 3–38), *Human Relations*, vol. 4, no. 1, 1951

Turnbull, G. *A History of the Calico Printing Industry of Great Britain*, Altrincham, 1951

Vroom, V. *Work and Motivation*, John Wiley, New York, 1964

Wallen, R. "Three types of executive personality", *Dun's Review*, December 1963

Walker, C. R. and Guest, R. H. *The Man on the Assembly Line*, Harvard University Press, 1952

Weber, M. *The Protestant Ethic and Spirit of Capitalism*, Scribner and Sons, New York, 1958

Whisler, T. L. *The Impact of Computers on Organisations* Praeger, New York, 1970

Woodward, J. *Industrial Organisation: Theory and Practice*, Oxford University Press, 1965

Index